My Father's Shadow

My Father's Shadow

Intergenerational Conflict in African American Men's Autobiography

David L. Dudley

UNIVERSITY OF PENNSYLVANIA PRESS   Philadelphia

Permission is acknowledged to reprint published material:

From W.E.B. Du Bois, *Dusk of Dawn: An Essay Toward an Autobiography of a Race Concept*. New York: Harcourt, Brace, 1940. Reprint Millwood, N.Y.: Kraus-Thomson Organization Limited, 1975. Reprinted by permission.

From Richard Wright, *Black Boy*. Copyright 1937, 1942, 1944, 1945 by Richard Wright. Reprinted by permission of Harper-Collins Publishers and Jonathan Cape.

From Joanne Braxton, *Black Women Writing Autobiography*. Philadelphia: Temple University Press, 1990. Copyright © 1990 by Temple University. Reprinted by permission of Temple University Press.

From Eldridge Cleaver, *Soul on Ice*. New York: McGraw-Hill, 1968. Copyright © 1968 by McGraw-Hill, Inc. Reprinted by permission of McGraw-Hill, Inc.

From Joseph Campbell, *The Hero with a Thousand Faces*, Bollingen Series 17. Copyright © 1949, renewed 1976, by Princeton University Press. Reprinted by permission.

From James Baldwin, "Notes of a Native Son." Copyright © 1955, renewed 1983, by James Baldwin. Reprinted by permission of Beacon Press.

From Malcolm X, with the assistance of Alex Haley, *The Autobiography of Malcolm X*. Copyright © 1964 by Alex Haley and Malcolm X. Copyright © 1965 by Alex Haley and Betty Shabazz. Reprinted by permission of Random House Inc. and Hutchinson.

Library of Congress Cataloging-in-Publication Data

Dudley, David L.
    My father's shadow : intergenerational conflict in African
American men's autobiography / David L. Dudley.
        p.   cm.
    Includes bibliographical references and index.
    ISBN 0-8122-3081-7
    1. American prose literature—Afro-American authors—History and criticism. 2. American prose literature—Men authors—History and criticism. 3. Intergenerational relations in literature. 4. Autobiography—Afro-American authors. 5. Afro-American men in literature. 6. Fathers and sons in literature. 7. Autobiography—Men authors.   I. Title.
PS366.A35D84 1991
818'.08—dc20   91-8377
                                                                          CIP

For Eileen

Proverbs 31:10
Philippians 4:13

Contents

Acknowledgments

I owe a great debt to Dr. James Olney, at Louisiana State University, Baton Rouge, who has offered unfailing encouragement and numerous insightful suggestions as this book evolved into its present form. With pride I call James Olney friend and colleague and thank him for his confidence in me.

My thanks also to Linda Grogan, secretary of the Department of English and Foreign Languages at the University of West Florida. Endlessly patient and good humored, she typed and retyped the manuscript in its many versions without ever voicing a word of complaint. She has saved me hundreds of hours of work.

Many other people have offered support and various kinds of help to me and my family during the past seven years. I extend grateful thanks to Steve Rinnert, Randy Nichols, Mike Hesse, Chuck Comella, Sandy Greene, Meredith and Bill Tumlin, Chuck and Jere Lewis, Marsha and Jack Layfield, Jerry and Claire Ogle, Rick and Dottie Culp, Maggie Gilmore, and Margie Metzger. Particular thanks to Dr. and Mrs. Bob Frank for the great help they have given my family.

Most of all, I extend thanks to my loving and patient wife, Eileen, who has believed in me when I doubted myself, encouraged me to continue my work even when it took me away from my family, and loved me when I was unlovable. My love to Eileen and my children, Chris, Joy, Michael, and William, who make my work worthwhile.

Introduction

This work began as a study of the structures of several African American autobiographies, taking as its starting point the "bondage-freedom" pattern Sidonie Smith identifies in her book *Where I'm Bound*.[1] I expanded Smith's two-part pattern to include a third element, flight, which Smith also implies in her book. My purpose was to trace the development of this three-part pattern from the slave narratives to the "Civil Rights" autobiographies of the 1960s and 1970s. As my study progressed, however, I began to notice another pattern in the texts—one that caught my imagination and that is the primary focus of this book.

My Father's Shadow examines a line of African American men's autobiographies from Frederick Douglass's work to Malcolm X's, including also works of Booker T. Washington, W.E.B. Du Bois, Richard Wright, James Baldwin, and Eldridge Cleaver. I identify among these writers a kind of Oedipal conflict wherein each rising writer faces and overcomes his predecessor in the tradition. This predecessor, besides having written an autobiography establishing a powerful "I" somehow threatening to the younger writer, often occupies a position of power in the black (and sometimes white) community that the younger man would like to have for himself. To use Harold Bloom's expression in *The Anxiety of Influence*, the young autobiographer must overcome the older in order to clear imaginative space for himself.[2] In this particular line, the space to be cleared is often more than imaginative; it may be defined in terms of political power or of the popular perception of the autobiographer in question as *the* leader of black culture.

I am not, of course, the first to recognize or study conflicts between prominent African American men of letters; two of their most celebrated disputes, those between Booker T. Washington and W.E.B. Du Bois and between Richard Wright and James Baldwin, have received copious scholarly attention. But *My Father's Shadow* is the first study, as far as I know, to trace an unbroken line of such conflict in autobiographies from Douglass to Malcolm X.

The Oedipal issue, often cheapened and over-simplified into a matter of family sexual taboo, centers, as the myth itself reminds us, on the crucial issue of identity. The male child who feels threatened by his father and who desires in some way to supplant his father in his mother's affections is seeking his identity in relation to the two most important others in his life. When self-identity, not sex, becomes the key issue of the Oedipal conflict, its relevance to autobiography is clear. An autobiographer seeking to displace an older writer whom he perceives as a father figure wrestles not only with the problem of making his own artistic space but also with the question of his identity in relation to the literary and cultural tradition in which he lives and writes.

Henry Louis Gates, Jr., asserts that literary traditions come into being "because writers read other writers and *ground* their representations of experience in models of language provided largely by other writers to whom they feel akin."[3] While I hesitate to claim that the autobiographers and their works that I study here form a literary *tradition* (the term *line* seems preferable to *tradition* because it suggests a narrower field), I do find Gates's definition applicable in an inverted sort of way. The kinship these writers experience is rooted not in family solidarity, nurture, and mutual support, but in discomfort resulting from "family" ties and lines of authority that they wish were not there at all. To use another metaphor, we might say that these writers, rather than building upon earlier works to create a single structure whose various parts complement one another, instead seek to knock down pre-existing structures in order to clear space for their own new edifices.

Although it is difficult to trace the intergenerational antagonism in this particular line of African American men's autobiography to any single root cause, I suggest that one origin lies in the disruption of their families when these writers were children—disruption that at least four of these men state was caused by a hostile and meddling white world. Douglass and Washington did not know who their fathers were, except that they were white men who did not marry their mothers—an almost unthinkable prospect in antebellum America. Du Bois, Wright, and Malcolm X lost their fathers early: Du Bois's and Wright's fathers deserted their families, and Malcolm's father, Earl Little, was killed by white men who disliked his espousal of the black pride and back-to-Africa philosophy of his hero, Marcus Garvey. Douglass also lost his mother when he was a child, but her white owner had years before separated her from her son so that he felt no emotion upon hearing of her untimely death. Both Wright and Malcolm "lost" their mothers to debilitating illnesses, and Malcolm does not hesitate to blame an uncaring white social service bureaucracy for his mother's mental collapse. All these writers grew up in homes that were dysfunctional because of the white world's injustices and interference, and all these men experienced conflict with father figures in their adult lives. Yet each man has been nationally and internationally renowned and has influenced thousands of black and white people not only in America but across the globe. This study contributes to our understanding of these writers' personal lives and mutual relationships and how these factors influenced their contributions to our world.

*   *   *

Many critics would undoubtedly argue that we have scant need for another study of African American male writers and their work based solely (or even primarily) on the assumption that male authors and a concern for male issues are sufficient warrant for such a study. As Calvin Hernton convincingly demonstrates, black men and their writing have long—too long—dominated the African American literary scene, but that power has at last been successfully challenged by black women.[4] (In this respect, at least, African American literary history parallels that of white American literary history; we continue to witness the restructuring of the literary canon to include women whose work has until recently been devalued and ignored.) Today, however, as Hernton's article also makes clear, we are in the midst of a joyous explosion of black women's writing in America and throughout the world, writing in fiction, poetry, drama, and the essay that is being widely published, read, and appreciated.

Besides the other ways in which women writers and critics are currently contributing to our literature, they are compelling teachers to re-examine their assumptions about the comparative value of the works they present in the classroom and treat in their scholarship. Hernton notes that in Richard Barksdale and Keneth Kinnamon's widely used anthology *Black Writers of America* (1972), subtitled *A Comprehensive Anthology*, no women writers are included in the subsection entitled "Racial Spokesmen."[5] Martin Luther King, Jr., Malcolm X, and Eldridge Cleaver are the three writers chosen. An examination of the anthology as a whole reveals that it includes the work of some sixty-eight men and seventeen women, a neat four-to-one ratio. An instructor may seek to correct this imbalance, as I have, through supplementary texts, but the point is clear: the black literary tradition has been male-dominated.

Literature by and about black men is in no way privileged by virtue of its "maleness"; if studies are produced solely about male writers, they can no longer be based on the assumption that such works constitute *the* black literary tradition or that any one tradition or line is inherently of greater value than another. Instead, works about male writers must examine these writers anew to discover those peculiarly male characteristics that differentiate them from female perspectives. That is the intention of this book. Stripped of the accretions that cling to any long-privileged tradition, black male literature (and autobiography in particular) is currently open to receive such reevaluation to reveal what it can about the experience of being both black and male in America.

The same is true, of course, about all men's writing. The Western literary canon has long centered on male writers, and the critical lenses through which it has been examined have been male-oriented, as well. In *The Anxiety of Influence*, published in 1973, Harold Bloom assumes that poetic history is the history of *male* writers, and he uses a masculine perspective, that of Freud's "family romance," as an important part of his theoretical framework. When Bloom pleads for an end to the New Critical project—"Let us give up the failed enterprise of seeking to 'understand' any single poem as an entity in itself"—and a turn to a consideration of a poet's personal history and relationship with earlier poets—"Let us pursue instead the quest of learning to read any poem as its poet's deliberate misinterpretation, *as a poet*, of a precursor poem or of poetry in general"—he is asking for a reinterpretation of the *male* tradition.[6] Today, however, any such study that limits itself exclusively to male authors and male-centered critical assumptions and procedures must consciously do so, seeking to discover in the texts it treats distinctively masculine perceptions and modes of expression while acknowledging the existence and equal value of women's writing.

The omission of texts by African American women from this book indicates no devaluation of those texts. Indeed, a comprehensive study of African American autobiography, which *My Father's Shadow* is not, demands the inclusion of women's writing, which forms a vitally important "tradition within a tradition," as Joanne Braxton expresses it in the subtitle of her book.[7] I omit texts by women because I cannot find among them the antagonistic intergenerational dynamic that is such a striking and disturbing feature of the men's texts included here. But while such a conflict is absent from women's texts, they do share with black men's autobiographies interrelated elements that join them with men's texts into the larger, comprehensive tradition of African American autobiography.

First, autobiographies by both black men and black women take as their goal the arousing of a complacent and ignorant America to the plight of its African American citizens. The numerous slave narratives of the antebellum years have this purpose; in ending his *Narrative*, the premiere male slave narrative, Frederick Douglass expresses the wish that "this little book may do something toward throwing light on the American slave system, and hastening the glad day of deliverance to the millions of my brethren in bonds."[8] Joanne Braxton notes that Harriet Jacobs's *Incidents in the Life of a Slave Girl* (the greatest female slave narrative) possesses a similar purpose, to alert white women in the North to the plight of black female slaves and to call white women to their aid.[9] The slave narratives of men and women begin a tradition in African American writing that repeatedly directs attention to the injustices suffered by the black community and also calls upon the nation to make good the promises of the Declaration of Independence and the Constitution for *all* Americans regardless of the color of their skin.

African American autobiography speaks with a rich variety of voices, but I agree with Roger Rosenblatt's contention that amid their diversity of expression exist two other common elements: first, the desire of these writers to live their lives as they choose, not as the dominant white environment dictates; second, a criticism, overt or implicit, of the society that has from its beginning sought to limit the freedom of blacks.[10]

It must be a rare African American autobiography that contains neither of these elements; I know of none. To read such works from any period of time is to take in hand a literature that exposes the gap between the ideals and the realities of American life and that, as a kind of national conscience, persistently calls the nation to honor its promises of equal opportunity, equal justice, and equal freedom.

Yet autobiographies by black men and women differ in some important ways, which may in part be traced to conditions under slavery. Valerie Smith notes that male slaves enjoyed greater freedom of movement than did female slaves and were more likely than women to be sold away from their families. Smith concludes, "Factors such as these underscore important differences between the nature of male and female slavery in the American South and suggest why male slave narrators would figure themselves as self-sustaining individuals."[11] The different ideas of self-identity inculcated into slaves found their way into the narratives of slave men and women and have been, I believe, passed down to later generations of African American autobiographers; the result is that black men still tend to view themselves as isolated characters striving alone to make their way in life, while women tend to see themselves in relation to others, particularly to their mothers, to their children, and to other women.

Despite the extraordinary circumstances of slavery, the American cultural tradition of acceptable male and female roles is perhaps the most important source of differences in African American men's and women's manners of self-definition. This work, like others before it, notes that black male autobiographers create selves that fit readily into a primary American myth—what Phyllis Cole and Deborah Lambert call "the solitary but representative male figure on the physical or metaphysical frontier of the new world."[12] This figure is typified in its white manifestations by the hunter, the trapper, and the cowboy—by pioneer heroes fictional and real from Natty Bumppo and Daniel Boone to Tom Mix and the Lone Ranger. Self-reliant, emotionally independent, and endlessly resourceful, such larger-than-life characters have been seen as explorers and tamers of the wilderness whose call is to make it safe for later, permanent settlers. This same figure, in his more sinister manifestations, has also been associated with what Stephen Butterfield calls "the worst aspects of our history: murder of the Indians, rampant capitalism, the exploitation of the poor and weak, the amassing of huge fortunes, and the imperialistic contempt for the cultures of other countries."[13] We might well add the enslavement of millions of black people to such a list. Even though this sometimes reckless drive toward dominance—an ugly underside to white American male mythology—helped enslave blacks, African American men have not been immune to the cultural model of what masculinity involves; indeed, because of the circumstances in which many black men have been raised—in poverty and broken homes—black men may be particularly susceptible to the lure of the myth of the self-made American male who rises above the emotionally and materially deprived circumstances of his youth to achieve freedom, fame, and material wealth. This male figure must make it on his own—and does. If young Benjamin Franklin arriving (alone) from Boston in Philadelphia epitomizes the white American version of the myth of the free man about to succeed in the land of unlimited opportunity, then Frederick Douglass and all male slaves who, like him, escaped slavery alone and made their way to the North represents the *African* American version of the same myth.[14] So powerful is this myth in American life that generation after generation of American autobiographers, both white and black, have told their stories according to such patterns. Consequently, Malcolm X's self in his autobiography shares with Douglass's Frederick of the *Narrative* so many similarities that we can readily see the two autobiographical selves as part of the same line of works.

If the myth of the American male centers on the lonely conquest of the frontier, then the myth of the American female has centered on home and family, with motherhood seen as the ideal role. If male mythology portrays the man off on solitary quest, then the mythology of the female shows the woman at home, tending the children, "keeping the fires burning" until her man returns. American women have experienced the difficulties of breaking this pattern as they have struggled over the years for the vote, for equal rights before the law, and for equal opportunity in the work place. In some ways, the myth has prevented women from realizing their freedom to live as they would like, just as male mythology has at times pushed some men into roles they have found uncongenial. On the other hand, as the male myth is obviously appropriate in some ways to the man's particular psycho-social and biological makeup (otherwise it would not have exercised such influence over men for so long), so is the female myth in certain ways both a reflection of women's unique capabilities and a source of women's individual and communal strength.

Robert Stepto, commenting upon the importance of freedom and the attainment of literacy as themes in "every major Afro-American text," identifies a "primary Afro-American archetype, the articulate hero."[15] This male figure, who through the acquisition of literacy and the "comprehension of his culture's tongues" discovers also his own individual voice, has been, for many years, the most-discussed figure in African American literature. Best represented by Frederick Douglass, who heads the line of autobiographies studied in this book, the articulate hero has been thought to embody the African American experience. All seven autobiographers in the line I discuss can readily be described as articulate heroes, men who, having found their voices, have used the power of their words to wield great influence. As black feminist critics have noted, however, the concentration upon the articulate male hero has resulted in the relative neglect of his female counterpart, the figure Joanne Braxton identifies as the "outraged mother."[16] This female figure is as imposing and powerful as her masculine partner and, like him, uses words (especially a form of indignant, barbed speech Braxton calls "sass") to maintain self-esteem and to protect herself and those in her care.[17]

I note immediately that the term "outraged *mother*" suggests that black women's quest for self-discovery and ultimate self-definition is bound to relationship with others in ways that the male's quest is not. A male hero may perform his exploits in splendid isolation, but a mother enacts her role as she lives in contact with others who are bound to her. Thus, the very terms used to describe the central mythic figure in the male and female lines of autobiography suggest one of the great differences in the two—differences that emerge in the texts: the male tends to be more self-absorbed, more concerned with solo combat against hostile forces, and the female more concerned with *communal* effort to overcome the enemy. Frederick Douglass's single combat with the slave-breaker Edward Covey is the archetypal scene of the male mythos; his victory marks the end of his self-identification as a slave and makes his later escape inevitable. The female equivalent of this scene resembles it in that its goal is the same—escape from slavery—but the means are different: the female narrator celebrates the cooperative effort of many people working together to effect the freedom not only of herself but of her children and sometimes of her parents.[18] Harriet Jacobs's *Incidents in the Life of a Slave Girl* exemplifies this dynamic; as Braxton notes, Jacobs's narrative "represents a celebration of community and the bonds of sisterhood that can only be forged in struggle against a common oppressor."[19] The male and female autobiographical traditions differ in another way. The male line, as we have noted, is marked by intergenerational conflict and by a series of ruptures in the autobiographers' perceptions about *how* African Americans should proceed individually and as a group to solve the problems and overcome the hostilities that face them. Because this theme is the substance of much of this book, I shall not pursue it in detail at this point. I would summarize, however, by stating that the articulate hero, as he pursues his solitary quest for freedom, invariably encounters a predecessor in that quest who has pursued a similar goal by different means; the result is conflict, sometimes bitter, with the younger man determined to expose the flaws in the older man's methods and to persuade his readers that his own way is the correct path, his own life the truly exemplary one for men to follow.

The dynamic among black women is different. Instead of intergenerational antagonism, we find intergenerational bonding between the female autobiographer and both her biological mother and grandmother and also her literary forebears in the feminine tradition. Writing about the black female autobiographers of the nineteenth century, Joanne Braxton declares that these women "made 'a way out of no way' for those who would follow, even as they built on the foundation they inherited from books, the oral tradition, and, indeed, their own mothers"—thereby neatly joining the biological and literary generations together.[20] Braxton strengthens her argument about the literary solidarity among black women when she notes that some of the texts we possess might not now be in existence, let alone in print, were it not for the efforts of black women to see to it that such texts were preserved. She mentions by way of example

Dr. Anna Julia Cooper's work on behalf of Charlotte Forten Grimké, and Alfreda M. Duster's editorship of her mother's autobiography, *Crusade for Justice: The Autobiography of Ida B. Wells*.[21] Braxton characterizes this dynamic among black female writers as one of "collectivity, cooperation, collaboration, and celebration"—a description alien to the black male autobiographical line examined here.

Finally, I would reemphasize a point made earlier: despite their differences, both male and female African American autobiographers share the common goal of personal and communal freedom, even if their means of attaining such goals are different. It should also be noted that the African American male autobiographer, despite his self-image as isolated loner, neither lives his life in social isolation nor ignores the needs of the larger community of which he feels a part, even though he may continue to struggle with feelings of psychic isolation. Thus, all the writers treated in this book have devoted their lives to helping the cause of African Americans, whether it be through writing, lecturing, sociological research, politics, education, or leadership in religion. The difficulties these men have endured have not fostered in them defeat or a retreat from facing social problems, but, on the contrary, impelled them into service, and Americans black and white owe them a debt. If black female autobiographers have not had as prominent a place in the literary, social, and political worlds of our nation, this is no reflection on their abilities or desire to contribute; we must note, as it is, the enormous contributions of Harriet Tubman, Sojourner Truth, Ida B. Wells, Zora Neale Hurston, and many other women, all of whom overcame prejudices and obstacles to emerge victorious in the struggle for personal and communal freedom. Such women, and countless thousands like them who have left no autobiographical record, have worked, often quietly, often unsung, to maintain the African American family and its traditions and have, to a greater extent than the men, determined to "bring their families with them" into freedom. The men, for their part, have brought countless others into freedom, if in a more impersonal way as the leaders of movements, inspiring and helping from a distance, yet leading the cause nonetheless.

In her book of essays *In Search of Our Mothers' Gardens*, Alice Walker writes with passion and warmth about her relationship to Zora Neale Hurston, a writer she never met, but whose work and personal career are obviously her model and her greatest inspiration. In the essay "Looking for Zora," Walker relates her quest to locate Hurston's burial place. To facilitate her search, Walker portrays herself as Hurston's niece, an identity that suits her well, for artistically and spiritually Walker is Hurston's younger relative.[22] In finding

Hurston, Walker also finds herself, and in having a fitting marker erected above Hurston's grave, Walker gives tangible tribute to the woman she reveres as an authentic American genius—and her own artistic mother. This relationship between two African American women who never met but who are nevertheless both part of Braxton's "mystical sisterhood" best exemplifies the black female autobiographical tradition as I understand it. Black women's autobiographies, while sharing a great deal in common with black men's writing, nevertheless differ in some important ways and so form a distinct tradition that rewards separate study as well as their examination alongside men's works. Because women's autobiographies lack the particular intergenerational conflict that is the specific focus of this book, I believe that such texts lie outside its scope; they are not, therefore, treated here. In subjecting seven autobiographers to detailed analysis, I keep in mind that their works do not express the full truth for black male writers, let alone for women, but I believe that the autobiographical line their works form merits individual study not only for the peculiar intergenerational dynamic at its center but also because these writers whose works are here examined have contributed so significantly to the life of the United States and of the world.

The related subtheme also treated in this book lies in this book's origins, as I have already noted, and has to do with the structure of African American men's autobiographies. I identify a three-part pattern of bondage, flight, and freedom as the prevalent pattern of men's writing. This structure was created by the slave narrators and is still widely employed by black men today, for it appropriately expresses what remains the shape of many black men's lives: a birth into social and economic bondage, a struggle to escape such constricting circumstances, and the shaping of a free adult self removed from the negative circumstances of childhood and youth. This structure well reflects what I believe to be the purpose of all genuine autobiography—the creation of that autobiographical "I" that is free to stand against all the forces in its past and present that would try to conform it to any shape unnatural to itself. Bondage, flight, and freedom express the patterns of many lives, not just those of black men, for all people are challenged to establish their own identities distinct from the communal identity of family and cultural group. If the three-part pattern is particularly appropriate to the experience of black men in America, it also applies on a broader level to all lives that aspire to intellectual, emotional, and spiritual freedom.

1: The Head of a Line: Frederick Douglass

The beginning of African American autobiography may be fixed at 1760 with the publication in Boston of Briton Hammon's impressively titled *A Narrative of the Uncommon Suffering, and Surprizing Deliverance of Briton Hammon, a Negro Man,—Servant to General Winslow, of Marshfield, in New England: Who Returned to Boston, after having been absent almost Thirteen Years*. The full title continues for another hundred or so words, relating, in the florid style of the time, an outline of the book's contents. A steady trickle of narratives by slaves, many of them relating their escape from slavery to freedom, became an overflowing stream by the 1830s; at least eighty such works were published between 1835 and 1865.

Not only were many slave narratives published; they also sold well. Josiah Henson's *Life*, published in 1849, is said to have sold 100,000 copies by 1878. Solomon Northup's *Twelve Years a Slave* (1853) sold 27,000 copies in two years, and Douglass's *Narrative* (1845) sold 13,000 copies in its first year, 30,000 copies by 1850.[1] The narratives were popular because they made exciting reading, telling of inhuman treatment (often accompanied by graphic and gory illustrations), escape plots, flight and pursuit, close calls and hairbreadth escapes, culminating in the traditional happy ending; the fugitive reaches safety and freedom. More importantly, however, the narratives were read because they indicted the slave system and supported, implicitly at least, the abolitionist movement. Indeed, the slave narratives provided much of the grist for the abolitionists' propaganda mill, which had enormous impact on public opinion in America and Europe (Great Britain particularly) in the thirty years before the Civil War.

Their sponsorship and use by the abolitionist movement would explain in part the similarities among the slave narratives. These works were often dictated by illiterate or semiliterate narrators to abolitionist hack editors who cast their tales into standardized form for publication. Certain formulae of language, plotting, and structure were quickly found effective and were repeated numerous times for a public that never seemed to tire of the same story over and over again. James Olney has drawn what he calls a "master outline" listing the conventions of the slave narrative—elements that recur repeatedly both in the format of the printed work and in the narrative itself.[2] He further explains the remarkable similarities among the narratives by recalling that they share a single focus—slavery—and a common audience and sponsors; in addition, the motives and uses of the narratives were recognized and shared by their authors, audiences, and sponsors as being directed toward one goal, the abolition of slavery.[3]

Although most of the slave narratives lack enduring literary value, no one can deny their important contribution to the cultural and political milieu of their time. Every narrative, whether dictated, ghost-written, or independently penned, was an act of rebellion against the status quo in the slaveholding states. Such works were understandably viewed with fury and fear in the South, where they were usually banned, for besides denouncing slavery, the narratives proved that flight was possible and that the defiant escapees indeed possessed feeling, memory, and hope—signs of their full humanity and arguments that they *should* be free.

When the slave narratives are viewed as revolutionary acts, struggle, as Benjamin Quarles remarks about Frederick Douglass's *Narrative*, can readily be claimed as their central theme.[4] I agree with Quarles's assessment and add freedom as a corollary, for the narratives deal specifically with the *struggle to be free*. Full freedom, however, is seldom realized, and even partial freedom comes at great cost, particularly to the slave narrator. The very act of writing a life, an act by which one ostensibly seeks to define and differentiate an "I" distinct from all others, actually tends to confine that "I" to "what the book says about it," and often thereafter limits the writer's power of redefinition. Strangely enough, autobiographers who wish to announce their freedom through the writing of their lives end up imprisoned by the very structure they had thought would grant them personal emancipation. This is certainly the case with Frederick Douglass, whose *Narrative*, universally regarded as a peerless assertion of freedom, ultimately ended up narrowly defining how the world would see Douglass—as a tireless champion of every kind of liberation—and how he came to view himself. He later sought to modify that image, with limited success.

If the struggle to be free is the dominant theme of the slave narrative, then Sidonie Smith's detection of a two-part structure in many of the works makes logical sense. Smith finds the ex-slaves telling of their break into a community that allows them to find authentic identity; this break occurs after the slaves have escaped from a community that prevents self-expression and relegates them to menial positions outside society.[5] I would amend this useful analysis slightly by expanding the structure to three parts: bondage, *flight*, and freedom. Smith implicitly acknowledges this three-part structure, for two of her chapters, "Flight" and "Flight Again," treat the transitional phase between bondage and freedom. Not all slave narratives include an extended section dealing with flight: Douglass's *Narrative*, the most celebrated, mentions scarcely any details of his actual escape from slavery, for reasons Douglass makes clear in the work itself. Flight becomes an important dynamic in later black autobiographies, however, sometimes being transformed to *fight*; so the three-part form is significant. African American autobiography's use of this pattern also reveals that genre's connection with autobiography as a whole. For more than two hundred years, black Americans have employed figures of bondage, flight, and freedom to describe their experience in the land that forcibly adopted them and then kept them as stepchildren. But every life can be cast into a similar pattern, for each individual must strive to throw off the shackles of parental and societal imperatives if he or she is to seek the elusive goal of emotional and intellectual independence.

* * *

Of the numerous slave narratives published before Emancipation, Frederick Douglass's *Narrative* has long been considered the greatest and has received the most critical attention. The work epitomizes the themes and structure of the slave narrative, and while it is part of a literature of *reaction*, a rejection of and rebellion against an entire social order, it also stands at the head of the autobiographical line examined in this book. Ironically, this revolutionary work later assumed an authoritative character itself, which made it vulnerable to challenge in its turn. Douglass, the hero who helped destroy the paternalistic enslaving culture of his youth, later became a formidable father figure in his own right, a power to be symbolically slain by the next generation of black male autobiographer.

Frederick Douglass made his escape from slavery to freedom on Monday, September 3, 1838. Using borrowed seaman's clothing and identification papers, Douglass boarded a train from Baltimore to Philadelphia, then continued on to New York City the following day.

A few days later, his fiancée, Anna Murray, joined him, and the two were married. Fearing for his safety even in New York, friends sent him on to New Bedford, Massachusetts, where for the next three years Douglass earned his living through various kinds of manual labor. During these years, Douglass found time to work for the church and to enlarge his reading. Already well acquainted with the Bible and *The Columbian Orator*, a book of speeches by orators such as Thomas Sheridan, William Pitt, and Charles Fox, Douglass added Sir Walter Scott, John Greenleaf Whittier, and Combe's "Constitution of Man" to the scope of his reading.[6] Most important, however, he began reading William Lloyd Garrison's *Liberator*, the abolitionist newspaper that, as Douglass himself wrote, "became my meat and my drink."[7] The *Liberator* itself first mentions Douglass's name in its March 29, 1839 edition, reporting on a meeting of black people in New Bedford. Douglass is reported to have spoken in favor of a resolution condemning slavery and commending Garrison.[8] We see, then, that Douglass became active in anti-slavery circles soon after his move to Massachusetts. A little more than two years later, on August 11 or 12, 1841, Douglass's public career as an anti-slavery spokesman began at a meeting in Nantucket. Asked by William C. Coffin to address a white audience, Douglass spoke briefly but powerfully of his experiences as a slave. Upon hearing Douglass's talk, Garrison followed with an impassioned address, and thus began a long, mutually influential relationship. As an agent of the abolitionist movement, Douglass traveled extensively, telling and retelling his story. Four years later, he published his *Narrative*, the book that first secured his fame and his reputation, but that also fixed the pattern for the rest of his life.

Although standing at the beginning of an autobiographical line, the *Narrative* did not—could not—spring from nothing. Douglass, admittedly gifted with a genius for self-expression, nevertheless neither wrote in the language of his youth, the slave's vernacular, nor created an entirely new voice for his autobiographies. Instead, drawing from the literary tradition of the white world, the only tradition available to him, he created a voice distinctly his own.

Determining precisely which items in Douglass's reading most influenced the style of the *Narrative* is now difficult. We do know that Douglass, by learning to read as a child, enjoyed an ability forbidden slaves; even more unusual, he obtained, at about the age of twelve, a copy of *The Columbian Orator*, a book whose anti-slavery speeches helped shape ideas he claims were already in his mind, awaiting words to give them expression. As Douglass writes, "These documents enabled me to utter my thoughts, and to meet the arguments brought forward to sustain slavery" (67). Douglass also knew the Bible, and sometimes uses its speech patterns, imagery, and stories, employing particularly the language and themes of the American jeremiad both to denounce the evils of the slavery system and to declare his belief that a cleansed America could still fulfill its promise.[9] Other slave narratives may have helped Douglass shape his own story, but this case for influence could more easily be argued the other way: Douglass's work antedates all the other narratives usually most highly regarded; those of William Wells Brown, Charles Ball, Henry Bibb, Josiah Henson, Solomon Northup, J.W.C. Pennington, and Moses Roper all were published after 1845.[10] We may conjecture that Douglass became familiar with some of the narratives circulating in abolitionist circles, but a strong, direct line of influence seems impossible to establish. Some critics of Douglass sense the presence of Puritan spiritual autobiography behind the *Narrative*, but again, whether Douglass knew Cotton Mather and company before 1845 is open to question. What does seem apparent, however, is the sense of the growth and maturation of the narrator in both the spiritual autobiographies of the Puritans and of Frederick in Douglass's work, a quality that places them, along with the autobiographies of Franklin and Henry Adams, in the larger tradition of American spiritual autobiography.[11]

Several sources clearly do inform Douglass's *Narrative*. The first is Garrison's *Liberator*, which Douglass first saw in 1839 and read regularly thereafter. From the paper Douglass learned the abolitionists' arguments against slavery, but largely escaped what today seem Garrisonian stylistic excesses. A comparison of Douglass's style and Garrison's, most easily made by reading Garrison's preface to the *Narrative* and then the *Narrative* itself, shows first the abolitionist's love of the rhetoric of exclamation—strings of short, declarative sentences liberally salted with exclamation marks, cry upon cry heaped up to create a cumulative effect of outrage:

Yet how deplorable was his situation! what terrible chastisements were inflicted upon his person! what still more shocking outrages were perpetrated upon his mind! with all his noble powers and sublime aspirations, how like a brute was he treated, even by those professing to have the same mind in them that was in Christ Jesus! (10)

Garrison's use of similar devices occurs in *The Liberator* as well; this passage, for example, comes from the May 31, 1844 issue and is excerpted from a piece titled "Address to the Friends of Freedom and Emancipation in the United States":

Three million of the American people are crushed under the American Union! They are held as slaves—trafficked as merchandise—registered as goods and chattels! The government gives them no protection—the government is their enemy—the government keeps them in chains![12]

After even a little Garrison, one finds Douglass's style a welcome relief, for it is by comparison spare, controlled, and less given to flights of shock and outrage. The passage in the *Narrative* most resembling the Garrisonian style is Frederick's celebrated apostrophe to the ships on the Chesapeake Bay:

You are loosed from your moorings, and are free; I am fast in my chains, and am a slave! You move merrily before the gentle gale, and I sadly before the bloody whip! You are freedom's swift-winged angels, that fly round the world; I am confined in bands of iron! O that I were free! O, that I were on one of your gallant decks, and under your protecting wing! Alas! betwixt me and you, the turbid waters roll! Go on, go on. O that I could also go! (96)

Although undeniably skillful in its use of antithesis, which Stephen Butterfield identifies as a hallmark of Douglass's style, this passage jars us because its rhetoric is clearly the language of Douglass the writer not Frederick the speaker.[13] Like all autobiographers, Douglass cannot help but impose his voice and perceptions at the time of writing upon the autobiographical self he is creating, even upon that self as a youth. Thus, the ideas and the words of young Frederick are shaped by his creator, the Frederick Douglass of 1845, a man infinitely better read than Frederick, more mature, experienced, and sophisticated—a different man altogether. How could such shaping ever be avoided? The autobiographer cannot escape the self he has become, even to recreate objectively the self he was. Yet skillful autobiographers (and Douglass ranks among the greatest) manage to conceal this tension from the reader to the extent that they can create a consistent, believable voice for their literary alter egos. It is a tribute to Douglass's ability that we tend to accept Frederick's words, few as they are, until we reach this passage. Then we realize that no fifteen-year-old speaks this way; in fact, no one speaks this way, except in books and unless she or he has been influenced by a writer like Garrison. Douglass, by reading those very works that gradually shaped his spoken and literary style, also gradually lost his original voice, the voice of the youthful slave. He himself probably never considered the change as loss nor lamented it as such, but the reader, coming on the scene of an adolescent slave boy standing at the edge of the Chesapeake Bay and longing for freedom, realizes that the words Douglass puts into his mouth are not the words the boy could have used. The fifteen-year-old Frederick's voice is lost forever, drowned out by the distinctive voice born of Douglass's reading and of his association with the white world after his escape, the voice that he felt to be appropriate not only for his own writing but for his autobiographical self.

A second source for the *Narrative* is Douglass himself, not in the sense that the work is truly his and not the product of a ghost-writer, but in the sense that it was the product of Douglass's telling and re-telling his story countless times between 1841 and 1845. During these years, Douglass traveled thousands of miles on behalf of the Massachusetts Anti-Slavery Society and the American Anti-Slavery Society, visiting Rhode Island, Vermont, New York, Pennsylvania, New Hampshire, Ohio, and Indiana. Urged at first simply to "tell his story," Douglass soon felt the need to interpret his experience, to wield his own story as a weapon against slavery rather than allowing others to do it for him. He writes, "It did not entirely satisfy me to *narrate* wrongs; I felt like *denouncing them*."[14] The *Narrative*'s straightforward style results also from its origins in spoken language as well as in abolitionist rhetoric. The product of the give and take of the lecture platform, the *Narrative* shows the polish of an experienced communicator. Butterfield shares this assessment and notes that the elements of Douglass's style—the accumulation of denunciatory adjectives, for example—is "a device learned and tempered at public meetings and speeches and suggests a direct verbal relationship with the audience."[15]

Abolitionist thought helps shape the *Narrative*, and Douglass's numerous retellings of his story help give his written account the forceful style of public speech. Additionally, at least three other sources influence the work. The first, *The Divine Comedy*, receives only brief explicit reference, but both its structure and theme inform Douglass's work.

Early in the *Narrative*, Douglass recounts the brutal beatings his Aunt Hester received at the hands of Captain Anthony. Witnessing one such beating profoundly affects young Frederick; Douglass recalls, "It struck me with awful force. It was the blood-stained gate, the entrance to the hell of slavery, through which I was about to pass" (28). The reference to the blood-stained gate of hell recalls Dante's description of hellgate in the *Inferno*, and Douglass sets himself up to be both our Virgil through his tour of the hell of Southern slavery and one of its victims. Additionally, invoking the *Divine Comedy* early in the *Narrative* allows Douglass to link the related images of blood and hell that together characterize his monolithic vision of slavery. Blood, beginning with the blood pouring from the back of Frederick's Aunt Hester, tied and scourged like a Christ, is a fitting symbol for the slave's fate. Hester's blood covers the hellgate through which Frederick himself must later pass, and Douglass unfailingly recalls such blood whenever he wishes to emphasize the full horror of slavery. Encounters between slaveowners and overseers and their black victims inevitably end with the shedding of black blood, as in Austin Gore's murder of the slave Demby or in Andrew Anthony's brutal treatment of Douglass's younger brother, whom he threw to the ground "and with the heel of his boot stamped upon his head till the blood gushed from his nose and ears" (47, 75).

Frederick's own bloody baptism comes at the hands of Edward Covey, who strikes him on the head with a hickory slat, causing the blood to run freely; Frederick runs away to his owner and presents himself in a kind of *ecce homo* tableau:

From the crown of my head to my feet, I was covered with blood. My hair was all clotted with dust and blood; my shirt was stiff with blood. My legs and feet were torn in sundry places with briers and thorns, and were also covered with blood. (100)

Douglass links this image of the bloodied slave with hell, the second recurring image in the *Narrative*. Blood saturates the hell of Southern slavery, a world, for the purposes of the *Narrative*, utterly antithetical to the opposing heaven of freedom. The opposition between the two is illustrated by the supercharged language of Frederick's address to the Chesapeake Bay boats in which he cries, "You move freely before the gentle gale, and I sadly before the bloody whip[.] . . . I am left in the hottest hell of unending slavery" (96). When Douglass has Frederick exclaim, in the same passage, "Alas! betwixt me and you, the turbid waters roll," he suggests, to this writer at least, the Lucan parable of the rich man and Lazarus (Luke 16: 19–31), in which the ungodly rich man calls out to Abraham from his agony in the flames to send Lazarus to come and cool his tongue with a drop of water. Abraham reminds the rich man that "between us and you a great chasm has been fixed" and that no one from heaven can cross to hell just as those in hell cannot escape their punishment. In slavery, Douglass sees a perversion of the just order expressed in the parable, for in the South the poor and innocent are confined to torment, while their evil oppressors go free.

The *Narrative* presents a vision of a just world order every bit as absolute as the Lucan parable's, except that in the *Narrative* the wrong people suffer. Because the abolition of slavery is his goal, Douglass can permit himself no other vision: Southern whites are almost without exception cruel and corrupted, their victims one and all dehumanized, kept from forming the natural human ties of family and destined, sooner or later, to undergo the bloody ordeal of beating. In his second autobiography, *My Bondage and My Freedom* (1855), Douglass softens his portrait of his early life considerably, including a more positive description of his relationship with the grandparents who raised him, but in the *Narrative* he is constrained at every turn by self-imposed absolutes: absolute good versus absolute evil, absolute justice versus absolute injustice, and absolute slavery versus absolute freedom. Douglass may have later come to realize that absolute freedom, if it exists, is nearly impossible to attain, but his judgments about slavery never changed.

Structurally, the *Narrative* follows the three-part plan of the *Comedy*, for Douglass's years as a slave are both his hell, a time of dreadful suffering, and his purgatory, the time of strengthening for the paradise of freedom. Thematically, the *Narrative* resembles the *Comedy*, for if Frederick is our Virgil and a hell-bound sufferer, he is also a kind of Dante, the hero who descends into the underworld but returns unexpectedly having gained wisdom to be shared with others. As I shall discuss in a moment, this linking of Frederick with the figure of the descending and ascending hero fits well with Douglass's unconscious portrayal of his autobiographical "I" as the protagonist in the primal myth of the hero.

The two American texts that Douglass draws upon both have had incalculable influence in American life and letters. Douglass handles them in similar ways, recounting his experience in terms of the earlier work, yet showing at the same time that neither text reveals the full truth of the American experience, particularly for African Americans, and that each, accordingly, is subject to revision.

The first text is Franklin's *Autobiography*. Although several critics have noted its influence on Booker T. Washington, only one that I know of has examined its relationship to the *Narrative*. John Seelye detects in the *Narrative* a structure that mirrors that of the *Autobiography*: both works connect their heroes' social rise with journeys to the city—Franklin's to Philadelphia and Douglass's to Baltimore.[16] But whereas Franklin discovers success, Frederick's taste of greater freedom is embittered by his realization of his own former ignorance, of the full weight of slavery even in this city so close to free territory, and of white prejudice not only against slaves but against free blacks. Both Franklin and Douglass write of difficulties to be overcome, but the *Narrative* stands in counterpoint to the *Autobiography*, reminding the reader that a person of intelligence and perseverance may still not end up realizing the Benjamin Franklin version of the American success story—particularly if his or her skin is black. Franklin's "comedy," as Seelye calls it, tells only part of the story; Douglass's darker tale recounts the other side.

The same interplay of texts marks Douglass's use of the Declaration of Independence, which itself may be considered the autobiography of a nation, and which, more than any other, created the American persona.

The likelihood that Douglass knew the Declaration by 1845 is great, given the resemblances between it and his autobiography. Reading the Declaration and the *Narrative* shows that the two works share common structural elements. The Declaration begins by stating that when a people needs to separate from another nation, the reasons for the division ought to be given. The body of the piece gives the colonies' reasons—a lengthy list of grievances against the King of England for his abuses of the American colonies. It states that the colonies should be "free and independent states," possessed of the rights and powers of such states. The document concludes with a sacred pledge by the signers to strive for freedom and is completed by the famous signatures. Much of Douglass's *Narrative* resembles the central section of the Declaration, for it is a list of grievances supporting his contention that his freedom is justified. In the appendix to the *Narrative*, Douglass brings his work to a fittingly stirring conclusion, making conscious use of the rhetoric of 1776:

Sincerely and earnestly hoping that this little book may do something toward throwing light on the American slave system, and hastening the glad day of deliverance to the millions of my brethren in bonds—faithfully relying upon the power of truth, love, and justice, for success in my humble efforts—and solemnly pledging myself anew to the sacred cause,—I subscribe myself, FREDERICK DOUGLASS. (163)

"I subscribe myself"—by thus affixing his signature to the *Narrative*, Douglass evokes the revolutionary patriots who declared their freedom, and he identifies himself as one with them. In this case, freedom for African Americans is the issue not only for Douglass but for those still in bondage. Douglass makes the *Narrative* a Declaration of Independence for himself and for his race, drawing upon the wealth of associations clustering around the earlier document to give his own work added force. Additionally, he shows that the Declaration needs to be fully realized for *all* Americans. Once again, the *Narrative*, by evoking a text that proclaims American ideals, reveals the failure of their fulfillment.

*   *   *

Despite its skillful appropriation of already extant literary traditions and texts and its turning of some of those texts for its own ironic purposes, the *Narrative of the Life of Frederick Douglass* is not unique in its structure or themes. Yet it is preeminent among slave narratives. Why? First we should mention the work's intrinsic literary merit, a quality long noted by critics. Benjamin Quarles praises its "readable prose style, simple and direct, with a feeling for words. It [is] absorbing in its sensitive description of persons and places."[17] Philip Foner calls it "by far the most effective" of all the autobiographies of fugitive slaves, and quotes from a review of the work that rings true today: "Considered merely as a narrative, we never read one more simple, true, coherent, and warm with genuine feeling."[18] Houston Baker calls the *Narrative* "a consciously literary work of the first order."[19] Butterfield asserts that Douglass used language and strategies common among slave narratives, "but did them more consistently and skillfully and with a more careful blend of content and form."[20] The unusual excellence of the *Narrative* becomes apparent when one compares it with some of the other "best" of the genre. Douglass's achievement becomes even more remarkably clear when one recalls that the *Narrative* is not ghost-written (no critic or historian has ever produced evidence to the contrary) but is the work of a man with little formal education who writes better than the white ghost writers who helped produce stilted "autobiographies" like Josiah Henson's.

Not only is Douglass's *Narrative* extraordinarily well written, but it also bears the distinguishing mark of genuine autobiography: the author's successful transformation of the bare facts of his or her life into a narrative delineating the intellectual, emotional, and moral growth of an autobiographical "I" that is his or her subject. Other slave narrators fail to achieve such a synthesis, but Douglass shapes the incidents of his life to reveal his transformation from slave to public figure, orator, and champion of human rights. Douglass can tell the external events by which this startling metamorphosis occurred, but he also traces the inner changes that produced the unexpected result—a man with his own mind and voice.

Related to this process of growth in the *Narrative* is a second quality essential to autobiography: unlike other slave narrators, Douglass distinguishes between the person written about, the Frederick Bailey of the *Narrative,* and the person writing; the Frederick Douglass of

1845 looks back at the man he was, but no longer is. This distinction is important because it highlights the process of growth that is a key element in autobiography. Other slave narratives lack these qualities and therefore hardly qualify as autobiography in the deepest meaning of the term.

Besides the *Narrative*'s widely acknowledged literary excellence and its superiority as autobiography, I find a third reason for its greatness, a quality I shall call *resonance*. Douglass's work stirs us as other slave accounts do not because it suggests other, greater meaning beyond itself in ways that Douglass consciously intended and also in (at least) one way of which he was unaware.

G. Thomas Couser treats the first of these resonances in *American Autobiography: The Prophetic Mode*. He interprets Douglass's *Narrative* as standing in the tradition of the spiritual autobiography with its roots in the Bible, *Pilgrim's Progress*, and sermonic rhetoric.[21] This interpretation places the *Narrative* within the conversion narrative genre so important and popular in early American literature. This conversion motif agrees with the view of the *Narrative* that sees it as a document revealing the spiritual growth of the narrator. Couser notes Douglass's use of conversion language in what is perhaps the work's central incident, Douglass's fight with, and victory over, Covey the slave-breaker. Of that struggle, Douglass writes:

I felt as I never felt before. It was a glorious resurrection, from the tomb of slavery, to the heaven of freedom. My long crushed spirit rose, cowardice departed, bold defiance took its place; and I now resolved that, however long I might remain a slave in form, the day had passed forever when I could be a slave in fact. (105)

Douglass describes this incident in language redolent of Christian conversion and thereby consciously awakens in the reader a deeper sense of the meaning of the event. The fight with Covey is more than physical, it is spiritual—the soul's victory over satanic forces and its rising to new life. (In Douglass's *My Bondage and My Freedom*, this motif is suggested all the more strongly through Douglass's repeated reference to Covey as "snake-like," thus identifying him as the devil [122].) By expanding the meaning of the incident from that merely of a slave fighting a vicious handler to the Christian soul battling Satan, Douglass deepens the meaning of the event and makes it universally applicable.

The second resonance in the *Narrative*, the one more than any other that gives the work its greatness and enduring importance, is one of which Douglass probably had little conscious awareness. In analyzing Douglass's autobiographical handling of his childhood from a psychoanalytical perspective, Steven Weissman notes how Otto Rank first pointed out the role of the Freudian "family romance"—particularly the conflict between father and son—in the ancient myth of the birth of the male hero.[22] Weissman describes in detail the mythic elements in Douglass's recounting of his childhood but restricts his discussion to that first phase of Douglass's life. Once mythic patterns are identified, however, one is prompted to investigate whether similar patterns recur throughout Douglass's autobiography. A comparison of the *Narrative* with the myth of the hero in its entirety reveals a remarkable phenomenon: the story of Frederick, as Douglass tells it, fits the myth of the hero again and again, thereby becoming mythic itself with its protagonist cast in the ancient, glorious mold.

Joseph Campbell's *The Hero with a Thousand Faces* remains the standard treatment of the "monomyth"—the story found in every culture throughout the world, the tale relating the exploits of a male hero who sets off on a quest, battles hostile forces, seizes a prize of immense worth, and returns to his people to share with them the fruit of his struggle.[23] Campbell anatomizes the myth into its component parts, illustrating each aspect with copious examples from world folklore, mythology, and religious writings. Frederick's career parallels that of the hero of the myth in so many ways that the similarities are worth noting in detail.

This mythological hero is invariably born under mysterious or unusual circumstances. He may be born in poverty to humble parents (Jesus, for example), or his father may be divine, a god who has impregnated the hero's mother while in some disguised form (as in the many amorous exploits of Zeus). Sometimes, the hero's birth has been foretold, and the ruling king, hearing the prophecy, seeks to destroy the child, for part of the prophecy proclaims that the child will one day overthrow the king and take his throne (Herod and the Slaughter of the Innocents, for instance). Frederick's birth has in it all three of these elements, for he is born to a slave woman, that is, among the poor and despised, and his father is a white man, perhaps even his own master, who has almost godlike authority over the mother. Most important, Frederick's birth presents a threat to his father and to all slaveowners even if they do not realize it until later, when a free Frederick begins his assault on slavery with the spoken and written word.

That Frederick's father is a white man and that Frederick's birth poses a threat to the very one who gave him life are facts of incalculable importance for this study, which centers on Oedipal conflicts between fathers and sons. In the Oedipus myth, Laius, Oedipus's father, is told that his son will kill him and seize the kingdom. To prevent this, the king has the child exposed, but he is rescued and raised in secret. Years later, Oedipus meets his father at a crossroads and after a quarrel, kills him, thus fulfilling the prophecy.

Although Frederick Douglass eventually became a kind of Laius, a father figure to be overcome by Booker T. Washington, his "son" in the autobiographical tradition, we must remember that the *Narrative*'s protagonist was himself first an Oedipus, the son destined to slay his father.

Douglass, in commenting upon his own racially mixed birth, describes the unusual position of the mulatto in Southern slave society. Such a child especially offends the white mistress, who sees it as the product of her husband's infidelity, of his preference for a black woman as his sexual partner. Upon the mistress's insistence, mulatto children are usually mistreated more than other slaves, and are often sold, repeating the banishment/exposure element of the myth.

Douglass goes further with the theme of the threat of the mixed race child to the slave system by noting that a certain Southern statesman had predicted "the downfall of the slavery by the inevitable laws of population" (27). Douglass continues:

Whether this *prophecy* [emphasis added] is ever fulfilled or not, it is nevertheless plain that a very different-looking class of people are now springing up at the south, and are now held in slavery, from those originally brought to this country from Africa; and if their increase will do no other good, it will do away the force of the argument that God cursed Ham, and therefore American slavery is right. If the lineal descendants of Ham [blacks, according to the Biblical exegesis of the time] are alone to be scripturally enslaved, it is certain that slavery at the south must soon become unscriptural, for thousands are ushered into the world, annually, who, like myself, owe their existence to white fathers, and those fathers most frequently their own masters. (27)

Douglass, by the sheer fact of his mixed blood, was perhaps part of the growing "threat" to the slave system, according to the strange scriptural "logic" he cites. Douglass seems never to have felt any tension at being a half-white man sworn to overthrow the system that both gave him half his blood and then kept his whole body in bondage, nor does he have Frederick express any such ambivalence. In the myth, a remorseful Oedipus blinds himself upon realizing that *he* is the murderer of Laius and the fulfiller of the prophecy. One can hardly imagine Douglass, on the other hand, batting an eye at the overthrow of his white father's world, let alone feeling any grief for helping destroy it. In this, neither he nor Frederick fits the mythic mold, perhaps because the white blood brings with it little sense of white identity. Douglass may adopt for himself a "white" literary voice and put "white" words into Frederick's mouth; he may assimilate the ideas of "good" white people; and he may later in life have felt some pangs at his harsh characterization of his third master, Thomas Auld, in his autobiographies; but Douglass's essential identity was as a black man, not a man of mixed race who belonged to neither. He was free of the racial uncertainty that has formed the theme of much fiction by both black and white authors—the white authors usually dealing with the subject as the "problem" of the miscegenation, the blacks handling it under the theme of "passing for white."

Despite Douglass's personal freedom from the crisis of identity brought about by his mixed parentage, the fact remains that his *Narrative* is a book by a man half white directed against the white world that bred and enslaved him. Thus Douglass's narrative, like other slave narratives, displays what Butterfield calls "a kind of cultural schizophrenia." Black or half-black writers, looking for their roots in a nation which rejects them as human beings, cannot identify themselves exclusively with blacks, for then they risk losing their true identity to a mask of grinning subservience. Neither can they throw in their lot with whites only, for then they risk alienation from their fellow blacks and risk becoming collaborators with whites against blacks.[24] The *Narrative* begins a history of conflict that is genuinely Oedipal in its implications, for when Frederick struggles to be free from his white masters and overseers, we witness the conflict of blood against like blood. This dynamic is repeated in a slightly varied form throughout the tradition as black men later combat other black men—their own flesh and blood—instead of directing their effort to be free against the more obvious antagonist, the white world that continued to devise ways to enslave the African American even after the legal ending of slavery.

* * *

After the myth describes the birth of the hero and some of the circumstances of his childhood, it tells of the hero's journeys. For Frederick, the adventure begins with his removal from his grandparents' home to the great Lloyd plantation. Most of the *Narrative* describes Frederick's life in the world of his adventures, and is complete with wondrous new landscapes (the opulent Lloyd plantation, the sea journey and the city of Baltimore), hostile forces (wicked overseers like Severe and Gore); his various masters (Aaron Anthony, Hugh

Auld, and Thomas Auld); a kind helper (Sophia Auld, who treats him as a son and begins teaching him to read and write until stopped by her cold-hearted husband, Hugh); and tests to be passed. As I and virtually all critics interpret it, however, the supreme event of Frederick's "wanderings" is his fight with the slave breaker, Covey.

Frederick's year with Covey marks the nadir of his early career, a time of never-ending physical toil such as Frederick has never known before and, for the first eight months, regular, severe beatings. As Douglass describes it, the situation between young Frederick and Covey (to whom he has been sent so that his spirit might be made tractable) comes to a head in August when Frederick suffers sunstroke while winnowing wheat. Unable to continue work, he is attacked by Covey, struck in the head with a heavy slat, and abandoned. Frederick flees seven miles back to his master, Thomas Auld, hoping for sympathy and relief, but is ordered to return to Covey. On his return to Covey's farm, Frederick meets a certain Sandy Jenkins, who might be seen in the role of helper who lends the hero magical aid, for Jenkins presents Douglass with a talisman—a root that, if Frederick will carry it on his right side, will prevent Covey, or any white, from whipping him (102). "Soon after, the virtue of the root was fully tested," as Douglass writes, for Covey ambushes Frederick in the barn and tries to tie his legs and hands in order to administer a beating. But Frederick resists and battles Covey in hand-to-hand combat for two hours, drawing blood from his oppressor's throat with his fingers, thus symbolically reversing the white-black relationship that exists in the *Narrative* to this point. Here, for the first time, the slave sheds the oppressor's blood. The battle ends only when Covey, exhausted, calls it to a halt. This is Frederick's supreme test, and his victory over Covey marks, as Douglass writes, "the turning-point in my career as a slave." Never again is Frederick whipped, although he remains a slave for four more years. More important, a great change comes over him. He writes: "I was a changed being after that fight. I was *nothing* before; I WAS A MAN NOW. It recalled to life my crushed self-respect and my self-confidence, and inspired me with a renewed determination to be a FREEMAN."[25] As Campbell might express it, Frederick, through his victory over Covey, wins the boon he has come into the world of slavery to attain: the prize is the expansion of consciousness from the self-image of slave to that of free man, an equal with others. From this point on, Frederick is essentially free, although he must still wear for a time the trappings of the slave.

The standard reading of Frederick's fight with Covey sees in it the central mythic event in Douglass's autobiography—and so it is. One could also argue that it is the primal scene in male African

American autobiography as a whole, for such struggle is endlessly repeated in varied forms as the black hero, held in bondage (literal, social, or economic), finally determines to fight his oppressors, almost always embodied by white men, who control the social order. The determination to fight asserts personhood, manhood; the act is seen to establish free adult identity.

A closer reading of Douglass's description of the incident reveals tensions and ironies passed over in the standard reading, however. True, Frederick wins a kind of freedom by fighting, but I suggest that this event marked the beginning of a new kind of bondage for Douglass even as it describes the conflict between whites and blacks through the imagery of an intimate yet antagonistic embrace.

In describing Frederick's fight with Covey, Douglass writes, "I seized Covey hard by the throat; and as I did so, I rose. *He held on to me, and I to him*" (103; emphasis added). Frederick and Covey, it appears, are engaged more in a wrestling match than in a fistfight; rather than trading blows, the two men grapple with one another, Covey to bring Frederick down so that he can be tied and beaten, Frederick to resist such an eventuality. For Frederick, the struggle is ironic because, in order to be free of Covey's beating, he must embrace him in a way he has never touched any white man. Frederick discovers, too, that once he has fastened his grip on Covey, he cannot or will not let him go. The match ends only when Covey cries enough; Frederick would have apparently held on to the death.

This wrestling match image is rich in mythic associations. Frederick's unbreakable hold on Covey (and Covey's on him) suggests the folk tale of Br'er Rabbit and the Tar Baby. The moment Br'er Rabbit touches the sticky image (made by Br'er Fox as a means of catching Br'er Rabbit), he is trapped. Only his wits save him from being killed and eaten. In a similar way, Frederick finds himself trapped in his hold on Covey, and the fight that he undertakes as a way toward freedom ends up, as I will show in a moment, to be a snare.

Frederick's encounter with Covey also recalls the Genesis account of Jacob and the Angel (Genesis 32:22–32), though Covey is more devilish than angelic. After Jacob wrestles with the angel all night, the angel touches the hollow of his thigh and puts it out of joint. This tactic might seem unfair, yet the angel acknowledges that Jacob has won the match, for in changing Jacob's name to Israel, the angel tells him, "you have striven with God and men, and have prevailed" (v. 28). This wrestling match marks a key moment in Jacob's life, as the name change indicates; in becoming Israel, Jacob is one step closer to fulfilling his destiny as the father of the twelve tribes. He prevails, yet he bears in his body the mark of his victory, for he leaves the place limping from his heaven-dealt injury.

I recall these mythic associations to underline my contention that although Frederick wins something crucially important by fighting Covey, he also loses something. True, he ceases to be a slave in his own mind and feels his manhood for the first time. Yet as Jacob's victory seals his destiny as the father of the nation of Israel, so does Frederick's victory seal his new identity. No longer a slave, he moves immediately from that discarded self toward that which he later fully assumes in the final scene of the *Narrative*: anti-slavery warrior, solemnly pledged to the "sacred cause." Douglass could have been or done nearly anything he chose, so manifold were his intellectual gifts. But I argue that from the moment of his triumph over Covey, this man was destined to assume only one identity: freedom fighter, a fulfillment as apparently satisfying and "right" as is his wrestling match victory. Just as we inwardly cheer when Frederick finally decides to resist Covey, so do we rejoice when, in the final tableau of the *Narrative*, we see Frederick on the platform, telling his story for the first time, wielding it as his most powerful weapon in the battle to destroy the world that kept him a slave.

What of Frederick Douglass, though, the creator of Frederick, his autobiographical alter ego? William Andrews suggests that Douglass wrote his second autobiography ten years after the first to free himself from the identification as a Garrisonian thinker that had held him for more than a decade.[26] Although Douglass fought for abolition until it was achieved, he was, even before 1855, chafing to fight on his own terms, not on those set by another man, not even his mentor and intellectual "father," William Lloyd Garrison.

After the Civil War, Douglass devoted his life to various liberation causes; he was, for example, an early champion of women's rights and fought for racial equality. While applauding the man's achievements, one cannot help wonder if, under different circumstances, he would have chosen another life for himself. One clue to Douglass's possible diffidence toward the direction his life took lies in his attitude, in later life, toward political power. Douglass never seized such power nor sought to woo those organizations that might have helped him win elective office. By the last decade of the century, Douglass was, as Robert Factor notes, opposed to the prevailing ideas of labor, capital, agriculture, national expansion, and racial thought: "[he] was an American at odds with his country, a Republican opposed to his party's policies."[27]

By resisting Edward Covey, Frederick frees himself from his birth identity—that of the slave, but by the same act he relinquishes his freedom to become whatever new self he chooses. Frederick could not have guessed this at the time and maybe Douglass did not know it in 1845, when he wrote his *Narrative*, but perhaps by the 1850s he had begun to understand his new bondage and tried to free himself. If this is true, the title of the second autobiography, *My Bondage and My Freedom*, takes on a meaning besides the obvious one: the years between 1838 (his escape to the North) and 1855 (publication of the second autobiography) might be years of both freedom and bondage concurrently. Free from his literal slavery, Douglass is nevertheless still in bondage to an identity he could not escape.

Douglass's *Narrative*, then, the famous testament of freedom, actually includes within it some ironic counterpointing between various kinds of freedom and bondage, summarized by Frederick's victory over Covey which ultimately seems to win him the freedom never to stop fighting to be free. Is that, however, true liberation?

According to the mythic pattern that Douglass's *Narrative* follows, Frederick's victory over Covey recalls the hero's supreme ordeal in the underworld of his adventure. At what Campbell calls "the nadir of the mythological round," the hero encounters an enemy, triumphs over it, and wins the prize for which he has been questing. He then returns, bringing with him the boon that restores life to the upper world. Frederick's self-understanding undergoes a fundamental change during his fight with Covey, and he sheds his slave identity; however, the flight from the hell of slavery into external freedom has yet to be made.

Douglass made two such attempts to reach external freedom through flight. The first was undertaken in April of 1836, in conjunction with a small group of fellow slaves. The plot was discovered before it could be enacted, and Douglass spent some time in jail, he could have been sold south (a common penalty for attempted escapees), but was sent instead back to Baltimore by Thomas Auld, who apparently sensed that Douglass was marked for better things than a field hand's life. Douglass's second escape attempt, this one successful, was accomplished virtually alone, as if the hero, having entered the underworld alone and having won his victory by himself, now had to find his means of escape through an act of self-dependence, as well. Douglass did have a helper, the black sailor who lent him clothes and papers, but Douglass undertook the short train ride from Baltimore to Philadelphia alone. In the *Narrative*, Douglass gives no details of his flight, explaining that to do so would jeopardize his fellow slaves still in bondage who might use the same means he did to get to freedom. Only later in his life, after the Civil War, did Douglass disclose the details, at a time when the information could neither harm a potential runaway nor help masters seeking to prevent their slaves from escaping or searching for any who had managed to flee north. Actually, though, the escape itself is of minor importance for the *Narrative* because the true break to freedom has already been accomplished and told in detail in Douglass's battle with Covey.

Once the hero has made his way from the fantastic realm of his adventure, he must return to the world of common experience. What Frederick expects in the North, however, can hardly be called ordinary. He has lived his life in what is repeatedly called the hell of slavery, and must think that New York City will, by contrast, be that "heaven" of freedom so long held in his imagination. Douglass recalls that, upon escape, he felt like an unarmed mariner rescued from pirates and like one "who had escaped a den of hungry lions." In other words, he feels himself brought to life after having escaped certain death. At first, however, the heaven of freedom proves a great disappointment. Frederick finds himself alone, penniless, and frightened in New York, suspicious of everyone, white or black, terrified of being captured by slave hunters. True, he is technically "free," but his freedom is bought at the cost of isolation and fear—"in total darkness as to what to do, where to go, or where to stay." Although Frederick's situation quickly improves—he is taken in hand by a man concerned for fugitive slaves and is fed, housed, and sent on his way farther north—his initial taste of freedom as an experience of loneliness and fear introduces an untidy element into the dichotomous vision of the *Narrative*. Frederick's physical freedom at first proves as burdensome and confining as his so-called identity as a "free" man later would, and even the improvement of his circumstances in New Bedford cannot completely erase the misery Frederick feels along with his taste of freedom.

As Douglass enters upon his freedom, he undergoes the rite of initiation long recognized and commented on by escaped slaves themselves and by critics of the slave narratives: he changes his name to reflect his new status as a free man. Like so many others before and after him, Douglass leaves old names behind him, changing from Frederick Augustus Washington Bailey to Frederick Johnson and finally to Frederick Douglass, taking his last name from a character in Walter Scott's *Lady of the Lake*. No longer does he have to accept a name given him by an owner—he can accept a name suggested by an abolitionist acquaintance, Nathan Johnson.[28]

The hero who has fulfilled his quest and returned to the world with his prize is often rewarded with a bride, as Campbell notes in his chapter "The Hero as Lover." After Frederick escapes to the North, he immediately sends for his betrothed, Anna Murray (a free black woman), and the two are married in New York before witnesses on September 15, 1838. Like the hero who proves his potency through his struggles against hostile forces, Frederick may now enjoy his masculine power in the bridal bed. The unexpected appearance of this never-before-mentioned bride takes a reader by surprise, however, as does her almost immediate disappearance after the wedding. Douglass was married twice, the second time to a white woman (this union called down much criticism on Douglass from whites whom he had considered his friends), but neither of his wives plays a part of the slightest significance in any of his three autobiographies. Mention of wives and the suggestion of the autobiographer's sexuality are absent not only in the works of Douglass but in most of the autobiographies examined in this book. Not only do Douglass's wives receive short shrift, but so do Booker T. Washington's three wives and W.E.B. Du Bois's two. Wright's *Black Boy* and *American Hunger* end before his first marriage, and Malcolm X, while discussing his courtship and marriage, does not credit fully the influence his wife Betty had on him or his growing dependence on her during the last months of his life. Only in the autobiographical essays of James Baldwin and in Eldridge Cleaver's *Soul on Ice* does the sexuality of the writer receive detailed treatment, and in each of those two cases that sexuality is unorthodox: Baldwin is a homosexual and Cleaver is obsessed with white women.

It may be that by the 1960s, when Baldwin and Cleaver wrote, the black man's sexuality was a subject black men could or would openly discuss, but earlier writers, from Douglass through Wright, seem to have been uncomfortable with the issue. This may be one reason why women, even black women united to black men in lawful matrimony, are conspicuously ignored in this particular autobiographical line. These autobiographers may have sensed that revealing themselves as sexual beings was simply too threatening to many of their white readers, so they omit all references to involvements with females except for their mothers and other female relatives.

Douglass, one notes, quotes verbatim the contents of Frederick's marriage certificate in his otherwise brief description of his wedding to Anna Murray. He may wish to show that Frederick's marriage is licit and so offers this document as proof, in much the same way that the *Narrative* as a whole is proof of his very existence and of the veracity of the story he had told so many times on the lecture circuit. More importantly, Douglass may be subtly suggesting to his readers (most of whom were white) that Frederick, although free, can keep his sexuality in bounds; quickly and properly married, he presents no threat to any woman, black or white. Douglass was surely aware of a

fear shared by Southern and Northern whites that, once emancipation was achieved, black men would begin demanding intermarriage—sexual access—to white women. (He later came to claim that
racial discrimination could be eradicated through mixed marriages
and backed up his contention by his marriage to Helen Pitts, his white
secretary.) Here, however, he seems at pains to assure his reader that
the freed black man, himself included, does not take freedom to include access to white women. Douglass, Washington, and Du Bois all
portray themselves as somehow sexless, married primarily to the various causes to which they devoted their lives. This may be canny strategy for writers who desire their autobiographies to be untainted by
anything that could antagonize a white readership, but it also results
in the neglect of the role of women to such an extent that these early
autobiographers seem somehow to have lived in exclusively masculine worlds. The absence of the female—the prize for which the son
fights and kills the father—in an autobiographical line so closely mir-
roring the Oedipal pattern seems peculiar indeed; however, the
woman is sacrificed so that the autobiographer, perhaps already fearful that he is overstepping what some may see as his "proper bounds"
by the self-assertion connected with writing an autobiography, may
not cause further problems through even a hint of sexual self-
assertion.

More important in Douglass's case than his role of hero as lover
is the role of hero as warrior. The victorious, returning hero may also
assume this guise; his mission as warrior is distinctly defined in the
myth:

For the mythological hero is the champion not of things become but of things
becoming; the dragon to be slain by him is precisely the monster of the status
quo: Holdfast, the keeper of the past. From obscurity the hero emerges but
the enemy is great and conspicuous in the seat of power; he is enemy,
dragon, tyrant because he turns to his own advantage the authority of his
position. He is Holdfast not because he keeps the *past* but because he *keeps*.[29]

Frederick Douglass's *Narrative* ends with Frederick the hero-as-
warrior poised at the beginning of his public career as combatant
against the Holdfast of his time: the institution of slavery personified
by the Southern slaveholder. Given that the wrestling match with
Covey is the pivotal event in Frederick's career, "Holdfast" is a sin-
gularly appropriate name both for the enemy and for Frederick's
means of combat. The Southern system *did* strive literally to "hold
fast" the slave, and Covey's grasp on Frederick symbolizes its clutch-
ing grasp. But Frederick clings just as tightly—first to Covey and, in

later years, to the cause of exterminating the slave system. The *Narrative* ends with the events of the summer of 1841; Emancipation was not achieved until 1863. Once committed to the cause, Frederick Douglass held on to his pledge for more than twenty years, years of tireless effort on behalf of abolition.

The final scene of the *Narrative* recounts Frederick's first speech before a white audience; urged by William Coffin, Frederick speaks briefly of some of his experiences as a slave. This act, as others have noted, is the logical conclusion toward which the work has been moving all along: the slave who has become a man, has educated himself, and has found his own voice finally speaks. Douglass's book proper ends at a beginning point—the inauguration of the public career, and Douglass skillfully closes the gap of time between that first speech in 1841 and the book's publication in 1845 with these words: "From that time until now, I have been engaged in pleading the cause of my brethren—with what success, and with what devotion, I leave those acquainted with my labors to decide" (153). Douglass of course knows full well that most of his early readers would have been thoroughly acquainted with his recent labors—labors whose chief fruit was the very book those readers held in their hands, one of the most popular best sellers of its time.

Although the *Narrative* proper ends with a satisfying sense of closure (the speech for which Frederick's whole life to that point has been but preparation) while simultaneously reminding the reader that Frederick/hero has undertaken further exploits since that time, a disquieting detail appears in Douglass's account of that speech. He writes: "But while attending an anti-slavery convention at Nantucket, . . . I felt strongly moved to speak. . . . It was a *severe cross*, and I took it up reluctantly. I felt myself a slave, and the idea of speaking to white people weighed me down" (153; emphasis added). Frederick's desire to speak conflicts with his sense of what actually making a speech means to him: "a severe cross." The reference to the words of Jesus (Matthew 16:24 and parallels) is certainly intentional; in the Gospel account, Jesus tells his disciples, "If any man would come after me, let him deny himself and take up his cross and follow me." Is Frederick's reluctance to shoulder the cross of public speaking rooted in his realization that self-denial is the price to be paid? Without pushing this point too far, I suggest that Frederick may feel a tension at this point of decision: he seems to realize that, as in the fight with Covey, once he commits himself to speak, he must accept the consequences. The self-denial may entail abandoning personal ambition in order to devote his life to the greater cause. Frederick could not have fully realized such things on that August day in 1841, but Frederick

Douglass writing the *Narrative* in 1845 surely did, and may give slight indication here that the work of the intervening years has not been completely free of conflicting personal desires—perhaps his need to fight for the abolitionist cause versus his desire for a private life.

The second disquieting note in this final scene is the admission that Frederick felt himself a slave and so was uneasy speaking before a white audience. This feeling appears to contradict Frederick's realization after the fight with Covey: "however long I might remain a slave in form, the day had passed forever when I could be a slave in fact" (105). But here, three years later, when confronted with a white audience, Frederick again feels himself a slave, reverting, for the moment, to the self-identity he thought he had left behind. Once again, the demarcation between slavery and freedom proves not as clear as the *Narrative*'s system of images would at first suggest, and again, Frederick's identity as a free man and warrior in the struggle for freedom is qualified. The free man on the verge of his illustrious public career inwardly feels himself a slave; the freedom fighter sees his call as a "severe cross," which he takes up reluctantly.

Douglass's *Narrative*, then, reveals a more complex vision of the relationship between bondage and freedom than a cursory reading first reveals. Its vision of freedom particularly turns out to be more troublesome than Douglass realized. The *Narrative*, however, cannot indicate what the later life of Frederick Douglass seems to bear out: namely, that the portrait of Frederick as a man destined for agonistic relationships later imposed itself upon Frederick's creator, Douglass himself. The pattern most strikingly shows itself in Douglass's relationship with William Lloyd Garrison, long Douglass's helper and friend and the author of the lengthy preface to the *Narrative*. As long as Douglass was content to live the role of Garrison's protégé and was willing to narrate the story of his life as a slave without interpreting its meaning, the two men's relationship went smoothly. But by 1847, when Douglass determined to print his own abolitionist newspaper, he had also come to oppose some of Garrison's most cherished principles. Douglass undertook the publication of his paper despite Garrison's opposition, thereby straining his friendship with the other man. The final break between them occurred in 1851 in a dispute about the advisability of political action to end slavery. Garrison was so incensed with Douglass that he thereafter refused to speak to him or even be in the same room with him. The abolitionist apparently resented Douglass's independence and seemed to believe that Douglass owed him loyalty for all he had done for him. A subtle paternalism, if not racism, was at work in Garrison, but Douglass, for his part, once set upon *his* course, would not change direction even to preserve his friendship with Garrison. The two men devoted to the same cause came into conflict in an ironic variation of Frederick's fight with Edward Covey in which two assailants also took hold of each other and refused to give up the fight.

In his conflict with Garrison, as with many of his later undertakings, Douglass assumed the heroic role that he first devised for Frederick in the *Narrative*. Douglass was, by all accounts, a strong personality, dominating other people (whether in hand-to-hand combat or on the speaking platform); himself (never shirking his call as spokesman, servant, and leader of his people however he may have struggled inwardly); and the literary form he chose to use (the slave narrative, which he perfected and in which no other writer surpassed his achievement). But in achieving dominance, he became a dominator himself, a potent father figure, a folk hero, for black Americans · of his own and succeeding generations. Douglass's growth into mythic stature has deep implications for later black writers, but even he seems somehow overwhelmed by his achievement in the *Narrative*. Douglass wrote two later autobiographies, *My Bondage and My Freedom* (1855) and *Life and Times of Frederick Douglass* (1881, revised 1892); neither, I believe, approaches the excellence of the *Narrative*. William L. Andrews, on the other hand, argues forcefully that *My Bondage and My Freedom* is much more than an expanded version of the *Narrative* and that in itself it embodies a vision quite different from that of the earlier work. Andrews speaks for several recent critics who, in re-evaluating Douglass's autobiographies, find hitherto unrecognized excellences in *My Bondage and My Freedom* while deploring its long neglect.[30] Douglass's second work, in Andrews's opinion, is his greatest. I do not find it so. More to the point, it is not *My Bondage and My Freedom*, with its vision of its protagonist seeking a place of belonging as the leader of a black community, that has created the autobiographical line that this book explores. It is Douglass's depiction of himself as "heroic loner," to use a term Andrews employs, that has roused later black male autobiographers either to react against that image and consciously portray themselves as leaders devoted to forming and leading community (as Booker T. Washington does) or to see themselves in a solitude similar to Douglass's (as do Du Bois in *Dusk of Dawn*, Wright in *Black Boy* and *American Hunger*, and Malcolm in *The Autobiography of Malcolm X*). All the protagonists in these works move into community for a time—Du Bois into the Niagara Movement and then into the NAACP, Wright into the Communist Party, and Malcolm in the Black Muslims—but each must eventually leave community and strike out on his own once again, for his vision has outgrown that of the group, and his presence threatens the communal life. Even Douglass, who devoted his entire adult life to the cause of the greater good of the American community both white and black, was always something of a loner, usually out of step with the tenor of his times. Douglass's persona in the *Narrative*, always in the world but never quite one with it, represents more fully the vision of self held by most autobiographers treated here than does Douglass's altered self in *My Bondage and My Freedom*.

2: Assuming the Mantle: Booker T. Washington

In 1856, one year after the publication of *My Bondage and My Freedom*, Booker T. Washington was born in Franklin County, Virginia. After Emancipation, his family moved to Malden, West Virginia, where Washington's stepfather had found work in a salt furnace. Booker himself worked first in the furnace and then in a coal mine before setting out, in 1872, for the Hampton Normal and Agricultural Institute in Hampton, Virginia, a school for blacks run by General Samuel C. Armstrong. Driven by an intense desire for knowledge and success, Booker worked his way through school, graduated, and after teaching in West Virginia for three years, attended seminary in Washington, D.C. before being called back to Hampton to work with Armstrong. In 1881 the Alabama legislature voted funds to establish a school on the model of Hampton in Tuskegee; the citizens of that town asked General Armstrong to send them a man to get the project under way. He sent Washington, and the saga of Washington and Tuskegee began.

Washington undertook his work with definite ideas about the kind of education the school should offer. He saw around him many poor, unskilled black women and men, and he determined to provide them training in practical arts as well as academics. Consequently, the institute developed a curriculum teaching among other things carpentry, blacksmithing, farming, tailoring, dairy farming, brick manufacturing, masonry, and home economics. Washington believed that African Americans should work their way up from the bottom of the heap where they found themselves; to make themselves indispensable to the economy of the nation, they must equip themselves with a host of skills. Through hard work, blacks would win the respect of their communities while improving themselves economically and socially. Washington propounded his philosophy of education, economics, and society many times, but nowhere more eloquently than in his address to the Atlanta Cotton Exposition in 1895. Speaking to a large audience composed primarily of white Southerners, Washington pleaded for a cooperative effort between white and black Southerners in all matters economic while omitting a call for full social equality between the races. The most famous and often-quoted sentence from the speech summarizes his view: "In all things that are purely social we can be as separate as fingers, yet one as the hand in all things essential to mutual progress."[1] This position, called accommodationist by Washington's critics because it seemed to open the door to social persecution of blacks in the South while attempting to placate Southern whites fearful of the intermixing of the races, resulted from a complicated set of forces at work on Washington. On the one hand, he believed in the appropriateness of the education Tuskegee was offering. He realized that most blacks would benefit more from industrial and agricultural education than from pure academics, for the community had only limited need of teachers, preachers, and other scholars. Second, he was willing to wait for social equality for blacks because he could afford to alienate neither his Southern neighbors nor his Northern benefactors, few of whom were ready to grant equal social status to blacks, no matter how well educated they were. Washington must have felt that social privileges were a fair trade-off for the moment if only his school and his programs could exist and continue their work. If Washington was later grieved by the abuses against his people (abuses brought about at least in part because of his accommodationist policies) and hurt by the severe criticism of a younger generation of black intelligentsia, he never publicly abandoned his policies or programs. He did, however, undertake a secret campaign on a limited scale to help blacks in trouble and worked privately to eliminate the scourge of lynching.

The year 1895 inaugurated Booker T. Washington's twenty-year reign as the most popular and powerful black man in the nation. It also marked a "passing of the colors" from one generation of black leadership to another, as Washington himself notes: "Frederick Douglass died in February, 1895. In September of the same year I delivered an address in Atlanta at the Cotton States Exposition."[2] In *My Larger Education*, his third autobiography (1911), Washington describes how surprised and embarrassed he felt at being encouraged, upon the death of Douglass, to take his place as the new "leader of the Negro people." Assuming the mythic role of the rustic naif who suddenly has greatness thrust upon him or her ("I was at that time merely a Negro school teacher in a rather obscure industrial school"), Washington underplays his qualifications for taking the mantle of

Frederick Douglass. But the assumption of the mantle appears inevitable, and nowhere does Washington hint that he seriously considered refusing it. His claim of ignorance about the "functions and duties of a leader" and of the expectations of the "coloured people or of the rest of the world" is followed immediately by his tacit acceptance of the office: "It was not long, however, before I began to find out what was expected of me in the new position" (*Education* 426).

The carefully modulated voice that Washington adopts for all his autobiographies dictates that his stance toward Douglass will be deferential and his reaction at being hailed Douglass's successor be self-effacing embarrassment. However, Washington's attitude toward Douglass, his "father" in the saga of African American leadership as well as in the autobiographical line here examined, is actually somewhat more complex than the respectfully subservient tone in these passages. Even in 1895, I suggest, Washington *wanted* to be recognized as Douglass's successor, an identity that became more and more important to him after the turn of the century, when he felt his position threatened by W.E.B. Du Bois. But besides desiring to identify himself with the renowned abolitionist, thereby strengthening his own place in the line of leadership, Washington offers himself and his autobiographies as correctives or replacements for Douglass's life and works. As Washington himself puts it, Douglass's great work had been abolition and the recognition of black women's and men's rights as individuals and as citizens, but this has not prepared Douglass for "the equally difficult task of fitting the Negro for the opportunities and responsibilities of freedom" (*Education* 424). A new leader with a new vision is needed; despite his modesty, Washington clearly sees himself as that leader. If the older generation of black leaders showed "something lacking in their public utterances," Washington would fill up the void with the sound of his own voice.

Washington acknowledges that Frederick Douglass influenced and inspired him from early childhood. In *My Larger Education* he writes:

> Even before I had learned to read books or newspapers, I remember hearing my mother and other coloured people in our part of the country speak about Frederick Douglass's wonderful life and achievements. I heard so much about Douglass when I was a boy that one of the reasons why I wanted to go to school and learn to read was that I might read for myself what he had written and done. (422)

It is hardly surprising that Douglass inspired Washington; he served as model for many African Americans of the generation that followed him. By the time of Emancipation, Douglass was internationally famed as author and lecturer, friend of politicians and humanitarians, and adviser to Abraham Lincoln himself. Well might a black child born into the poverty and degradation of slavery look to Douglass as the model of the black who had successfully lifted her or himself from the lowest rung of American society to the highest.

By the 1880s, when Washington was building Tuskegee and the nation as a whole was beginning to focus on the ruthless capitalist and expansionist goals that flowered in the Gilded Age of the nineties, Douglass must have begun to seem a revered relic of the past to the younger generation of ambitious black men. Robert Factor notes the apparent contradiction between Douglass's popularity and prestige, which never waned during his lifetime and have hardly been tarnished since then, and his disaffection from the powerful organizations and popular ideas of the late nineteenth century.[3] But as it turns out, Washington still easily drew a connection between himself and Douglass, thereby establishing himself as Douglass's logical successor, for even before Washington's birth, Douglass had expressed his thinking about the freed black American's economic and educational needs in words that could have been penned by Washington.

In his first autobiography, *The Story of My Life and Work* (1900), Washington notes the visit of Douglass to the Tuskegee campus to deliver the commencement address of 1892. Although Washington does not mention it, the subject of the address was one that Douglass had used on the lecture circuit for years: "Self-Made Men"—a topic that accorded well with the philosophy of the school's president. Washington takes care to note the similarities between Douglass's thought and his own:

Mr. Douglass had the same idea concerning the importance and value of industrial education that I have tried to emphasize. . . . In fact, the more I have studied the life of Mr. Douglass *the more I have been surprised to find his far-reaching and generous grasp of the whole condition and needs of the Negro race.* [emphasis added][4]

Washington's "surprise" at Douglass's acuity is slightly patronizing, but Washington underlines Douglass's early agreement with his own ideas of industrial education by quoting at great length from a letter Douglass wrote to Harriet Beecher Stowe in 1853 advocating the establishment of an "INDUSTRIAL COLLEGE in which shall be taught several important branches of the mechanical arts" (*Life and Work* 58). Douglass continues to assert that "colored men must learn trades; must find new employments; new modes of usefulness to society, or . . . they must decay under the pressing wants to which their condition is rapidly bringing them" (*Life and Work* 50).

Those who claim that Washington represents an aberrance in the militant line of black leadership that by rights should move directly from Douglass to W.E.B. Du Bois apparently neglect both Douglass's and Du Bois's recognition, years apart, of the necessity that black Americans learn trades as well as academic subjects and that they establish themselves economically at the same time that they strive for full civil rights. That Douglass agreed with the work of Washington and Tuskegee is demonstrated not only by the contents of the letter he wrote three years before Washington's birth but also by his willingness to speak at Tuskegee in 1892. The year before, Douglass had addressed a dinner honoring Washington; in turn, Washington sponsored three banquets honoring Douglass, contributing one hundred dollars on each occasion.[5] Douglass endorsed Washington when he addressed the Bethel Literary and Historical Society in Washington, D.C., and advocated Washington's policies before its intellectual and influential members.[6] The two men obviously agreed on some basic principles of self-help for the black American.

It is important to Washington, then, to establish Douglass's agreement with and approval of his own philosophy of industrial education and its embodiment at Tuskegee Institute. The endorsement of the most famous and respected black American must certainly have seemed, in Washington's eyes, to help legitimize his program and his own succession to the leadership of African Americans. Washington also seeks, however, to establish a link between Douglass's self-image and the persona he had adopted for himself. Here Washington's need to serve as a corrective for the life of Douglass begins to be apparent. Uncomfortable with the militant, rebellious portrait of Frederick drawn in the *Narrative*, Washington prefers to concentrate on the persona of Douglass's later autobiographies—attempting, perhaps, to suggest that the Frederick of the *Narrative* is not Douglass's "finished" or even "true" self, but a provisional self created to survive the pressure of slavery days and then abandoned with relief when freedom arrived.

As we have noted, Washington acknowledged Douglass's influence over him in *My Larger Education*. After remarking that he had heard of Douglass early in his life and wanted to attend school to read for himself what Douglass had written and said, Washington continues: "In fact, one of the first books that I remember reading was his own story of his life, which Mr. Douglass published under the title of 'My Life and Times.' This book made a deep impression upon me, and I read it many times" (*Education* 422–23). This passage is noteworthy because it catches Washington in a slip of memory. He states that the book he read and reread was *My Life and Times*. Frederick Douglass did write a book with a similar title—his third autobiography, first published in 1881 and reprinted and updated in 1892. But by 1881, the year of the book's first appearance, Washington would have been twenty-five years old and just beginning his career at Tuskegee. The book Washington knew as a young man was either Douglass's 1845 *Narrative* or *My Bondage and My Freedom* (1855). The similarity of titles—*My Life and Times* (actually, the title is *Life and Times of Frederick Douglass*) and *My Bondage and My Freedom*—leads me to believe that it was *My Bondage and My Freedom* that Washington probably thought he had read as a boy. But why confuse the title? Washington certainly knew the *Life and Times of Frederick Douglass* as well as the earlier autobiographies, so he may have inadvertently supplied a garbled title, confusing a book more recently read with one read many years earlier. But if Washington is caught by a faulty memory, there may be a good reason why he unconsciously claims to have been deeply impressed by "My Life and Times." This Douglass autobiography best fits how Washington preferred to look at Douglass; the book also presents a portrait of a self-made man turned public servant that supplies the model Washington would have felt most comfortable with himself.

Life and Times of Frederick Douglass was written partly to make money for its author, but it did not. Despite Stephen Butterfield's praise for its rhetorical polish, it is an unsatisfying book, particularly for those who know the *Narrative* and *My Bondage and My Freedom*. Douglass was never averse to quoting verbatim passages from his earlier autobiographies in his later ones: in *My Bondage and My Freedom*, he does this several times and unabashedly informs the reader when he does so. The first two autobiographies differ in many ways, as William Andrews has shown. But the differences between *My Bondage and My Freedom* and *Life and Times* are few and insignificant. Douglass abridges the narrative of his early life to make room for events in the latter part, but the reader does not sense any reshaping of Douglass's vision of his childhood and youth. *Life and Times* virtually quotes *My Bondage and My Freedom* with some stylistic changes and omissions. The earlier book is not rewritten; it is *copied* into the later autobiography. We can assume either that Douglass had wearied of retelling his early life (how many times did he tell the tale while on the abolitionists' lecture circuit?) or that he was well satisfied with the written form of the account as it appeared in *My Bondage and My Freedom*. At any rate, the first part of *Life and Times* is a repeat of the earlier book.

When Douglass begins to recount his life after about 1854, the last year covered by his second autobiography, the reader detects a change in the writing. Gone is the intense passion that sparked the *Narrative*; gone, too, is the heroic imagery that holds the *Narrative* together and still informs, though to a lesser degree, *My Bondage and My Freedom*. These losses are perhaps inevitable, for Douglass, writing in 1881, is recalling events from many years earlier. Although he tells stories of stirring events and famous people, the fire is largely gone. Additionally, *Life and Times* was written after the end of slavery, and Douglass's greatest work, it can be argued, was on behalf of abolition. When he wrote his two earlier autobiographies, slavery was intact, and his works still served as weapons against it. By the year *Life and Times* was published, slavery was a thing of the past—the war had been fought, and the abolitionists' cause had proved victorious. The plight of many Southern blacks was still desperate, but their literal enslavement was ended.

Two other factors may account for the quality of the second half of *Life and Times*. Douglass's recollection of his later life begins to read like a list of honors received and positions held; because Douglass did rise to the pinnacle of national fame, he could hardly tell his story without mentioning the public offices he held and the recognition he received. If *Life and Times* begins to sound like "first I did this, then I held that post, then I traveled there," it is because Douglass's later life was characterized by such constant activity. But the practice of listing—one event strung after another without any shape except for that of chronology—may result from another phenomenon occurring frequently in autobiographies of older writers as they move forward in time toward their most recent experiences. Many autobiographies degenerate into chaos (Rousseau's *Confessions* is a prime example) because the writer is too close to the events being narrated to be able to give them shape. An ordering metaphor is lost, and the works lapse into a series of events ordered only by time. This happens to Douglass with an attendant loss of form and interest. The young Douglass was able to write his *Narrative* as a cohesive whole, united by the mythic element, but the older Douglass was unable to achieve a similar vision in his final autobiography.

Douglass's *Life and Times* is his least satisfactory autobiography, but I believe it is the one Booker T. Washington felt most comfortable with, for the image of Douglass portrayed in it—the underprivileged youth who rises to prominence and devotes himself to a life of public service in the manner of Benjamin Franklin—was the image Washington adopted for himself and worked to maintain all his adult life.

Washington's identification with and favoring of the persona in Douglass's later autobiographies suggest, as I have stated, a corrective stance toward the *Narrative*. Washington's most famous autobiography, *Up from Slavery*, is, in both content and style, a "corrective rewrite" of Douglass's masterpiece, as I shall argue in a moment. As a way of introducing *Up from Slavery* and its implicit stance vis-à-vis the *Narrative*, I begin with an episode from his work that states explicitly how Washington sees himself and his life in relationship to the career and accomplishments of Frederick Douglass.

*   *   *

In 1899, Washington and his wife were given a trip to Europe as a gift from some admirers. He mentions meeting in England some of the men and women who had, years earlier, "known and honoured the late William Lloyd Garrison, the Hon. Frederick Douglass, and other abolitionists." Thus Washington deftly reminds the reader that Douglass, too, had traveled to Europe and had met prominent people. On his return trip, Washington has an experience that further connects him with Douglass and that he uses to make a point about his relationship with the other man and between the two different times in which they lived:

After three months in Europe we sailed from Southampton in the steamship *St. Louis*. On this steamer there was a fine library that had been presented to the ship by the citizens of St. Louis, Mo. In this library I found a life of Frederick Douglass, which I began reading. I became especially interested in Mr. Douglass's description of the way he was treated on shipboard during his first or second visit to England. In this description he told how he was not permitted to enter the cabin, but had to confine himself to the deck of the ship. A few minutes after I had finished reading this description I was waited on by a committee of ladies and gentlemen with the request that I deliver an address at a concert which was to be given the following evening. And yet there are people who are bold enough to say that race feeling in America is not growing less intense! (*Up from Slavery* 368)

In *My Bondage and My Freedom*, Frederick Douglass does indeed relate an incident such as Washington describes. On his first journey to England, in 1845, he was prevented from sailing as a cabin passenger because of the objections of some Americans on board. Consigned to the second cabin, Douglass soon was visited by many of the white passengers, his case a minor *cause célèbre* during the voyage. The intended insult became an opportunity for a moral triumph and is narrated as such by Douglass.

Forty-four years later, this incident is nothing more than an old tale in a book shelved in a ship's library, where it is found by another black man whose circumstances are somewhat similar. One is struck by the coincidental perfection of the scene as Washington relates it: he "happens" upon a life of Douglass, he "happens" to be reading of Douglass's shipboard experience (some 250 pages into the account), and he just happens, at that very moment, to be invited to address the entire ship—an invitation that throws into sharp contrast the situations of the two men. Douglass was allowed on ship, but not offered first-class accommodations; Washington is free to have whatever rooms he wishes and is given the honor of speaking to the assembled passengers. "How far we have come!" is the message, the message Washington wishes to convey when he evokes Douglass. The moral victory of Douglass is glossed over; improved race relations are more important for Washington's purposes. Douglass is relegated to his book, an historic curiosity, manageable, something that can be taken up and put down at will. In this case, Douglass is put back on the shelf so that his successor may receive another honor. The past gives way to the present, where everything is improving every day in every way.

The optimistic tone Washington adopts in his recollection of his ocean voyage—such a different experience from Douglass's years earlier—is the first thing that strikes a reader who comes to *Up from Slavery* after Douglass's *Narrative*. Both autobiographers begin their works with a description of their childhoods in slavery, but Washington seems to have lived in a world different from the one in which Douglass suffered, or at least Washington is determined to offer up to his readers a vastly different view of that world. Washington's world view softens the horrors of slavery as Douglass describes them and portrays the South of the Reconstruction era and the Gilded Age as an idyllic pastoral world populated by hard-working blacks and friendly, encouraging whites. Such a view has in some quarters earned Washington criticism since *Up from Slavery* was published and has subjected him to almost universal scorn since the rise of the Civil Rights Movement in the late 1950s. Yet, as Houston Baker suggests, there is more to Washington and to his autobiography than our current view of African American history readily allows. Baker asserts (rightly, I believe) that Washington intentionally adopts the "minstrel mode" of rhetorical discourse, a mode complete with black stock characters, situations, jokes, and dialect borrowed from the popular minstrel show entertainments of his time.[7] He employs this mode, so offensive today but so popular at the turn of the century, not because it is the only style and tone available to him (Washington could write standard English as well as anyone could), but because he understands that the only way to be heard is to speak in a voice acceptable to the largely white readership of *Up from Slavery*.

This point must be recognized in any account of Washington if we want to find in him more than a subservient accommodationist to the turn-of-the-century whites' agenda for African Americans. (Washington is not altogether innocent of such charges, a fact few would dispute.) However, those who are offended by *Up from Slavery*—and I count myself among them—finding its world view hopelessly (sometimes laughably) optimistic and blind to the realities of its era and seeing in Booker, its protagonist, a character too virtuous, too eager to please, in short, too good to be true, readers who much prefer the "tougher" style of the *Narrative* and its rebellious hero, who seems somehow more current a figure than Booker, those readers, I claim, need to place much of the blame for *Up from Slavery*'s offensiveness not on Washington but on the exigencies of his time. Washington read, better than we can, perhaps, the reality of late-nineteenth-century America, a time when some progressive humanitarians wanted to see the African American "rise" economically if not socially. But the mood of the era also dictated that black Americans should "keep their place"—and their place, in many eyes, was as laborers dedicated to helping the nation and the South particularly expand and develop economically. If the nation would not accept an autobiography from the newly acknowledged leader of the black race in an angry, militant style reminiscent of Frederick Douglass's, then the blame must lie primarily with the mood of the time, not with Booker T. Washington. It is true that Washington could have refused to write in the ingratiating style he chooses for his autobiography; it is also true, though, that a radically different *Up from Slavery* might not have been published or, if it had, might have alienated the very people whose contributions kept the Tuskegee Institute solvent. A Booker Washington in the style of the Frederick of Douglass's *Narrative* would also, I believe, have conflicted with Washington's genuine sense of himself; by every indication, the Booker of *Up from Slavery* actually does accord in most ways with the character of Washington as it revealed itself in the man's public and private utterances and in the conduct of his life. By adopting the tone and style he uses in *Up from Slavery*, Washington knowingly involved himself in a trade-off: tell the public what it wants to hear in a way it finds acceptable so that the public will accept and support the philosophy and implementation of the philosophy of Booker T. Washington and the Tuskegee Institute. Critics from W.E.B. Du Bois to our own time have castigated Washington for his willingness to make this concession, and the controversy over his choice will not soon be resolved. Washington's severest critics point, with justification, to his apparent willingness to accommodate himself to the horrendous abuses of African Americans' civil rights during the period now known as "the nadir" of black American life in this country; they must also, however, acknowledge the nearly miraculous accomplishments of Washington in creating from three abandoned plantation outbuildings a full scale industrial and agricultural college constructed by its own students with bricks they made themselves—a feat Washington with some justification compares to the achievement of the ancient Israelites who worked in Egypt under similarly harsh conditions.

The very tone of *Up from Slavery* serves as a corrective of Douglass's *Narrative*, as if Washington declares from the opening paragraphs that a new day and time demands a new telling of the African Americans' past and of their present. At the same time, Washington wants to identify himself with Frederick Douglass and the line of black leadership, as his use of the forms established by Douglass and the other slave narrators shows.

A reader who turns to *Up from Slavery* after having read other slave narratives, Douglass's in particular, is immediately struck by the many ways Washington casts his first paragraphs into pre-established molds. Houston Baker notices the similarities, stating that the first chapter of *Up from Slavery* is "almost an imitation of Douglass's *Narrative*."[8] Indeed, Washington covers much of the same information found in the first chapter of the *Narrative*. Like Douglass, he begins, "I was born," and proceeds to tell the place of his birth, his ignorance of the exact date because accurate records were not kept for slaves, and something about his parents—that his mother was a black slave and his father a white man of unknown identity. The kind of information given in Washington's first chapter recalls Douglass, but the tone is different, as noted by Henry Louis Gates, Jr.:

Douglass's neatly structured, uncompromising antitheses and his multiple use of the trope of chiasmus become qualified in Washington's saga by curiously compromising and demeaning parenthetical "explanations" of his assertions.

"My life had its beginning in the midst of the most miserable, desolate, and discouraging surroundings," Washington assertively enough begins his second paragraph. Then he qualifies this: "This was so, however, not because my owners were especially cruel, for they were not, as compared with many others." Furthermore, in his first paragraph, Washington transforms Douglass's magnificently determinant rhetorical gesture into a poor attempt to amuse. Douglass writes, "I was born in Tuckahoe, near Hillsborough, and about twelve miles from Easton, in Talbot County, Maryland. I have no accurate knowledge of my age, never having seen any authentic record containing it. By far the larger part of the slaves know as little of their ages as horses know of theirs, and it is the wish of most masters within my knowledge to keep their slave thus ignorant." Washington's revision confirms the presence of a drastically altered rhetorical principle: "I was born a slave on a plantation in Franklin County, Virginia. I am not sure of the exact place or exact date of my birth, but at any rate I suspect I must have been born somewhere at sometime."[9]

Gates's close analysis identifies the "drastically altered rhetorical principle" that informs *Up from Slavery*: Washington adapts Douglass's forms, but time after time recasts the content, everywhere softening the harshness, downplaying the brutality, flattening the emotion. He seems to be correcting the strong anti-slavery views of the earlier writer, replacing them with a milder version of the institution of slavery, a vision popularized by later writers of romantic Southern fiction. Although Washington's first chapter tells of harsh living conditions—life in a primitive, cold cabin, long hours of hard work, poor and insufficient food—he studiously avoids mention of physical violence perpetrated by whites against black slaves. Having been only nine years old when slavery was abolished, Washington may have witnessed few violent acts or remembered few that he may have seen, but his opening chapter contrasts sharply with Douglass's in his recollection of the relationship between blacks and whites in the antebellum South. Douglass's central metaphor for the relationship between the blacks and whites is bloody violence, introduced and epitomized by Aaron Anthony's beating of Frederick's Aunt Hester. But when Washington comes to describe the relationship between the races in his first chapter, we find something quite different from Douglass's account of brutality. Washington asserts that there was no bitterness among the blacks on his plantation toward their white owners and that the majority of slaves in the South who were treated decently did not feel bitter toward whites (*Up from Slavery* 220). He goes on to tell tales of slaves mourning the deaths of their white owners lost in the war, of slaves protecting the white women on the plantations when the men were absent, even of former slaves helping with the education of the children of former owners. Washington takes pains to assert the trustworthiness of slaves and the reluctance of some to accept emancipation when it arrived. He crowns his musing on the relationship of blacks and whites in pre-war days with these words: "Ever since I have been old enough to think for myself, I have entertained the idea that, notwithstanding the cruel wrongs inflicted upon us, the black man got nearly as much out of slavery as the white man did." Thus does Washington summarize, with perfectly deadpan "minstrel show nonsense" the whites' fantasy of life in the antebellum South. Those whites who needed to maintain, for whatever private or public reason, that blacks did not really fare so badly under slavery, find here a black man's testimony that their position is valid. Those whites who denounced slavery could also take comfort in reading that the conditions they once deplored were not as bad as they had thought. Granted that Washington's experience of slavery was much more limited than Douglass's, and granted that one could find authentic instances of every case of tender feelings between owner and slave related by Washington, one today is still disconcerted at reading Washington's first chapter. The form recalls Douglass, but imagine Douglass ever asserting that blacks got nearly as much from slavery as whites did. Only when we understand Washington's strategy in *Up from Slavery* do some of the absurdities (there are worse ones to come) make sense.

If some of Washington's stories about the relationships between blacks and their white owners as described in the first chapter of *Up from Slavery* strike the reader as selective at best and intentionally misleading at worst, they nevertheless sound like things that could have actually happened. But in his effort to put the best construction on race relations in the post-war South, Washington is at his most rhetorically daring: in his account of the Ku Klux Klan, he verges on the absurd, taking minstrelsy, as Baker might express it, to a new height. In Chapter 4 of *Up from Slavery*, Washington describes the activity of the Klan in West Virginia in the late 1870s, when he was teaching school before going to Washington, D.C. for seminary training. In a comic description of Klan purpose and activity, he writes, "The 'Ku Klux' were bands of men who had joined themselves together for the purpose of regulating the conduct of the coloured people, especially with the object of preventing the members of the race from exercising any influence in politics" (254). "Regulating the conduct of the coloured people" is Washington's euphemism for the terrorizing of blacks by whites, the threats, the burnings, the beatings, and the lynchings. He does admit that some churches were burned, that "many innocent people were made to suffer," and even that "during the period not a few coloured people lost their lives," but again we find the technique by which Washington is able both to register a wrong and to understate it to a remarkable degree. Here again, as with his description of blacks' conditions under slavery, Washington carefully reminds the reader that Klan violence is a thing of the past:

I have referred to this unpleasant part of the history of the South simply for the purpose of calling attention to the great change that has taken place since the days of the "Ku Klux." Today there are no such organizations in the South, and the fact that such ever existed is almost forgotten by both races. There are few places in the South now where public sentiment would permit such organizations to exist. (255)

Washington's statement about the end of Klan activity is correct: by the 1870s the organization had largely disappeared. But the Klan did not go out of business because race relations had dramatically improved. It stopped its reign of terror because its goal—the subjection of Southern blacks—had been realized. A younger generation might have had no first-hand knowledge of Klan tactics, but hundreds of older men and women would never and could never forget it had existed: it still existed in their minds, for the memories of terror and death do not quickly fade. Washington here shows his determination to recreate the South to fit his vision of what it should ideally be—a paradise of racial harmony where black and white would work together but live separately. Ironically, the Klan, whose disappearance Washington seizes as a sign of progress in Southern race relations, was reactivated in 1915, the year of his death.

    *   *   *

Thus far I have suggested that Booker T. Washington wishes to identify himself with Frederick Douglass and to be recognized as Douglass's rightful heir in the line of African American leadership. At the same time, Washington offers his own life and his autobiography as correctives to Douglass's outdated rhetoric and self-image. Washington's autobiography itself embodies these strategies, for by adopting Douglass's forms, he suggests the link between the *Narrative* and *Up from Slavery*; the latter work is intended to be regarded as the next entry into the black autobiographical tradition. Washington's book, however, like Washington's life, amends the tone of Douglass's. Washington changes an angry, defiant tone to an ingratiating one, puts the best construction on events and character, and replaces Douglass's determination not to be anyone's slave with his own dedication to be servant of all.

For all his attempts to join Douglass in the pantheon of African American heroes, Washington at heart does not regard Douglass as his true spiritual father even though he assumed Douglass's mantle just as Elisha had taken the prophetic authority from Elijah. The Frederick of the *Narrative* takes as his credo "I will not serve," and he brings that contention to life by his escape from slavery. A rebellious persona, even one whose rebellion is justified, could never fit the self Washington creates in *Up from Slavery*; even the more tractable Frederick of the two later Douglass autobiographies, although now a figure dedicated to serving the nation and his race, has clinging to him some of the aura of the runaway, the person who serves only when, where, and *whom* he chooses. Washington, who in creating Booker molds perhaps the most accommodating autobiographical persona in American letters, cannot adopt Frederick or Frederick Douglass as his true father. Two white Americans, one identified explicitly, the other present implicitly throughout *Up from Slavery*, stand as Washington's true fathers, the men who shaped his thinking and his identity.

The first of these venerable figures is General Samuel C. Armstrong, the white man who founded the Hampton Institute, where Washington received his education. Once we get beyond Washington's Victorian niceties of tribute that today ring so hollow ("I have not spoken of that which made the greatest and most lasting impression upon me, and that was a great man—the noblest, rarest human being that it has ever been my privilege to meet"), we see that Washington puts Armstrong to good thematic use in his book, a fact that might have pleased the General, whose philosophy seems to have been "be useful." Truly, however, Washington's affection and respect for Armstrong are more than rhetorical ploys manufactured for his own purposes, and there is no doubt that Armstrong's was the decisive influence in Washington's life. (After all, it was Armstrong who handpicked Washington to go to Tuskegee; no Armstrong, no Booker T. Washington as we know him.)

Washington manages to illustrate several of his primary points in *Up from Slavery* through the character of Armstrong, the embodiment of selflessness and of the determination to let the past rest while working to build a better nation:

I never saw a man who so completely lost sight of himself. I do not think he ever had a selfish thought. He was just as happy in trying to assist some other institution in the South as he was working for Hampton. Although he fought the southern white man in the Civil War, I never heard him utter a bitter word against him afterward. On the other hand, he was constantly seeking to find ways by which he could be of service to the Southern whites. (243)

Armstrong personifies the determination to serve others no matter how daunting the odds. Toward the end of his life, when he suffered nearly total paralysis, Armstrong asks to visit Tuskegee. As a guest in Washington's house for two months, Armstrong symbolizes a total lack of racial prejudice (many whites would not have stayed in a black home) and an ongoing drive to serve:

> Although almost wholly without the use of voice or limb, he spent nearly every hour in devising ways and means to help the South. Time and time again he said to me, during this visit, that it is not only the duty of the country to assist in elevating the Negro of the South, but the poor white man as well. (372)

Armstrong's visit to Tuskegee also illustrates a "pattern of completion" that occurs repeatedly throughout *Up from Slavery*. Washington often shows Booker returning in triumph to places and situations once marked by uncertainty and deprivation. The incident of his reading the Douglass autobiography on board the Atlantic steamship and then being invited to address all the passengers—so different from Douglass's experience of shipboard ostracism—illustrates this pattern. So does the book's ending: the final words are written, "not by design," Washington coyly asserts, in Richmond where, he reminds us, "about twenty-five years ago, because of my poverty I slept night after night under a sidewalk" (385). Armstrong's dying visit to Tuskegee "completes" Booker's first trip to Hampton. When Booker made the trip, it was the young black man who needed help that Armstrong could give him; now Armstrong comes to Booker, but this time it is the older man who is in reduced physical circumstances, an invalid literally needing assistance in the Washington household. He comes to Tuskegee to see what his protégé has accomplished and to offer, even in his paralysis, whatever help he can. Thus he personifies what Washington wants his white readers to see as the ideal stance of whites in their relationship to African Americans: all along, Washington contends that if black Americans can make themselves indispensable to the nation, then white America will come to their door seeking what they have to offer.

To be useful, then, is Washington's ideal, and he creates Booker as a pre-eminently useful protagonist. But it is not from General Armstrong alone that Washington and his Booker absorb the gospel of living for others; this myth is also embodied in the autobiography of Washington's other true spiritual father, Benjamin Franklin. Franklin's *Autobiography*, one of the most influential of all American books, embodies, like Douglass's *Narrative*, a myth with broad appeal. But whereas Douglass unconsciously taps the monomyth that touches universal human issues, Franklin gives words to the peculiarly American version of the myth of the hero—its domesticated embodiment in the person of the Self-Made Man who, after he has attained wealth and status in his community, devotes himself to a life of public service. In Franklin, Washington finds a kindred spirit.

Franklin's story is well known. In a famous passage, he describes his arrival in Philadelphia—a young man with little money and no friends in the great city, looking for work and hoping to make his fortune. The mythic hero begins his quest, away from home and in a strange place populated by potentially hostile strangers; he must, by his wits, luck, and hard work, find his fortune and establish himself in society. But if the pattern is recognizable, the stakes involved are deflated: instead of exotic landscapes filled with terrifying monsters, we find a city populated by greedy merchants and snobbish aristocrats who look down upon hicks from the country. Instead of the prize beyond price—self-knowledge, divine wisdom, or (as in Douglass's case) freedom and the realization "I am a man"—we find material wealth and social respectability the boons to be won. Instead of a message of universal spiritual truths, we have Poor Richard's homely advice and a list of virtues to be followed if one is to be successful. Franklin preaches thrift, cleanliness, and honesty, but often for self-interested purposes.

Franklin demonstrated by his own life that the virtues he practiced and preached could lead to success, American style. He became the most prominent citizen of the town he entered as a naive boy. His *Autobiography* traces his rise from obscurity to fame and offers the picture of the self-made man who, having attained success through virtuous living, crowns his virtues with those of public service. Once he becomes financially secure and socially prominent, even though he may walk over others to do so, the hero of this American saga freely devotes himself to helping others, to living a "useful" life.

Booker T. Washington knew Franklin's *Autobiography* and consciously connected his life with that of the earlier man. Sidonie Smith notes how Washington echoes Franklin's entry into Philadelphia in his description of his own entry into Richmond on his way from West Virginia to Hampton.[10] Washington carefully points out that he arrived in Richmond with even less than Franklin had when he came to Philadelphia. This makes his rise even more spectacular than his predecessor's: the reader, of course, knows that Washington has another burden to bear that Franklin did not—his blackness. Washington draws another parallel between Franklin and himself when he uses some of Franklin's famous Thirteen Virtues as guiding principles for himself and for his students at Tuskegee. In an article that draws many parallels between Washington and Franklin, Stephen Whitfield notes how Washington stresses, as did Franklin, industry and prudence, humility, sincerity, and cleanliness as keys to success personal and public (409). Clearly, as Sidonie Smith states, Washington is giving us "the black version of a well-known formula."[11]

Washington's vision of himself as a self-made American in the line of Benjamin Franklin served him well and fit comfortably with the age in which he lived. The last decades of the nineteenth century saw the rise of many self-made Americans and the establishment of great fortunes based upon hard work, tenacity, shrewd dealing, and—sometimes—corruption and exploitation. Men who became wealthy and powerful could (and would) resort to whatever means necessary to reach the top and stay there. Franklin might have been horrified at the abuses to which his prescriptions for success were subjected in the 1880s and 1890s, but he would have had to admit his part in forming the values of a later century. Washington, naturally gifted with qualities necessary for success in his age, cultivated those qualities and used them to maintain the power he had gradually amassed. In the standard biography of Washington, Louis R. Harlan explores at length the machinations Washington used to extend his influence into every area of black American life as well as into many areas of white life. If the resulting portrait of Washington is not altogether flattering, it does acknowledge the man's devotion to his cause and testifies to his truly amazing success as a shaper of the black community. Like Franklin, Washington presents a public image of community servant, an image he worked hard to maintain, believing, as I have stated, that he and other African Americans had to keep the aura of usefulness about them if they were to be accepted by the white community.

Although Washington may have at heart felt a closer philosophical kinship with Franklin than he did with Frederick Douglass, his desire to identify himself with Douglass may explain why he chose Douglass's *Narrative,* not Franklin's *Autobiography,* as his model. James Cox draws a distinction between the true literary author who struggles against the conventions of autobiography as he or she writes his or her own life story and the "nonwriter" or naive autobiographer who sees autobiography as a mold "into which he can empty the experience he confidently believes that he has had."[12] Cox sees Washington as this naive autobiographer who picks up forms readily at hand; Cox believes that *Up from Slavery* is modeled after Franklin's *Autobiography* and not Douglass's *Narrative*; I would say it thematically follows Franklin while formally mimicking Douglass. As Gates has convincingly demonstrated, *Up from Slavery* carefully follows (while it rewrites) Douglass; the overall structure of the autobiography also can be described in terms of the three-part structure of the slave narrative—bondage, flight, and freedom.

*   *   *

For Washington, bondage is actual slavery, the state in which he lived for the first nine years of his life, but it is also enslavement to ignorance and poverty, conditions that did not magically disappear after emancipation. He did not have to escape slavery by fleeing north, as did Douglass and hundreds of others born earlier; Washington received freedom when emancipation was decreed. He did have to achieve mental and material freedom by working to educate himself: this process comprises the large central section of his work, including his description of his early years at Tuskegee, during which he had to teach himself how to create and sustain the school of which he found himself head. The "freedom" section of *Up from Slavery* could be said to commence with chapter 14, "The Atlanta Exposition Address," Washington's recounting of the speech that brought him fame and that convinced him that he had finally "arrived." No one could now deny Washington's success or take from him what he had attained for himself through long, arduous labor. He had worked for, and received, the freedom to interact with white America as an equal and to express his opinions without fear. He had followed Franklin's advice and had been duly rewarded.

The tripartite structure is present, but the central metaphor of *Up from Slavery* sits uneasily upon it. In the slave narratives, flight links bondage and freedom as a rite of passage from one state to its opposite. In some cases, in the narrative of William and Ellen Craft, for instance, flight is shown to require cunning, determination, and nerves of steel. In others, Douglass's primarily, flight is a mental and emotional process as much as a physical one and involves *fight*, if necessary: Douglass's passage from slave mentality to thinking of himself as a free man comes after he has fought Covey. In these cases, flight forces the slave to take a stand against the desires of his or her master. If their masters want William and Ellen Craft to remain slaves, the Crafts refuse and break for freedom. If Covey wishes Douglass to submit passively to a brutal beating, Douglass will fight back. The slave must assert her or himself and take a stand opposing the wishes of others. But Washington's central metaphor is not one of resistance; it is one of at least seeming compliance, acquiescence.

When Booker T. Washington arrived at the Hampton Institute, he had no money to pay tuition. Upon applying to the head teacher, a Miss Mackie, for admission, he was at first put off: the woman would neither accept nor refuse him. As Washington puts it, he "continued to linger about her, and to impress her in all the ways I could with my worthiness" (*Up from Slavery* 241). After some time, the teacher requests Booker take a broom and sweep a recitation room. This he does, three times, then proceeds to dust the room four times, cleaning every place where dust could possibly hide. Miss Mackie gives the room a thorough inspection and, in Washington's words, "When she was unable to find one bit of dirt on the floor, or a particle of dust on any of the furniture, she quietly remarked, 'I guess you will do to enter this institution' " (241). Washington relates the meaning of the event for him:

I was one of the happiest souls on earth. The sweeping of that room was my college entrance examination, and never did any youth pass an examination for entrance into Harvard or Yale that gave him more genuine satisfaction. I have passed several examinations since then, but I have always felt that this was the best one I ever passed. (241)

Albert E. Stone notes this event, the cleaning of a room to meet the stringent standards of a white "Yankee" woman, as announcing Washington's essential mythic identity.[13] Washington sees himself not as the hero, the warrior, but as the servant who wins a place of trust and honor through faithful and superior service. If Douglass's credo can be said to be "I will fight," Washington's is "ego serviam," "I will serve." The act of service—in this case, sweeping a room—replaces the heroic flight/fight as the central event in Washington's personal drama. Douglass wins his manhood, his sense of self, by resisting the will of another; Washington discovers his by obeying the wishes of another—that other, be it noted, a white person. Thus Washington summarizes in this episode the character of his autobiographical persona; unlike the heroic loner of Douglass's *Narrative*, Washington creates an "I" that desperately wants to fit into communal life and will go to extreme lengths to do so. This, after all, represents Washington's goal for himself and for all African Americans—to win a place in the greater American community. Washington lived his life and created his self-portrait in *Up from Slavery* to convince the white world that he and other African Americans were indeed worthy of such inclusion.

One question remains, however. William Andrews claims that the persona of Douglass in *My Bondage and My Freedom* discovers that freedom also brings loneliness; accordingly, *this* Frederick longs for a welcoming community, not isolation.[14] This image of self—not the isolated hero of the *Narrative*—best accords with Washington's "I" in *Up from Slavery*. Why, then, does not Washington shape his autobiography along the lines of *My Bondage and My Freedom* instead of the *Narrative*? We have demonstrated that Washington sought and found connections between his world view and Douglass's, but perhaps in the end he realized that, for all their apparent similarities of thought, he and the older man were at heart very different and that the image of the splendid *isolato* truly did define Douglass's mythic identity. If so, such an image had to be overcome, for Washington prized above all the greater good of the group, even at the expense of individual rights.

Washington's central metaphor of self fits poorly, then, on the heroic bondage-flight/fight-freedom pattern that Douglass uses and perfects. Washington believes that faithful service is the way of his present moment, that the struggles of the past are no longer necessary nor desirable. Yet he wants to identify himself with those struggles, and this further explains the use of Douglass's *Narrative* as a model. If he had simply needed a mold into which he could pour his experience, Franklin's *Autobiography* was available (and more in line with Washington's self-image)—he need not have evoked Douglass at all. The evocation is made, however, with the resulting uneasy mixture of heroic form and mundane content. Washington may wish to be seen primarily as a latter-day Frederick Douglass, but his true identity remains that of a black Benjamin Franklin.

*   *   *

Up from Slavery does not satisfactorily embody the myth of the hero, but it does embody myths: not only the myth of the self-made man but also the myth of progress—racial, social, and economic. *Up from Slavery* strongly asserts that the past is gone and, with it, hatred, oppression, and violence. A new day has dawned, one in which whites and blacks can live and work together in peace. But for this day to come fully to light, whites and blacks must forgive and forget. Washington carefully shows that he and like-minded people like General Armstrong have done both. From the beginning of his autobiography, he emphasizes the absence of bitterness in himself and in other blacks: he asserts that most slaves were neither hostile to their white owners nor bitter about slavery as an institution. Of himself, Washington writes:

I believe that I have completely rid myself of any ill feeling toward the Southern white man for any wrong that he may have inflicted upon my race. I am made to feel just as happy now when I am rendering service to Southern white men as when the service is rendered to a member of my own race. I pity from the bottom of my heart any individual who is so unfortunate as to get into the habit of holding race prejudice. (303)

Washington adds humility and a love of labor to the ability to forgive as necessary components any person—black or white—needs to succeed. These three traits Washington actively pursued as facets of his public persona; any resentment, anger, or frustration he may have felt toward the reality of race relations in the South he kept carefully to himself.

The myth of progress must have been difficult for Washington to sustain during the latter years of the nineteenth century, for these years marked the low point in race relations in the United States and saw African Americans stripped of many of the legal rights granted them after the Civil War. The Supreme Court's 1883 ruling that the Civil Rights Law of 1875 was unconstitutional, for example, opened the door for the disenfranchisement of blacks in the South. The states began systematic oppression of their black citizens, compelling them to live without the vote for many years, then having to fight to regain it in the 1960s and 1970s. But these harsher realities are glossed over in *Up from Slavery*. Instead, the book closes with a glowing description of the visit of President William McKinley to Tuskegee on December 16, 1898. Many of the citizens of Tuskegee, white and black alike, worked together to make the town and the school presentable for the President's visit. A parade and exhibitions were organized to show the chief of state and his entourage the work being done at the school. Washington quotes part of the President's speech that day, and then quotes an excerpt from an address by John D. Long, Secretary of the Navy:

I cannot make a speech today. My heart is too full—full of hope, admiration, and pride for my countrymen of both sections and both colours. I am filled with gratitude and admiration for your work, and from this time forward I shall have absolute confidence in your progress and in the solution of the problem in which you are engaged.

The problem, I say, has been solved. A picture has been presented today which should be put upon canvas with the pictures of Washington and Lincoln, and transmitted to future time and generations—a picture which the press of the country should spread broadcast over the land, a most dramatic picture, and that picture is this: The President of the United States standing on this platform; on one side the Governor of Alabama, on the other, completing the trinity, a representative of a race only a few years ago in bondage, the coloured President of the Tuskegee Normal and Industrial Institute. (379–80)

Long's heart obviously was *not* too full that day to make a pretty speech, and one, certainly, that vindicated the world-view Washington had worked long and diligently to bring into being. Washington himself could not have better expressed what the day meant to him, and he preserves Long's words so that his readers can know that meaning, too. The description of the three men standing on the platform—McKinley, the governor of Alabama, and Washington himself, tricked out in patriotic and religious language (Washington, Lincoln, and the Trinity) presents the myth of American racial progress in one remarkable image.

The McKinley visit to Tuskegee would be a fitting climax to Washington's work, and it is the next to last image Washington gives us. He concludes, however, with a picture of Tuskegee not during an exceptional event but as the school existed and functioned on a day-to-day basis. The picture is, by any account, impressive.

In 1901, Tuskegee had a twenty-three-hundred-acre campus, seven hundred cultivated; forty buildings, all but four erected by the students themselves; twenty-eight industrial departments; eleven hundred students; and eighty-six officers and instructors (*Up from Slavery* 381–82). The value of Tuskegee's property and endowment was $500,000; its annual operating budget was $80,000, most of which, Washington tells us, he raised "by going from door to door and from house to house." The property was mortgage free. Most remarkably, Washington had accomplished the creation of such an institution in only twenty years' time, having begun with no money, two or three dilapidated buildings, one teacher, and thirty students. For any person of any race to have done under any circumstances what Washington did would have been unusual; for Washington, a black man working in the South, it was nearly miraculous.

Washington's pride in Tuskegee is understandable; one can see why he presents the school as an edenic oasis of beauty, industry, and order. He describes Sunday afternoon walks with his family in the woods near his home where "we can live for a while near the heart of nature, where no one can disturb or vex us, surrounded by pure air, the trees, the shrubbery, the flowers, and the sweet fragrance that springs from a hundred plants, enjoying the chirp of the crickets and the songs of the birds" (355). His personal garden gives him an opportunity for some of the little leisure time he enjoys, and he takes great pleasure in the domestic stock he keeps: "few things are more satisfactory to me than a high-grade Berkshire or Poland China pig" (356). Meanwhile, the school runs efficiently, the students following a daily regimen that makes university life today sound sybaritic by

comparison (382–83). And at the center of it all is Washington himself, who assures us that he knows (by way of a system of reports that
must have been difficult to produce and deliver in the days before
rapid communication and computers) every day of the year, whether
he is at Tuskegee or not, what the school's income is, how much milk
and butter the dairy produces, what meat and vegetables are served
in the dining room, and who has attended class or not. Imagine any
university president knowing or caring about such details today.

But we can almost believe that the figure Washington creates in
Up from Slavery both knows and cares about the minutest details of
the institution he created, for Tuskegee is, in a real sense, an extension of its founder. A man who lives to be useful, whose creed is care-
fulness because he knows the world—particularly the white world—
is watching his every move, might reasonably make it his business to
know, even while traveling in Europe, the daily milk production from
his dairy back home. That such a concern implies an obsessive need
for control was not lost on Washington's contemporary critics, who
felt that Washington wanted to run not only Tuskegee but every
black person in America as well. We know from Washington's private
papers that he made it his business to learn what he felt he needed to
know, so that he even used a spy network to watch over those he
perceived as his enemies. This side of the man, only hinted at in *Up
from Slavery*, greatly troubled W.E.B. Du Bois and will be discussed in
the next chapter.

Washington consciously permits no hint of personal or institu-
tional troubles to tarnish the idealized portrait of a "completed" Tuskegee that he offers up in his autobiography. True, he does not
hesitate to describe the difficulties the school experienced during its
early years, but these, like all unpleasantnesses in *Up from Slavery,* are
passed over lightly, relegated to the past. As Washington presents it
(and as he undoubtedly believed it), Tuskegee is *the* solution to the
needs of the African American of Washington's day; Washington
claims, implicitly, that every thinking person will realize this. The ragged "aunty" who has lived most of her life in slavery, deprived of
education and opportunity, realizes it when she brings her six eggs as
her "widow's mite" for the advancement of the school: "I wants you
to put dese six eggs into de eddication of dese boys an' gals" (285);
the good white people of Tuskegee realize it and show it by their
support for and involvement with the institute; wealthy Northern
philanthropists realize it and show their support with large financial
gifts; elected officials know it, and so do other institutions of higher
learning like Harvard, which grants Booker an honorary degree.
Those who do *not* grasp that Tuskegee is the way of the future for

the African American are to be pitied; such are the foolish young black men and women who have gone to the cities looking for a "free ride." Among these are the young men who spend half a week's salary on one buggy ride down Pennsylvania Avenue in Washington, D.C., so that they can impress others into believing they are rich. Such are the young women with six or eight years of "book education" whose learning has fitted them for no remunerative occupation but has given them a taste for life's luxuries that they cannot afford. Washington states, darkly and ambiguously, "in too many cases that the girls went to the bad" (262). They could have been saved had their mental training been supplemented with "the latest and best methods of laundrying and other kindred occupations" (262).

Such a vision sounds simplistic today, and it sounded so to some of Washington's contemporaries, who were troubled, by the time *Up from Slavery* was published, by Washington's apparent devaluation of academic education. But Washington felt as if he spoke with authority about the needs of his people. He had sound basis for his claim: unlike many of his critics, he actually lived and worked among the poor and uneducated blacks of the South and saw first-hand their ignorance and their misconceptions about what academic education could do for them. Many felt that book learning was the way out of the hard physical labor of farming; others who had acquired some rudiments of education ("they could locate the Desert of Sahara or the capital of China on an artificial globe") could not do practical things like set a dinner table properly. Because he traveled extensively throughout the South to advertise Tuskegee and to raise funds, Booker felt a connection with these people and their needs and created Tuskegee, as he writes at the end of *Up from Slavery*, to educate the student "to meet conditions as they exist *now*, in the part of the South where he lives—in a word, to be able to do the thing which the world wants done" (381).

In his chapter entitled "The Secrets of Success in Public Speaking," Washington writes that he does not believe in public speaking for its own sake but only for delivering a message the speaker feels deeply moved in his or her heart to convey. When this conviction of the need to speak comes over a person, he or she ought to deliver his or her message without overmuch concern for "the artificial rules of elocution." Washington's principles for public speaking apply also to his writing in *Up from Slavery*, for the work obviously contains a message about which Washington felt deeply, and it puts forth that message without excessive care for the "rules" of formal speech; its informal tone, complete with humor, folksy sayings, stock black characters recognizable to turn-of-the century readers from the minstrel shows, and even jokes at blacks' expense all show the skill of a speaker and writer who assesses his hearers and tailors his speech to suit them. Washington claims he can also spot the unsympathetic listener in a crowd and that he goes straight at such a listener, trying to win him or her over; he uses the same tactic with *Up from Slavery*, aiming the book at the most hardened opponent of black progress, knowing that if his severest critics can be persuaded by his ingratiating, eager-to-please approach, so will thousands of others already more in sympathy to his program.

In his discussion on public speaking, Washington continues: "Although there are certain things, such as pauses, breathing, and pitch of voice, that are very important, none of these can take the place of *soul* in an address" (344). *Soul*, that elusive quality that we understand without being able to precisely define, and that has been so important in describing the African American experience ("soul music," "soul food," and "soul brother" come to mind), is precisely what Washington claims *he* has. Perhaps *soul* did not mean to him all that it does to us, but if it has anything to do with an individual's sense of the pulse of the masses of the people and his or her ability to sympathetically intuit their needs, hopes, and dreams, then Washington would say he possesses it. Tuskegee is the result of "soul" in practice, the tangible answer to the needs of the people. No one can question Washington's courage in envisioning Tuskegee and creating it in the deep South, nor can anyone deny that Washington believed he had touched the soul of the majority of the people through his work.

Nevertheless, many have argued that Washington gave away too much so that his dream could come to its startling fulfillment. Du Bois criticized what he perceived to be the narrowness of Washington's educational philosophy in his 1901 review of *Up from Slavery*; he repeated and expanded his charges in the now-famous essay in *The Souls of Black Folks* (the book in which he too claims to have tapped into the souls of his people). Most later critics also fault Washington for not striving for full social and civil rights for African Americans, and those who have written during the Civil Rights Movement have been hardest of all, scorning Washington as the one who gave away the rights of others that were not his to give, rights that had to be bought with more blood in the 1960s and after.

The controversy over Washington and his program is not settled and probably never will be. Over against the failures of the man and the limitations of his educational and social vision for the black American must be set what he did accomplish. Perhaps we cheat ourselves if we believe that we must be exclusive in our choices: why must we embrace the militancy of Douglass and Du Bois and reject Washington altogether, or favor Washington and denigrate the view of those who came before and after him? Although Washington saw himself and his work as correctives and replacements for Douglass, and Du Bois believed he had to combat Washington's errors, we can now see these figures as complementary whereas they and many later critics have seen them as exclusively antagonistic. Philip Foner, for example, who admires Douglass and despises Washington, concludes his biography of Douglass with a contrast between the two men, one that praises Douglass for his uncompromising stand against segregation and condemns Washington for playing into the hands of racists. Of Douglass, Foner writes:

In his phenomenal rise above some of the restrictions of the American caste system, Douglass consistently fought for those who were trapped in its tentacles. He bitterly denounced the unjust and brutal treatment of the mass of his people. Never fearing whom it might offend, he unflinchingly raised the cry for equality.[15]

But of Washington, he writes that "[he] recommended acquiescence or at least 'no open agitation,' for civil and political rights. The Negro could be happy in the South as long as he was subservient."[16] Foner goes on to relate an anecdote that, for him, summarizes the difference in philosophy between Douglass and Washington:

In the early days of 1895, a young Negro student living in New England journeyed to Providence, Rhode Island, to seek the advice of the aged Frederick Douglass who was visiting that city. As their interview drew to a close the youth said, " 'Mr. Douglass, you have lived in both the old and the new dispensations. What have you to say to a young Negro just starting out? What should he do?' The patriarch lifted his head and replied, 'Agitate! Agitate! Agitate!' "

In 1899 the same youth posed the identical question to Booker T. Washington who answered, " 'Work! Work! Work! Be patient and win by superior service.' "[17]

These two positions are simplistic, for Douglass also valued education for blacks and Washington worked behind the scenes for racial justice, but the anecdote illustrates how many people have come to view the differences in belief between the two men. Douglass believed in the integration of the races (his second wife was his white secretary, Helen Pitts) and predicted equality through intermarriage. Washington, on the other hand, worked to avoid antagonizing whites and genuinely seemed more content to wait for equality to come more through a natural evolution than through force. Those who revere

Douglass and despise Washington, as Foner does, can almost suggest that Washington kept his true beliefs under wraps until Douglass was dead, then sprang his doctrine on the country at the same moment that he took the leadership of African Americans upon himself. This scenario is certainly too Machiavellian to be completely accurate, but the close coincidence between the passing of the older leader and the ascendancy of the younger remains a tantalizing development. Did Washington feel free after Douglass's death to espouse his own economic and racial views? Would the Atlanta Exposition speech have been different if Washington had known that Frederick Douglass would read it? We cannot say, but certainly 1895 marked the passing of an old order and the rise of a new.

In recent years, we have witnessed a similar transition, and just as the differences between Douglass's vision and Washington's can be viewed as either antagonistic or complementary, depending upon how one interprets them, so can the changes in the mood and priorities of the black community be variously interpreted today. The militancy of the 1960s has largely disappeared, much to the disappointment of some; others, however, see the battle as having rightly shifted from the fight for equal rights under law and equal access to public accommodations to equal economic and educational opportunity. The "war" has moved from the streets into places of business and into the schools, and many African American leaders today would agree with Booker T. Washington that the black community needs jobs and skills to help people make decent livings and escape poverty, crime, and dependence upon government programs. People like Jesse Jackson, who once marched with Martin Luther King, Jr., today work to build the economic base for the black community and to create bridges across the racial barriers that still exist between blacks and whites. Jackson seems aware that there is a time to fight and a time to pursue other means; this was Washington's awareness, too. That Washington's vision was restricted and restricting few would now dispute; that he traded away too much for Tuskegee's right to exist most now agree. But for all that, Washington does not stand outside the line of black leadership, but raises a voice worthy to be heard alongside the more militant cries of his predecessors and successors.

3: The Struggle for Paternal Authority: Washington and W.E.B. Du Bois

The years 1895 to 1912 were the "glory years" of Booker T. Washington's reign as the most powerful black man in America. *Up from Slavery*, Washington's best-known expression of his social and economic credo, quickly established itself as "a work of near-Biblical inspiration and authority," almost universally hailed.[1] William Dean Howells's fulsome review typifies the praise heaped upon the autobiography; he extols Washington's "simple" and "charming" style, his "winning yet manly personality," and his "ideal of self-devotion [that] must endear him to every reader of his book."[2] Neither Howells nor other readers of *Up from Slavery* realized that the book had been ghost-written and that its "simple prose . . . of sterling worth" and "sweet brave humor" were the products, at least in part, of the efforts of two white men, Max Bennett Thrasher and Lyman Abbott, the first a paid writer of Tuskegee, the second a friend and adviser of Washington.

Amid the laudatory reviews of *Up from Slavery*, one dissenting voice made itself heard. W.E.B. Du Bois's short essay, "The Evolution of Negro Leadership," appearing in *The Dial* on July 16, 1901, was the opening shot in a protracted battle for leadership among African Americans that would last until Washington's death fifteen years later. Du Bois himself would go on to occupy a place of power and influence in the nation and would in time write two full-length autobiographies, as Washington had done. The earlier of these, *Dusk of Dawn* (1941), will be treated in this chapter. First, however, I shall deal with Du Bois's *Dial* review of *Up from Slavery*, his essay "Of Mr. Booker T. Washington and Others" (1903), and the controversy of which these articles signaled the beginning.

"The Evolution of Negro Leadership" seeks first to place Booker T. Washington into historical perspective by reviewing the various ways African Americans—"the imprisoned group"—had sought to deal with their situation. Revolution, adjustment and accommodation, and self-development in the face of discouraging circumstances had all been attempted. The fortunes of black people, so low during the long years of slavery, were suddenly and dramatically raised with Emancipation, ascended to the heights during Reconstruction, but met with reversal in the last years of the nineteenth century. As Du Bois puts it:

War memories and ideals rapidly passed, and a period of astonishing commercial development and expansion ensued. A time of doubt and hesitation, of storm and stress, overtook the freedmen's sons; and then it was that Booker T. Washington's leadership began. Mr. Washington came with a clear simple programme, at the psychological moment, at a time when the nation was a little ashamed of having bestowed so much sentiment on Negroes and was concentrating its energies on Dollars. The industrial training of Negro youth was not an idea originating with Mr. Washington, nor was the policy of conciliating the white South wholly his. But he first put life, unlimited energy, and perfect faith into this programme; he changed it from a by-path into a veritable Way of Life.[3]

Du Bois's review acknowledges Washington's considerable achievements, particularly his "conquest of the South" and his "gaining consideration in the North." But his success has been won at the expense of values that, while admittedly not commercially profitable, are nevertheless vital to people's spiritual health:

He [Washington] learned so thoroughly the speech and thought of triumphant commercialism and the ideals of material prosperity that he pictures as the height of absurdity a black boy studying a French grammar in the midst of weeds and dirt. One wonders how Socrates or St. Francis of Assisi would receive this! (54)

Having subjected Washington's view to implied criticism (the reader is meant to know very well how Socrates or Francis would have viewed Washington's "gospel of Work and Money"), Du Bois goes on to note that "singleness of vision and thorough oneness with his age is a mark of the successful man." Yet not all agree with Washington's program: those who founded the black academic schools of the South chafe under criticism from the Hampton-Tuskegee coalition; others distrust Washington for being so friendly with Southern whites. Still others, a group including eminent African Americans such as Paul Laurence Dunbar, Charles Waddell Chesnutt, and Charlotte and Francis Grimké, can agree with Washington and the policies of industrial education to a point but believe that the program by itself is too limiting and that blacks should be able to advance themselves in whatever areas of self-development they choose. Further, these critics of Washington insist that blacks must have suffrage on the same terms as whites.

Du Bois stresses two things in his short review. First, he points out that not all African Americans give wholehearted support to Washington although most can honor and support him to some extent. Second, he identifies the concerns that unite this group of which he himself was part and that he was soon to lead. Those blacks who opposed Washington tended to be well-educated individuals who had received academic, not industrial, education at Southern schools like Fisk in Nashville and Atlanta University or (in Du Bois's case) at Northern schools like Harvard. They recognized the value of traditional college training for those qualified to benefit from it—the "Talented Tenth" who would be the race's future leaders. They resented the fact that black schools like Fisk and Atlanta University were receiving less and less funding from Northern philanthropists, who were succumbing to Tuskegee propaganda, which claimed that African Americans needed training in industrial skills, not the arts and sciences. This group also deplored Washington's accommodationist policies and watched with concern, then horror, as civil rights for blacks in the South continued to decay even as Washington preached patience, hard work, and segregation.

Washington's reaction to Du Bois's review, if he read it, is not known. In 1901, the two men were on cordial terms; they camped with some other black leaders in West Virginia in September of that year. Surely Washington knew he had critics, yet neither he nor Du Bois could have guessed in 1901 that a rift would soon open between them that would result in a political struggle to determine the future direction of African Americans' fight for equal rights. At stake, too, was the mantle of Frederick Douglass which Booker Washington had worn by default since 1895 and which a younger generation now sought to take upon itself. Du Bois and his associates saw themselves as the true descendants of the militant Douglass and determined to continue his efforts for full freedom for their people.

* * *

Du Bois's essay "Of Mr. Booker T. Washington and Others," which first appeared in a collection of his short works, *The Souls of*

Black Folk, marked the beginning of the formal breach between Du Bois and Washington. Du Bois had already in 1901 expressed his reservations about Washington's program, and even earlier, in 1900, had chastised those African Americans who forget that "life is more than meat and the body more than raiment."[4] But now, the reservations had become open, pointed criticism. Why Du Bois became bolder in his attack is somewhat uncertain. Francis Broderick suggests some possibilities. Maybe Du Bois had gained confidence from the favorable reception his earlier critiques had elicited. He may have been inspired by William Monroe Trotter's attacks on Washington in his paper, the *Guardian*. He may have been angered by the decrease in funds received by Atlanta University in the face of the devaluation of academic education by the Tuskegee "Machine." Or he may have realized that his strategy of quiet scholarship designed to elicit change through a rational presentation of the truth was not going to be enough: open agitation would be necessary to win African Americans' rights.[5]

In *Dusk of Dawn*, his first full-length autobiography, Du Bois himself gives some indication of his motives for publishing "Of Mr. Booker T. Washington and Others." Just before he describes how *The Souls of Black Folk* came to be assembled, he mentions how Washington had invited him to participate in a conference to discuss the problems of African Americans. Du Bois notes his enthusiasm for the conference as well as his frustration that it took so long for the meeting to be organized:

. . . it seemed to me that I ought to make my own position clearer than I had hitherto. I was increasingly uncomfortable under the statements of Mr. Washington's position: his depreciation of the value of the vote; his evident dislike of Negro colleges; and his general attitude which seemed to place the onus of blame for the status of Negroes upon the Negroes themselves rather than upon the whites. And above all, I resented the Tuskegee Machine.[6]

Du Bois further notes that *The Souls of Black Folk* was a collection of pieces he had already written; when asked by the A. C. McClurg Company for a book of his essays, he took what he already had, added the chapter on Washington which he wrote for the occasion, and submitted the lot for publication.

Much of Du Bois's 1901 *Dial* review of *Up from Slavery* is incorporated into "Of Mr. Booker T. Washington and Others." The earlier essay's overview of black Americans' reaction to their history of oppression is repeated and expanded, but this time, Washington is said to be outside the line of self-assertive black leadership, a line centering in Frederick Douglass, "the greatest of American Negro leaders." Du Bois recalls that Douglass, throughout his long career, never changed the terms of his confrontation with white America: "Douglass, in his old age, still bravely stood for the ideals of his early manhood—ultimate assimilation *through* self-assertion, and on no other terms."[7] Washington, in contrast, is a compromiser who arouses the resentment of African Americans whose civil rights are thrown away by this man without authority to do so. He is criticized particularly for his "attitude of adjustment and submission," for almost accepting alleged black inferiority, and for asking blacks to give up, at least for the moment, political power, civil rights, and higher education for the young. During his tenure as leader of America's black community, that community has been disenfranchised, reduced by unfair laws to a status of legal civil inferiority, and has had its institutions of higher learning stripped of funding (*Souls* 50–51). Du Bois then asks:

Is it possible, and probable, that nine millions of men can make effective progress in economic lines if they are deprived of political rights, made a servile caste, and allowed only the most meager chance for developing their exceptional men? (*Souls* 51)

The answer is, of course, no. Further, Washington's policies involve him in a triple paradox: (1) He seeks to make blacks into business persons and property owners, but such people cannot hold and defend their place in society without suffrage. (2) He insists on self-respect, but no one can hold his or her self-esteem when systematically relegated to a socially inferior position. (3) He favors industrial education and deprecates higher learning, but the trade schools he favors need college-trained instructors to staff them (*Souls* 52).

These points, so telling because of the calm, analytical manner of their presentation, must have roused the ire of Washington and his circle. Du Bois's insistence that Washington's critics admire him for his positive achievements and his assertion of their responsibility to voice their own opinion probably did little to prevent an angry reaction. When Du Bois states that he and *his* circle stand unequivocally for the right to vote, civil equality, and education for black youth according to ability, the Tuskegee people must have known that the gauntlet had been formally thrown down. Du Bois was challenging an entire system of thought and action and was criticizing that system for giving white America the mistaken impression that it was justified in its oppression of blacks. The South, particularly, needed to be told the truth about its role in causing African Americans' problems and of its moral responsibility to help mend a situation it had caused.

Washington had, according to Du Bois, aided the national detour from its proper path—a path paved in earlier days by Frederick Douglass and others. A return must now be made, and Du Bois and his associates would attempt to take upon themselves Douglass's role in renewing the fight for full civil rights for black Americans.

*   *   *

True to his style, Booker T. Washington did not respond publicly to Du Bois's essay in *The Souls of Black Folk*. He often silenced his critics by ignoring them, thus depriving them of the publicity that would keep their causes before the public. He may also not have wished to antagonize Du Bois, who was teaching summer school at Tuskegee in 1903. Moreover, the two men were involved in negotiations for a conference of black leaders to be held in the early part of 1904. (The meeting, held at Carnegie Hall in New York City in January, 1904, had as its announced purpose the unification of black leadership and publication of a statement of common goals for the race; Washington viewed it as his opportunity to win his critics to *his* side.)[8]

Furthermore, Washington did not have to defend himself against criticism: many journals friendly to him both vigorously supported his program and viciously attacked Du Bois. An editorial in *Outlook* contrasted *The Souls of Black Folk* and Washington's *The Future of the American Negro*. Taking the two books as texts for reflections on "two parties or tendencies or influences in the negro race," it claimed:

One of these parties [Du Bois's] is ashamed of the race, the other [Washington's] is proud of it; one makes the white man the standard, the other seeks the standard in its own race ideals; one demands social equality, or at least resents social inequality; the other is too self-respecting to do either; one seeks to push the negro into a higher place, the other to make him a larger man; one demands for him the right to ride in the white man's car, the other seeks to make the black man's car clean and respectable; one demands the ballot for ignorant black men because ignorant white men have the ballot; the other asks opportunity to make the black man competent for the duties of citizenship, and wishes no man to vote, white or colored, who is not competent; . . . one wishes to teach the negro to read the Ten Commandments in Hebrew, the other wishes first to teach him to obey them in English; to one labor is barely more honorable than idleness and the education which makes "laborers and nothing more" is regarded with ill-concealed contempt; to the other industry is the basic virtue, and the education which makes industry intelligent is the foundation of civilization. (*Papers* 7, 150–51)

This characterization of Du Bois's position is grossly unfair; his policies are made to sound ridiculous through deliberate over-simplification and by a refusal to treat them in context. But as one sided as it is, the article reveals the depth of feeling evoked by the publication of *The Souls of Black Folk*.

Another publication favorable to Washington and Tuskegee, the Washington, D.C. *Colored American*, urged Horace Bumstead, president of Atlanta University, where Du Bois taught, to silence the professor. It said:

If Atlanta University intends to stand for Du Bois' outgivings, if it means to seek to destroy Tuskegee Institute, so that its own work can have success, it is engaged in poor business to start with; and in the next place, the assurance can safely be given that it will avail them nothing. Tuskegee will go on. It will succeed. Booker Washington will still loom large on the horizon, notwithstanding the petty annoyances of Du Bois and his ilk . . . Let him [Bumstead] prove himself by curbing the outgivings and ill-advised criticisms of the learned Doctor who is now in his employ; that is, if Du Bois does not really represent him and the sentiment of Atlanta University.[9]

In July of 1903 emotions on both sides of the rising controversy were heightened by events in Boston. Washington was scheduled to address the National Negro Business League in that city, which was the stronghold of the anti-Tuskegee movement, for it was the home of William Monroe Trotter's *Guardian*, the most outspokenly anti-Washington black newspaper in the nation. When Washington tried to address a packed auditorium, Trotter and an associate rose and directed prepared questions at him, which Washington tried to ignore. The audience erupted in hisses, someone threw pepper toward the platform, and police were summoned. Some in the crowd attempted to leave, and in the ensuing crush, one policeman had his uniform torn, another was stuck with a hatpin, and several women fainted. One young man, a supporter of Trotter, was stabbed.[10] Trotter himself was arrested and spent time in jail. This event, which came to be known as the Boston "riot," convinced some of Washington's critics that his Tuskegee Machine would go to great lengths to silence the opposition. Trotter's case for inciting to riot was vigorously prosecuted by a Tuskegee-picked lawyer who won an unusually harsh sentence on what appeared to many to be trumped up charges.

Du Bois was not involved in the "riot," for he was en route to Boston from Tuskegee at the time. Initially irritated with Trotter for provoking the Washington contingent, Du Bois later became sympathetic to Trotter when he learned the riot was probably triggered by

Assistant United States Attorney W. H. Lewis (a personal friend of Washington's), who presided at the meeting, and by the Boston police, who mishandled the arrest.[11] One historian believes that this event finally brought Du Bois—who had up to this point tried to stay away from active involvement in the fight against Washington—to a position of "active leadership of the Radicals."[12] From then on, Du Bois became more vocal and pointed in his criticisms; Washington, for his part, came to distrust Du Bois. In a letter to Robert Curtis Ogden, dated October 20, 1903, he wrote,

In connection with our conversation when I last saw you, I think I ought to say to you that I have evidence which is indisputable showing that Dr. Du Bois is very largely behind the mean and underhand attacks that have been made upon me during the last six months. (*Papers* 7, 298)

Washington apparently refers here to the Boston Riot, although as the editors of his letters point out, he probably had no such evidence of Du Bois's involvement, nor, as nearly as can be determined, was there any. Yet because Du Bois publicly sympathized with Trotter's victimization at the hands of Washington's forces, Washington may have felt justified in claiming that Du Bois was somehow involved (*Papers* 7, 298). At any rate, after the publication of "Of Mr. Booker T. Washington and Others," relations between Washington and his opponents worsened. His forces rallied behind him to attack Du Bois in print and Trotter in person, and Washington, although having to deal with Du Bois publicly to organize the Carnegie Hall Conference, privately blamed him for the attacks of 1903.

The Carnegie Hall Conference took place January 6–8, 1904. The attendees drafted an eight-point document addressing issues such as suffrage, segregation laws, lynching and due process, and race relations. An unusual spirit of cooperation characterized the conference and the document it produced. The conference appointed Washington, Du Bois, and Hugh Browne, president of Cheyney Institute in Pennsylvania, to select nine other men to serve with them on a committee of twelve to gather information and handle race relations on a national scale. But when illness kept Du Bois from attending the first meeting of the committee, Washington held it anyway; Du Bois then resigned. The Carnegie Hall Compromise had lasted only a few months.[13] Du Bois now felt that Washington was completely untrustworthy, and his personal dislike of the man increased. Alain Locke later wrote, "The third time I saw him [Du Bois], he suddenly launched into a philippic against Washington. I made no comment, but really, he ranted like a sibyl and prophesied the direct consequences."[14]

* * *

The break between Washington and Du Bois was complete by 1904. The two waged a paper war over the next few years, highlighted by Du Bois's charges in 1905 that the Tuskegee Machine used extensive bribery to influence the black press in its favor. His charges were probably true, but because Du Bois had only circumstantial evidence, nothing came of them (*Papers* 8, 224 ff). Washington's office at Tuskegee produced an editorial denouncing Du Bois ("A Base Slander of the Afro-American Press") and distributed it for publication in African American papers (*Papers* 8, 212–4). By 1905, Tuskegee was also monitoring the activities of Du Bois and his friends: on February 20, 1905, Emmett Jay Scott, Washington's private secretary, wrote to Charles William Anderson, a longtime friend and political ally of Washington's, asking him to be in Washington for Theodore Roosevelt's second inauguration in order to spy on Du Bois:

> You were sent a wire today advising you to be in Washington during the inauguration so as to keep your eyes on the enemy. . . . Hershaw is arranging to resuscitate the Pen and Pencil Club for a banquet during inaugural week, and of course will be very anxious to feature your little Atlanta friend [Du Bois, whose small stature Scott here ridicules] as a big attraction. The Wizard [Washington] believes that it would be well for you to be on hand and if possible, as you easily can, secure an invitation . . . so as to meet the enemy on any ground that may be offered. (*Papers* 8, 195)

Similar spying activities were undertaken at Washington's direct order later in 1905 when Du Bois and a group of like-minded blacks met at Niagara Falls to organize a movement against Tuskegee formally. Anderson was again involved, as were other Washington spies (*Papers* 8, 321, 326, 327). Anderson was still involved in covert surveillance of Du Bois in February of 1907 (*Papers* 9, 233).

Coupled with his efforts to spy on Du Bois, Washington continued to use his tactic of attempting to silence his opponents by denying them publicity. Emmett Scott wrote to an associate in July, 1905:

> I have just wired you today to the effect that a conference of our friends thinks it wisest to in every way ignore absolutely the Niagara Movement. . . . The best of the white newspapers in the North have absolutely ignored it and have taken no account of its meetings or its protestations. I think, then, as I have intimated, if we shall consistently refuse to take the slightest notice of them that the whole thing will die a-borning. (*Papers* 9, 331)

But try as he would, after a decade of dominance by the Tuskegee Machine, Washington was unable to stem the growing tide of opposition to his policies. Du Bois represented a view whose moment
had arrived. Once again, the leadership of African Americans was at
issue. Washington had seized that role in 1895 just after the death of
Douglass; now Du Bois and his associates were attempting to assume
leadership themselves, but their position was much more difficult
than Washington's had been. Washington had had no living leader
from whom to take control; Du Bois was up against not only a living
man but an extremely popular, powerful, and shrewd leader who to
all appearances occupied an unassailable position in American life.
Du Bois's courage and depth of commitment are the more remarkable given the apparently limitless influence and resources of the
Tuskegee Machine.

Hovering over the Booker T. Washington–W.E.B. Du Bois de-
bate were the spirit and authority of Frederick Douglass. Both con-
testants in the struggle realized they were fighting to see which truly
stood in Douglass's line. In a 1904 essay, "The Parting of the Ways,"
Du Bois again pointedly contrasts Washington's leadership with that
of former leaders such as Alexander Crummell, James Forten, and
Douglass.[15] *They* had believed in the broadest scope of education possible, in the ballot, in civil rights, and in the assertion of personal
rights even at the cost of civic strife. Washington, by contrast,
preaches the gospel of money, the uselessness of black universities,
and the expendability of the vote and civil rights. Du Bois ends with
ringing words directly at odds with the Tuskegee policy of accommodation: "The rights of humanity are worth fighting for. Those
that deserve them in the long run get them. The way for black men
to-day to make these rights the heritage of their children is to struggle for them unceasingly, and if they fail, die trying" (523).

Realizing that his position in the line of the great black leaders
was being undermined, Washington fought to re-identify himself
with the person and ideals of Frederick Douglass. A new building at
Tuskegee was named Frederick Douglass Hall; Lewis Douglass, son
of the great man, delivered the dedication address. Washington began a campaign in 1906 to clear the mortgage and to do restoration
work at Cedar Hill, Douglass's home in Anacostia Heights, Washington, D.C.[16] Most important, Washington fought, beginning in 1904,
to receive rights to write a biography of Douglass for the American
Crisis series of biographies of well-known Americans. The publisher
had originally asked Du Bois to write the book, but when Washington
protested, he was granted the privilege. This must have seemed a
double victory to him: he both deprived his rival of writing Douglass's

life and of putting his own "radical" interpretative emphases into the biography and also obtained the chance to identify himself with Douglass in print and to narrate the life of the famous leader in a way that would emphasize the similarities between Douglass's ideals and his own. Here was a perfect opportunity to "control" his predecessor, to identify himself with him, and to defeat his own would-be successor by wresting away a choice literary prize. This struggle between the two men, so reminiscent of sibling rivalry for the power of the father, recalls the Genesis account of Jacob and Esau striving against one another for the blessing of Isaac. Cast in terms of the Oedipus myth, the Washington-Du Bois relationship recalls the battle between the king's sons, Eteocles and Polyneices, to determine the rule of Thebes. The story of how Washington came to write *Frederick Douglass* is an intriguing, if minor, episode in the history of African American letters and bears further investigation. The finished product, largely ghost-written by Robert Park, Washington's much-employed white assistant, is an undistinguished piece of work, adding little to the two biographies of Douglass then in print. Producing it under his name, however, must have given Washington the satisfaction of someone whose power wins the day.

*   *   *

Although deprived of the authorship of *Frederick Douglass*, W.E.B. Du Bois continued to work actively in other areas to implement his own social programs. In 1905, he helped organize the Niagara Movement, an organization designed to attack the problems of black Americans through a program of "organized determination and aggressive action on the part of men who believe in Negro freedom and growth" (*Dusk of Dawn* 89). In 1909, the Niagara Movement gave up its independent existence, and many of its members joined the newly created NAACP, of which Du Bois served as director of publicity and research from 1910 until 1934. The year 1910 also saw the first volume of the organization's official magazine, *The Crisis*, which Du Bois edited. In 1934, he left the NAACP because his ideology had moved to the left while the organization's had remained more conservative; he returned to Atlanta University, where he was working when his first full-length autobiography, *Dusk of Dawn*, appeared in 1940.

By 1940, Booker T. Washington had been dead twenty-five years. He spent his last years vigorously promoting the same policies that had brought him fame and success, but he also was involved in three incidents that may well have caused him to question privately the validity of his public utterances. In 1911, after Washington purchased a small estate near Huntington, Long Island, his new white neighbors took a collection among themselves and offered him a thousand dollars profit if he would sell the home and leave the area. That same year, some Southern whites sued the Pullman Company and the Cotton Belt Railroad for allowing Mrs. Washington to ride in a Pullman car to Memphis.[17] Third, and most devastating, in 1911 Washington himself was attacked and beaten by a white man in a lower class neighborhood of New York City. The white attacker claimed he beat Washington for making an improper advance to a white woman. Washington lost his court case against his assailant, and he never fully explained his presence in the neighborhood. Washington may have asked himself how far African Americans had really come under his leadership if he himself could be attacked just because he was a black man in the wrong place at the wrong time.

Whatever Washington's feelings about the events of the inauspicious year of 1911, he never dramatically altered his public stance; he did, however, speak out more forcefully against lynching after his own beating. The following year brought another defeat to Tuskegee: the election of Woodrow Wilson, the presidential candidate supported by Du Bois and most of Washington's opponents, spelled the end of political patronage from Republican administrations toward Tuskegee. The school quickly ceased to be a political clearing-house for all affairs treating African Americans and returned to its original status as an institution of learning. Washington continued to travel, to raise funds, to speak publicly, and to write. His death in 1915 was attributed partially to sheer exhaustion.

Events after Washington's death and leading up to the civil rights struggles of the 1950s, 1960s, and early 1970s would prove the narrowness of Washington's programs, but during the height of his career, he was the most powerful and respected black man in the country, his policies received as gospel truth by millions. In historical perspective, however, Washington appears to be an obstacle in the road to freedom of all sorts—social, political, legal, and literary. The NAACP fought against Washington's legacy in court case after court case, finally triumphing in 1954. In the years that followed the Supreme Court's desegregation ruling, though, even the NAACP seemed too conservative and too cautious to many blacks, and the organization found itself criticized by a new generation of radicals in a way reminiscent of its own former criticism of the Tuskegee Machine.

W.E.B. Du Bois lived through it all, reaching the age of ninety-five before dying August 27, 1963. Significantly, Du Bois died during the famous 1963 March on Washington that witnessed Dr. Martin

Luther King, Jr.'s "I Have a Dream" speech. When Du Bois's death was announced to the gathered crowd, a time of silence was observed for the longtime leader of the black race. Du Bois did live to see some of the goals toward which he had worked all his life finally become reality in the land of his birth.

*   *   *

In 1940, looking back on more than seventy years of life, Du Bois published *Dusk of Dawn: An Essay Toward an Autobiography of a Race Concept*, the first of his two autobiographies. The full title of the book, read along with its opening "Apology" and brief first chapter, reveals immediately what a different kind of work this is from Washington's *Up from Slavery*, how different its author's world view is from Washington's, and how unlike Washington's is Du Bois's vision of his autobiographical self.

In the "Apology" of *Dusk of Dawn*, Du Bois looks back over thirty-seven years to 1903 and the publication of *The Souls of Black Folk*, which Du Bois calls "a cry at midnight thick within the veil, when none rightly knew the coming day" (vii). The present volume "started to record dimly but consciously that subtle sense of coming day"—the "day," as Du Bois makes clear, being the new era of racial equality for African Americans. After laboring for that equality for half a century, Du Bois senses that perhaps at long last his goal may be attained, the "dawn" may finally come. His two earlier books on the race problem, *The Souls of Black Folk* and *Darkwater* (c. 1920), penned to help hasten the day, "were written in tears and blood"; Du Bois continues, "this [present book] is set down no less determinedly but yet with wider hope in some more benign fluid. Wherefore I have not hesitated in calling it 'Dusk of Dawn' " (viii).

I suggest that the "benign fluid" Du Bois has in mind is sweat, thus completing the "blood, sweat, and tears" triad that he begins when he states that his earlier books were written in tears and blood. The sweat is Du Bois's own, the symbol of a lifetime of labor on behalf of black equality, labor now put into perspective by a seventieth birthday celebrated during the writing of the autobiography. The "dawn" of his title is the dawn of the new day of freedom for which he has worked, but the "dusk" is the twilight of his own life. This juxtaposition of images—the birth of a new dawn signifying life and hope played against the image of dark with its suggestions of death and loss—sets the tone for the autobiography. Unlike *Up from Slavery*, whose title adverb and preposition signify a life's forward movement away from a terrible personal and communal past, *Dusk of Dawn*'s title links the past to the future and perhaps suggests that the dawning day rises at the cost of the dying day: without the "dusk," the spent life of one who has given oneself to the cause, there can be no dawn. *Dusk of Dawn*, unlike *Up from Slavery*, is introspective in tone, even elegiac, as Du Bois reflects on his tireless labors, which have not been able to end his continued isolation from the mainstream of American life despite his manifold contribution to the nation. If the dawn is about to appear, dusk remains a present reality; Du Bois's own life is in eclipse (he was to live twenty-three more years, but he did not know that in 1940), and the possibility remains that the promised dawn may fade without ever coming fully to light. What Du Bois believes he sees may prove only a false hope, the ending (dusk) of the new day (dawn) before it fully comes to light. In contrast with the dauntless optimism that saturates *Up from Slavery*, *Dusk of Dawn* presents a more measured, cautious view of African Americans' position in their country, dwelling persistently on harsh realities that Washington chooses to ignore.

The subtitle of Du Bois's autobiography warrants close attention. By calling his work *An Essay Toward an Autobiography of a Race Concept*, Du Bois means two things: first, that in his own history can be seen a kind of compressed history of blacks in America; second, that his life story is the chronicle of his maturing understanding of the meaning of that complex and elusive term *race*. Du Bois's first meaning is stated in the "Apology":

But in my experience, autobiographies have had little lure; repeatedly they assume too much or too little: too much in dreaming that one's own life has greatly influenced the world; too little in the reticences, repressions and distortions which come because men do not dare to be absolutely frank. My life had its significance and its only deep significance because it was part of a Problem; but that problem, was, as I continue to think, the central problem of the greatest of the world's democracies and so the Problem of the future world. (viii)

The problem of which Du Bois writes is race, a problem that he locates in the subconscious and that he calls, of all the issues facing the world, "one of the most unyielding and threatening." Commenting on the same subject later in *Dusk of Dawn*, Du Bois restates his thesis:

My discussions of the concept of race, and of the white and colored worlds, are not to be regarded as digressions from the history of my life; rather my autobiography is a digressive illustration or exemplification of what race has meant in the world in the nineteenth and twentieth centuries. It is for this reason that I have named and tried to make this book an autobiography of race rather than merely a personal reminiscence, with the idea that peculiar racial situations and problems could best be explained in the life history of one who has lived them. My living gains its importance from the problems and not the problems from me. (221)

From these brief sections of his autobiography, we realize that Du Bois's concept of his autobiographical "I" is much different from Douglass's or Washington's. In both of the earlier writers' work, the "I" is foregrounded in the narrative; without Frederick or Booker, there would be no story to tell. In *Up from Slavery*, particularly, the "I" is presented as *the* controlling power, born into deprivation, but overcoming every obstacle—indeed, facing no power that for a moment seriously threatens its upward path to international fame. As a result, Washington's autobiography is egocentric beyond the ordinary even in a genre that would seem incapable of producing a work that does not focus primarily on the self.

Because Washington views his autobiographical alter ego as a man virtually always in control of his own life and his external circumstances, he largely ignores questions of national and international economics, politics, and history; such matters are mentioned only to the extent that they present obstacles to be overcome. Du Bois, on the other hand, whose life and work met with much more opposition than did Washington's (much of that opposition coming, ironically, not from the white world but from the Washington-controlled Tuskegee Machine), presents himself as a comparatively diminished player on a stage infinitely vaster than Washington's. Despite his many contributions to the cause of civil rights over the span of a long, active career, Du Bois never presents his life as the solution to the global problem of race. He asserts, "Little indeed did I do, or could I conceivably have done, to make this problem or to loose it" (3). This is a far cry from Washington's self-offering as an example of those attitudes and behaviors that can at least solve America's racial troubles. Instead, Du Bois portrays his autobiographical self in a strangely un-Western manner, depreciating his individual achievements and stressing how he is a speck nearly lost in the whirl of the universe: "Crucified on the vast wheel of time, I flew round and round with the Zeitgeist, waving my pen and lifting faint voices to explain, expound and exhort; to see, foresee and prophesy, to the few who could or would listen" (3–4).

In contrast to Washington, who presents himself as a man who has risen above the accident of his birth to fulfill the promise of the American Dream, Du Bois sees himself as a powerless pawn in a cosmic drama played out on a level far beyond his control. The helplessness he feels is revealed when he writes of his situation as a black person in a white nation, for then Du Bois tends to use strings of past participles, creating sentences whose passive tone reflects the image of a self more acted upon than taking initiative. Describing his life from 1868 to 1940, Du Bois writes, "in the folds of this European civilization I was born and shall die, *imprisoned, conditioned, depressed, exalted and inspired*" (3; emphasis added). Later, writing about race, which he calls "the chief fact" of his life, Du Bois states, "Into the spiritual provincialism of this belief I have been born and this fact has guided, embittered, illuminated and enshrouded my life" (140–41). Such a tone of helplessness, of fatality, seems ironic in a man whose long life was replete with accomplishments in many fields, but no number of achievements seemed able to compensate Du Bois for the isolation he felt simply because he was a black man in America. Contemplating this dynamic, one sees in Du Bois an image of the self-as-exile, a far cry from Washington's satisfied sense of self-integration into the deepest weave of American society.

The exiled self is a new element in the black autobiographical tradition, one that sets Du Bois and his successors apart from Washington and Douglass. Beginning with Du Bois, one sees the increasing frustration of black autobiographers trying to cope with their "crime" of being born black. If Douglass and Washington could find a place of belonging in America, one sees in Du Bois a growing sense of alienation that eventually led him—not to mention Wright, Baldwin, and Cleaver—to actual physical "exile" from America. (Du Bois joined the American Communist Party in 1961 and took up residence in Ghana in that same year. He became a citizen of Ghana shortly before his death in 1963, thus formalizing the estrangement from America that he had long felt.) Radical political and social views also characterize Du Bois's successors in this black autobiographical line, manifesting themselves in various ways—Wright's involvement with Communism, Baldwin's homosexuality and expatriation to France, Cleaver's "insurrectionary" rapes and involvement with the Black Panther Party, and Malcolm X's leadership in the Nation of Islam.

Dusk of Dawn, then, is not intended to be a standard autobiography, nor is the "I" it portrays a usual one, for Du Bois prefers to tell the story of his race during the years of his life rather than telling his individual story. Accordingly, sections of the work relating facts of his own life are interspersed with sections treating in general terms the idea of race, the situation of African Americans, and the attitudes of white Americans toward blacks. Du Bois omits most details of his personal life—his marriage, children, friendships—in favor of aspects of his life that do somehow comment on the broader racial situation of his time. Thus, when Du Bois decides to tell of his ancestry, he does not assume his readers' interest in the subject itself. Instead, as he declares, he desires to show how strenuously white America has suppressed the study of racial intermixture although America is one of the countries of the world that has experienced the greatest blending of the races. He writes:

We have not only not studied race and race mixture in America, but we have tried almost by legal process to stop such study. It is for this reason that it has occurred to me just here to illustrate the way in which Africa and Europe have been united in my family. (103)

There follows an intriguing account of Du Bois's family, the line traced on the paternal side back to French Huguenots and on the maternal side to an African named Tom, who was born about 1730 and served in the Revolutionary War. Du Bois seems to mistrust the intrinsic interest of what he writes, although he elsewhere tells his family history without apology. In *Dusk of Dawn*, however, he makes his personal history serve a larger purpose. His ancestry has brought him blood from several nations and from two races; his ancestors, like those of all but Native Americans, have come to this country from other places, yet have "made it" and have won the right to be called Americans. But because black blood runs in his veins, Du Bois is an outcast; despite his light skin, excellent mind, and superlative education, he remains part of America's "problem." Because of his black blood, he has inherited slavery, discrimination, and insult, and he feels himself bound not only to other black Americans but to the enslaved peoples of Africa and Asia. Du Bois's family history thus leads him to tell of his spiritual affinity with Africa and of his visit to his ancestral continent. This narrative, in turn, extols the beauty of the land and of its people and praises the harmonious and unhurried quality of life missing in Western culture. Where the white world has denigrated the dark races, Du Bois lauds them and shows that the whole white, Western concept of race is built upon lies that even many black women and men have been made to believe.

* * *

As Du Bois notes in the "Apology," he sees his life as significant because it was part of the race problem of his day. The injustice in white America's treatment of its black citizens is always his central theme. He uses his own example as an individual case illustrating a general truth: he possesses a superior education, an extraordinarily perceptive mind, and a highly cultured sensibility; his scholarly works are published and praised; but because he is a black man, America has declared him "nigger" and relegated him, literally and figuratively, to the Jim Crow car. With Frederick Douglass, Du Bois sees his own life as an expression of the victimization of millions of men and women because of one elusive "fact"—race. Du Bois takes pains in *Dusk of Dawn* to demolish traditional prejudices against the black race, especially its supposed mental and cultural inferiority. With Douglass, he declares "I am a man" and denounces the wrongs done him. In this respect, *Dusk of Dawn* offers specific criticisms of Booker Washington and his policies, but the entire book and Du Bois's self-perception also refute Washington's program in a general way.

Booker T. Washington's self-portrait in *Up from Slavery* paints his life as a solution to the American racial problem, and his book stands as an "annotated guide" to racial issues and their proper resolution. His message runs, "Learn a trade, get a job, make money, and you will receive your rights in due time. Look at my example—I have won my respected place through hard work and determination." Du Bois's autobiography refutes that philosophy. He declares:

I was not an American; I was not a man; I was by long education and continual compulsion and daily reminder, a colored man in a white world; and that white world often existed primarily, so far as I was concerned, to see with sleepless vigilance that I was kept within bounds. . . . How I traveled and where, what work I did, what income I received, where I ate, where I slept, with whom I talked, where I sought recreation, where I studied, what I wrote and what I could get published—all this depended and depended primarily upon an overwhelming mass of my fellow citizens in the United States from whose society I was excluded. (136)

This is Du Bois's most emphatic statement of his sense of double exile; Du Bois is both "kept within bounds," that is, restricted in his activities and also excluded from the privileges white Americans assume to be theirs by divine fiat. Du Bois is further isolated because he is a black man raised in rural, Puritan New England and so is out of touch with the black masses of the South and the urban North; additionally, his extraordinary intellectual gifts set him aside as part of the "Talented Tenth"—an individual fit, by native ability, education, and personality, more for a quiet, scholarly life than for the aggressive role of racial activist and propagandist that he reluctantly took upon himself.

Du Bois's sense of exile would look something like the diagram.

The White World

The Barrier: Race, and the System That Enforces Racial Separation

---

minorities, especially blacks

the masses   Du Bois

Du Bois takes this reality of exile with utmost seriousness, and reinforces his claim of the danger the white world presents to blacks by
his repeated references to lynching, the weapon the white world uses
to maintain racial barriers. The threat of lynching runs through *Dusk
of Dawn* as an ominous ground bass, always present, occasionally rising to the surface in images of horror. Descriptions of lynchings and
statistics about lynchings of African Americans during the thirty-four-
year period between 1885 and 1910 appear at least eleven times in
Dusk of Dawn, perhaps nowhere more powerfully than this account of
a 1917 killing in Tennessee:

The mobbing and burning were publicly advertised in the press beforehand.
Three thousand automobiles brought the audience, including mothers carrying children. Ten gallons of gasoline were poured over the wretch and he
was burned alive, while hundreds fought for bits of his body, clothing, and
the rope. (251)

The statistics are equally shocking: 1,700 lynchings between 1885 and
1894, with 235 in 1892, the "high tide" of lynching; 327 between 1910
and 1914; 100 in 1915; and 77 in 1919, including a woman and
eleven soldiers, of whom fourteen were publicly burned, eleven of
them alive (29, 48, 223, 264).

How far we are from Booker T. Washington's vision of America
as set forth in *Up from Slavery*. Washington sees America as an open
door through which any person with determination may walk with
impunity; Du Bois perceives the white world existing behind a nearly

insurmountable barrier that it protects by its ability publicly, horribly, and (technically, at least) illegally to kill black people. We usually associate the name of Richard Wright with a black autobiographer's overwhelming sense of the danger of the white world, but Du Bois, picking up the theme from Frederick Douglass's descriptions of the bloody beatings slaves endured at the hands of their white owners, establishes danger as a theme in these autobiographies. We note, too, that the lynchings Du Bois describes are altogether more horrible than anything to be found in Douglass's *Narrative*, for lynching implies the impersonal savagery and unreasoning hatred of the mob, forces even more dangerous than the power of individual slaveowners over their slaves.

The violence of lynching used to enforce African Americans' "internal exile" in America links well with the theme of exile inherent in the Oedipal myth. The newborn child, perceived as a threat to his father, whom he is predicted to slay, is subjected to physical violence (the piercing through the feet) and left to die outside the city. Unexpectedly saved, the child lives in exile far from the seat of power and his rightful inheritance. In the same way, black Americans have been violently expelled from their rightful place, set apart to wander in exile, threatened by violent death lest they attempt to claim their birthright. An added horror, for Du Bois, at least, is his perception that not only is the white world his enemy, but so is the leadership of his own race, for it has aligned itself, knowingly or not, with the enemy.

Du Bois's description of himself in *Dusk of Dawn* as an outcast, written twenty-five years after the death of Booker T. Washington, is more an indictment of Washington's philosophy than any direct criticism of his life and work. Washington's self-portrait in *Up from Slavery* presents a man of action whose hard work, determination, and tact, together with heaven's blessing (Washington never misses an opportunity to compare Tuskegee with the chosen people and himself with Moses) all combine into an unstoppable formula for success. Du Bois, however, just as dedicated as Washington, better educated than he and certainly his intellectual superior, is forced into a life not of action, but of reaction—reaction to the constraints an unjust world places upon him because he dares to demand his full freedom. If Washington worked at times to show that the Frederick Douglass approach to race relations was outdated, destined to give way to a more "enlightened" path suited to an era of capitalist expansion, then Du Bois spent his life countering the abuses that Washington's policies invited. The Niagara Movement, which Du Bois began, and the

NAACP, of which he was a leader for nearly twenty-five years, were created as direct responses to the Tuskegee Machine.

In his treatment of Booker T. Washington in *Dusk of Dawn*, Du Bois specifically faults Washington for decrying political activities among blacks while playing power politics himself, and he deplores Washington's policy of accommodation to the increasingly oppressive laws disenfranchising blacks and relegating them to second-class treatment in public services. But even more serious, in Du Bois's opinion, is Washington's power over others; the Tuskegee leader could make or break a career simply by giving or withholding approval of an appointment or of a plan of individual enterprise. Du Bois notes the case of Will Benson, who tried to organize a black town as an independent economic unit in the South. Benson appealed to Northern philanthropists for financial assistance. When, according to custom, Washington was consulted for his opinion about the project, he simply remained silent. Benson did not receive the needed help; Du Bois writes that he died young, "Of overwork, worry, and a broken heart."

Above all, however, Du Bois resents Booker Washington's determination to squelch opposition to his policies:

Contrary to most opinion, the controversy as it developed was not entirely against Mr. Washington's ideas, but became the insistence upon the right of other Negroes to have and express their ideas. Things came to such a pass than when any Negro complained or advocated a course of action, he was silenced with the remark that Mr. Washington did not agree with this. Naturally, the bumptious, irritated, young black intelligentsia of the day declared, "I don't care a damn what Booker Washington thinks! This is what I think, and *I have a right to think.*" (75)

Du Bois furthers his criticism of the Tuskegee Machine by noting that it was not the creation of blacks alone. Whites had an interest in Tuskegee and its accommodationist policies. The so-called philanthropists who funded Tuskegee had some self-interest in the success of the institution; being businessmen, they saw Southern blacks as a vast potential pool of semiskilled labor unlikely to agitate for the rights that the white labor unions of the North were seeking for their members. To keep Southern blacks acquiescent to this scheme, they must have their ambition curtailed. Washington's policies fit with the plan of Northern capitalists who "proposed by building up his prestige and power to control the Negro group." Du Bois concludes, "This was the real force back of the Tuskegee Machine. It had money and it had opportunity, and it found in Tuskegee tools to do its bidding" (74).

The implication that Washington was involved, even if unwittingly, in a subtle but pervasive plot against blacks makes him appear as more than misguided; Washington is a traitor to his race, willing to sell its birthright for a mess of personal power. Washington has "sold out" to the white world, thereby placing himself on the other side of the racial barrier that whites have erected to keep blacks from achieving the privileges America promises. This suggestion also ties in with Du Bois's theory of history, which he espouses throughout *Dusk of Dawn* and which he states succinctly at the end of the chapter treating his controversy with Washington:

> That history [of the West in the nineteenth and twentieth centuries] may be epitomized in one word—Empire; the domination of white Europe over black Africa and yellow Asia, through political power built on the economic control of labor, income, and ideas. The echo of this industrial imperialism in America was the expulsion of black men from American democracy, their subjection to caste control and wage slavery. This ideology was triumphant in 1910. (96)

Du Bois insists upon the reality of racial conflicts behind the great historical movements of his time, and he repeats this theme throughout *Dusk of Dawn*. For him, the colonization of Africa and Asia by the European powers results from the white race's contempt for the darker races combined with the white race's determination to exploit the raw materials and labor forces in lands inhabited by dark-skinned peoples. His determination to find a racial root for every one of the world's problems comes to sound strained, and it forces Du Bois into some simplistic reasoning. He must ignore other forces active in history in order to highlight racial injustice; but if it seems exaggerated to claim that World War I was fought for reasons having to do more with race than with entangling political alliances, one realizes how Du Bois, speaking on behalf of one of the world's largest oppressed minorities, can see racial prejudice as the supreme evil of his time. Du Bois actually takes up here a theme sounded by Frederick Douglass, who saw slavery as the great cancer eating away at antebellum America. For Douglass, slavery was an evil that adversely affected white slave owners as much as it harmed their black chattel: recall how he details the deterioration of the spirit and character of Sophia Auld once she became Douglass's owner, turning from a woman kind and compassionate into a petty and cruel tyrant because of her power over another human being. But if Douglass deals with the deleterious effects of bondage upon both races on the national scale, Du Bois expands the issue to the global. He elevates to the nth degree the bondage theme already observed in Douglass and Washington;

Du Bois looks at the history of the nineteenth and twentieth centuries and sees the enslavement of two of the world's three races by its third race as the era's dominant historical fact. This enslavement has resulted from economic forces, to be sure, and has been carried out with premeditated malice in many instances. But Du Bois detects other, harder-to-explain motives behind racial persecution; his changing understanding of the causes of racism and of the means necessary to combat them forms the second great theme of the autobiography. Early in his life, he assumed that prejudice was the result of ignorance: "The world was thinking wrong about race, because it did not know. The ultimate evil was stupidity. The cure for it was knowledge based on scientific investigation" (58). Well-equipped by his sociological training at a time when sociology was a fledgling discipline, Du Bois devoted years to producing studies that would, by telling the "truth" about blacks, change the attitudes of the white race. But as he grew older, Du Bois came to realize how naive his earlier view had been. Racial prejudice is not simply a matter of ignorance, but rather

is rooted in the irrational nature of man, buried in his unconscious, perpetuated by the folkways and mores of a whole culture. It is "the result of inherited customs of those irrational and partly subconscious actions of men which control so large a proportion of their needs."[18]

A realization of the irrational bases of race prejudice altered the course of W.E.B. Du Bois's career. Suited by training and temperament for an academic career, he became uncomfortable in his ivory tower "while negroes were lynched, murdered, and starved." He realized how few people were actually interested in the sociological truths he was uncovering, least of all the white racists who were, as he thought, most in need of them. Furthermore, the realization that prejudice and oppression are rooted in unconscious forces showed Du Bois the futility, the ridiculousness, of the programs of Booker T. Washington. Even a generous reading of Washington's motives would show them misguided, for his policies were designed not to change the white race's basic opinion of blacks but to equip blacks to step into cultural and economic roles acceptable to the prejudicial world view of whites. In training blacks to be skilled workers, Washington was only fitting them for exploitation on a slightly higher level than the one they had known. His advice to blacks to accommodate themselves temporarily to the status quo was doomed to fail, for the white world would never accept fundamental social change as long as unconscious attitudes remained intact. Through his controversy with

Washington and the Tuskegee Machine, Du Bois realized that, just as whites were not going to be persuaded by the facts, neither was Washington going to be moved by appeals to reason; another kind of tactic was in order. So Du Bois reluctantly left his work at Atlanta University (where his continued presence was making life uncomfortable for an administration under attack by Tuskegee for harboring him) and went to war full time against "physical, biological and psychological forces; habits, conventions and enactments" (96). As he says, "My career as a scientist was to be swallowed up in my role as master of propaganda" (94). Here again, Du Bois portrays himself not so much as actor but as reactor, compelled by his growing realization of the truth to alter the course of his life. Although he continued his scholarly work, Du Bois's life after 1910 moved from the narrow confines of academic study into the broader arena of activism, creating an inner tension in a man who was not naturally gregarious. His job with the NAACP, his role as editor of the *Crisis*, and his constant writing were all facets of his new sense of purpose in life, begun after his fortieth birthday and continuing into his nineties.

*   *   *

W.E.B. Du Bois's decision to devote his life to direct combat against racism marks his way of trying to solve the problems associated with bondage and exile. Frederick Douglass used both *fight* and *flight* as weapons against his oppressors; Washington's program of industrial education and temporary accommodation to the cultural milieu of his day was *his* way of fighting the economic and social plight of African Americans; now Du Bois, in his turn, would use propaganda against the unconscious racism he detected as the major historical force of his time. Each of these men lived in the flight/fight dimension of the three-part pattern, and each wrote of this dynamic in his autobiographies. But whereas Douglass and Washington both relied on narration of actual events in their lives, Du Bois not only employs a description of his career as worker on behalf of the black race but also creates an encounter with a fictional personification of white racist ideology to describe his fight against the racial bondage of which he himself was a representative victim.

"The White World," which includes Du Bois's imaginary conversation with a "friendly" white antagonist whom he dubs Roger Van Dieman, occupies the central place in *Dusk of Dawn*. It consists of two sections, the first a discussion between Du Bois and his "friend," the second, a description of the difficulties another fictional but representative white man faces as he tries to reconcile in himself the conflicting roles of Christian, gentleman, and white American. I have

already noted that *Dusk of Dawn* is no typical autobiography, containing, as it does, chapters that are essays on subjects related to Du Bois's
themes; "The White World," however, differs from these other chapters in its use of fictional characters and situations to make thematic
points. We shall see in the next chapter that Richard Wright is the
master of the fictionalized autobiography, creating scenes that never
occurred but that nevertheless possess emotional truth. Du Bois does
not go as far as Wright does, for Du Bois tells us plainly that he is
fabricating his conversation with Roger Van Dieman, perhaps to illustrate his conviction about the fictive nature of the concept of race
through an imagined discussion.

In this fanciful tête-à-tête, the two men take as their subject the
relative inferiority or superiority of the white and black races. Van
Dieman naturally assumes the superiority of whites, claiming them to
be physically more beautiful than blacks, mentally superior, and more
advanced culturally. Du Bois, for his part, accepts none of these assumptions and argues for the superiority of blacks in every particular. As the two men banter, the reader senses the futility of the black
man's arguments—sometimes teasing, sometimes serious—in moving
the white man away from his deeply ingrained (and unexamined) assumptions. Furthermore, the ways in which blacks are superior to
whites—their appreciation of beauty, their ability to laugh, their love
of land and family—are not assets in the industrialized, capitalist so-
cieties whites have created. The two men are as far apart in their
beliefs at the end of the conversation as they were at the beginning;
Du Bois thus shows the great difficulty, if not futility, in his chosen
life's work. If he cannot persuade Van Dieman, who is basically sympathetic, of the value of the black races, what chance does Du Bois
have against the masses of whites, who stand to gain wealth and
power from the continued oppression of blacks?

Toward the end of their conversation, after Du Bois has ham-
mered away at Van Dieman's simplistic notion of race by pointing out
how much race mixture has occurred over the years (so much that
clear demarcations among the races, even if they can be made, often
seem arbitrary at best), Van Dieman, exasperated, remarks, "you are
not black; you are no Negro." Thinking of the mixture of yellow and
black blood that has infused Europe over the years, Du Bois silently
answers Van Dieman, "You are no white." But if the generally accepted concepts of race are invalid as Du Bois has sought to demonstrate, then Van Dieman wants to know what all the arguments of
relative racial superiority or inferiority are about. He asks Du Bois to
identify the black race, if he can:

"But what is this group; and how do you differentiate it and how can you call it 'black' when you admit it is not black?"

[Du Bois replies,]

I recognize it quite easily and with full legal sanction; the black man is a person who must ride "Jim Crow" in Georgia. (153)

The absurdity and arbitrariness of racial distinctions and the cultural practices based upon them are shown in this fanciful conversation Du Bois constructs. The last part of the dialogue also expresses succinctly a paradox in Du Bois's thinking about himself and about the issue of race. On the one hand, he claims that race and racial identity do not exist. On the other hand, he and everyone he meets seem acutely aware of their individual racial identity: the Roger Van Diemans of the world are every bit as aware of their "whiteness" and its implications as Du Bois is of his "blackness" and what that means. Whereas Du Bois would prefer to look at himself as an individual with unique physical and mental endowments, with particular intellectual gifts, the environing world in which he lives insists that he is first and foremost a member of a particular "race," a fact he must reluctantly accept despite the impossibility of discovering precisely what "race" means. Consequently, he suffers an inner division, about which he had written years before *Dusk of Dawn* but that he still feels when he comes to pen his autobiography. In "Of Our Spiritual Strivings," the first essay in *The Souls of Black Folk*, Du Bois notes:

After the Egyptian and Indian, the Greek and Roman, the Teuton and Mongolian, the Negro is a sort of seventh son, born with a veil, and gifted with second sight in this American world,—a world which yields him no true self-consciousness, but only lets him see himself through the revelation of the other world. It is a peculiar sensation, this double-consciousness, this sense of always looking at one's self through the eyes of others, of measuring one's soul by the tape of a world that looks on in amused contempt and pity. One ever feels his two-ness—an American, a Negro; two souls, two thoughts, two unreconciled strivings; two warring ideals in one dark body, whose dogged strength alone keeps it from being torn asunder. (3)

African Americans, already suffering psychic division, are up against more than the Van Diemans of the white world; they stand also under the power of whites described in the second part of the chapter, the white male Americans who see themselves as Christians and who try to live by New Testament precepts. These individuals view themselves as gentlemen, too, but this only complicates an already muddled set of values that conflict within them. Du Bois charts the codes of conduct that war within such men (*Dusk of Dawn* 163):

Christian	Gentleman	American	White Man
Peace	Justice	Defense	War
Good Will	Manners	Caste	Hate
Golden Rule	Exclusiveness	Propaganda	Suspicion
Liberty	Police	Patriotism	Exploitation
Poverty	Wealth	Power	Empire

Try as he will to nurture in himself the Christian virtues preached to him and to combine with them some of the positive qualities of the gentleman, the white American will when threatened revert to those codes found in the categories *American* and *white man*. Since the white man naturally feels threatened by the rise of the dark races that, he believes, will want to take over his wealth and power and intermarry with his white women, even the well-meaning white man's attitude toward blacks is at bottom hostile, for he knows deep down that blacks hate their lot and *do* wish their share of the life that whites enjoy.

In *Dusk of Dawn*, then, Du Bois presents an "I" subject to inner tension as it strives to understand itself, desiring to be accepted simply as a person, yet unable to forget the racial factor that has, more than any other single power, molded its self-concept. But this divided self seems reasonably integrated compared to the confused white psyches represented by Roger Van Dieman, a man pulled in many directions at once. Du Bois is not the first black autobiographer to note the contradictions in the character of white Americans, particularly those who profess to be Christians; Douglass attacks the hypocrisy of such people in the Appendix of his *Narrative*. Later autobiographers, Wright, Cleaver, and Malcolm X among them, also note the disparities in the white world's view of itself and of blacks; no other writer, however, recognizes as clearly as does Du Bois that the white person's confusion, which often results in irrational behavior toward blacks, lies rooted in the unconscious. Prone to these inner conflicts which they themselves little understand, the whites are all the more difficult to deal with.

Booker T. Washington presents a self blessedly uncomplicated when compared to the self in *Dusk of Dawn*; the "others" in *Up from Slavery* are also viewed in a similarly simplistic manner. The world that Booker encounters may be harsh, demanding, and even unfair at times, but the "others" who comprise that world can be handled and won over if dealt with reasonably. The world with which Du Bois collides in *Dusk of Dawn*, summed up by Van Dieman, is not so tractable and does not respond to reason. By virtue of his native intellect and training, Du Bois perceives the subtleties and complexities both in himself and in others that escape Washington, or which he chooses to ignore, in *Up from Slavery*. The ultimate failure of Washington's programs may be attributed to his lack of insight into the unconscious forces behind American racism; Du Bois's successes are attributable in part to his deeper awareness of the nature of his opponent. His frustrations lie in his own imperfect understanding—usually growing, but often not quickly enough, as Du Bois sees it—of how the unconscious attitudes, values, and beliefs of the white world can best be overcome.

Du Bois, then, has chosen to fight against subtle but formidable forces. Rooted in the unconscious, they rise as a kind of reflex action in the white world whenever it feels its privileged position at risk. Frederick Douglass could engage in hand-to-hand combat with Edward Covey and win exemption from further beatings; later, he could board a northbound train and escape bondage. Booker T. Washington could secure an education and rise to a position of prominence so that he could train other blacks and manipulate both whites and blacks. These accomplishments, impressive in themselves, pale in comparison to the task Du Bois sees facing the black race, the task to which he devotes his life. The scope of bondage has become infinitely greater and the hope of success proportionately diminished. No wonder, then, that Du Bois is less optimistic than Washington about the chances for success. Yet he believes freedom, the third element in the pervasive three-part pattern of African American life and writing, is worth striving for.

Dusk of Dawn discusses some of the varied ways blacks have fought for their freedom and the difficulties attendant on each of those ways. The program of the Niagara Movement and the NAACP—which features "ceaseless agitation and insistent demand for equality" and "the use of force of every sort: moral suasion, propaganda and where possible even physical resistance"—is flawed because it fails to enlist the majority of blacks themselves in the fight for equality. The nation is to enact the programs and the blacks merely to receive them. Additionally, such a program would call for more unanimity among African Americans than exists (193). To criticize the programs to which he has devoted his life shows an unusual degree of objectivity and unusual commitment even in the face of perceived flaws in the approach. But Du Bois thinks his activities have at least been more realistic than a second solution sometimes proposed for black liberation. Du Bois scorns the "back to Africa" movements for their impracticality; there are no uninhabited regions of the earth suitable for mass migrations. Other migration schemes, whether from the American South to the North, the West, or just to the cities, do in fact bring physical relocation but also new segregation and op-pression in different locales. Du Bois has a third proposal for black freedom, one to which he has obviously devoted a good deal of thought. He envisions a huge network of black businesses working together in a kind of cooperative. Black people would buy from one another and sell to one another to create an inner and partially in-dependent economy in America. Ironically, Du Bois ends up espous-ing a plan of self-help for African Americans that sounds not very different from Booker T. Washington's. Admittedly, Du Bois does allow for the use of propaganda and agitation along with his eco-nomic program, but the description of his proposal is something Washington could have supported:

> The object of that plan would be two-fold: first to make it possible for the Negro group to await its ultimate emancipation with reasoned patience, with equitable temper and with every possible effort to raise the social status and increase the efficiency of the group. And secondly and just as important, the ultimate object of the plan is to obtain admission of the colored group to cooperation and incorporation into the white group on the best possible terms. (200)

We should not be surprised that Du Bois seeks the solutions to the racial injustices of his times in economic programs; he had be-come interested in the Russian Revolution and socialism in the 1920s. A visit to the Soviet Union in 1926 increased his curiosity about the ways socialism could aid African Americans. Increasingly, Du Bois came to believe that socialism was the way of the future. He joined the American Communist Party at the end of his life.

Dusk of Dawn ends with a chapter describing Du Bois's work with the NAACP during and after World War I up until his resignation from the organization in 1934 and his return to teaching. The goals for which he had given his life had yet to be realized; freedom had yet to be obtained. Yet Du Bois's energetic activity at the age of sev-enty is an indication of his lasting belief that, despite the bondage that still existed, the fight was valid because freedom could be obtained. In this respect, Du Bois's viewpoint is similar to Booker T. Washing-ton's, if somewhat more cautious.

Twenty years later, at the age of ninety, Du Bois closes his second autobiography in a vein rather more pessimistic than anything found in *Dusk of Dawn.* During the two decades separating the two works, Du Bois had experienced great personal trials. In 1950 and 1951 he had been indicted, tried, and acquitted of the charge of being an "un-registered foreign agent" because of his connection with the Peace Information Center. His well-known sympathy for socialism and the

Soviet Union undoubtedly made him a target of the rampant paranoia of the McCarthy era. His persecution at the hands of the federal
government certainly helped sour Du Bois on the United States. But
whatever the reasons, he closes *The Autobiography of W.E.B. Du Bois*
with a "postlude" that mourns for an America that has squandered
much of its glorious possibility. It has reduced life to buying and selling; everything falls to the desire for profit. Democracy has been
shown to be unworkable; cheating exists in all facets of economic and
political life; wealth and power are the ultimate gods. On the international scene, America is the great arms dealer, and it prepares for
more wars. The nation can yet be saved, "but it is selling its birthright.
It is betraying its mighty destiny." Du Bois asserts that he has served
his homeland all his life even though much of his calling has been
that of the prophet destined to preach an unpopular message of the
nation's failings. At the end of his life, Du Bois sums up his faith this
way: "I believe in socialism. I seek a world where the ideals of communism will triumph—to each according to his need, from each according to his ability. For this I will work as long as I live. And I still
live."[19]

* * *

Dusk of Dawn is an unusual work and in some ways an unsatisfying one. It lacks the narrative drive of Douglass's best work, Washington's skillful way with anecdotes, and Richard Wright's descriptive
power. Nevertheless, *Dusk of Dawn* accomplishes something no other
black autobiography attempts so consistently and on such a sweeping
scale: the demonstrable connection between the history of a distinct
group of people (Du Bois's argument against the validity of the concept of race notwithstanding) and one representative member of the
group whose individual life characterizes and mirrors the communal
experience. In this matter, Du Bois's autobiographical strategy contrasts, for example, with Richard Wright's. Wright strives in *Black Boy*
to demonstrate how different he is from other blacks living under
similar circumstances: his unique identity as artist sets him apart from
both the black and white communities and propels him on his quest
for freedom. Du Bois, on the other hand, although equally exceptional, insists on linking his life with the lives of other African Americans, discovering his identity not solely in his uniqueness but in his
oneness with others.

For this reason, *Dusk of Dawn* consistently recounts national and
world events, especially as they affect blacks, as background to the
events in Du Bois's own life. Digressions in the narrative serve a similar purpose, to help explain the forces in the world of Du Bois's time

that influenced him. Through this expansive approach to his life story, Du Bois manages to reveal himself in much the same way that Montaigne leaves us a lively self-portrait through the far-reaching subject matter of the *Essays*. (One wonders if Du Bois had Montaigne in mind when he subtitled his autobiography "An *Essay* Toward Autobiography of a Race Concept" [emphasis added].)

Most black autobiographers show, to some extent, how external events shape their lives; Douglass's birth into slavery is the determinative fact of his young life just as his escape is the incident that sets the course for his adulthood. Du Bois, then, is not alone in forging links between world events and his own life. No other black autobiographer is as insistent, though, on seeing her or himself as epitomizing the experience of a group. On first thought, such a vision seems antithetical to the very concept of autobiography, which is to reveal the development of a single life, not of a group of people. Du Bois knew himself to be far from average or typical in intellectual endowment and accomplishment; his insistence on his solidarity with all African Americans therefore serves to underline all the more the absurdity of treating a group of people as if they were all alike, which is precisely the way many whites seem to have regarded blacks during Du Bois's lifetime. Du Bois's individualism—any woman or man's individualism—is denied and eroded when all members of a group are regarded as one. Du Bois thus identifies a commonly recognized problem of modern life, one treated at length by other artists: the loss of individuality. He does not, however, lose his own individualism by insisting that his life is simply another example of the communal life of black Americans. To the contrary, he emerges from *Dusk of Dawn* as a man of singular compassion and dedication who could have lived, by virtue of his gifts and achievements, in splendid isolation, far removed from the problems facing the great majority of blacks. He manages to identify himself with the masses without falling prey to the condescension so often present in the idea of *noblesse oblige*. This lack of pretension does much to make sympathetic a personality that otherwise might be easily dismissed as cool and aloof.

If *Dusk of Dawn* carries to an unusual extreme this practice of viewing one's life as somehow typical of a group under the influence of external forces, it stands alone, as far as I can tell, in tracing its protagonist's growing consciousness in terms of a maturing understanding of the concept of race. Other black autobiographers probe into the mystery of their blackness—one thinks of James Baldwin's and Eldridge Cleaver's work—but none makes the idea of racial identity the key to his or her own development.[20] Du Bois also links this

changing awareness to his assertion of racial solidarity with other African Americans. What he came to realize, many others did too: the
concept of race is not a problem solvable by educating the ignorant;
it is a force rooted deeply in the unconscious and therefore combat-
table only by subtle and determined propaganda. That others came to
share Du Bois's new insights is demonstrated first by the formation
of the Niagara Movement and then by the creation of the NAACP.
Du Bois's views undoubtedly influenced other black leaders, but their
receptivity to his realizations shows that blacks as a group were moving in the same direction as Du Bois was.

Du Bois's gradual change from seeing the racial problems of his
day as merely the product of ignorance that could be remedied by a
presentation of the "truth" to an understanding of the unconscious
forces at work in both whites and blacks helps account for his relationship both with Frederick Douglass and with Booker T. Washington, his two forebears in black American politics and autobiography.

Du Bois identified himself and his life's work with Douglass, the
man he never met; conversely, he disagreed strongly (and eloquently)
with Washington, a man he evidently disliked personally and whose
policies and power he spent years combatting. To Du Bois, Washington was an interloper in the "true" line of black leaders; accordingly,
he and his works had to be expunged from the record. Because Du
Bois lived to such a great age, he had the satisfaction of seeing most
black Americans turn away from the Washington-Tuskegee philosophy of race relations and embrace a much more assertive program,
one that he himself helped bring into being.

In 1903, however, when the publication of "Of Mr. Booker T.
Washington and Others" inaugurated the Washington-Du Bois controversy, the task of redirecting American race relations must have
seemed daunting. Not only was the Washington-Tuskegee coalition
in full control, but Du Bois's still immature understanding of the true
nature of racial attitudes prevented his forming the most effective
plan for combatting Washington as well as white racism. Du Bois's
instincts about the problem facing African Americans were basically
sound even as early as 1901, and the evidence of black people's de-
teriorating economic and social position was available for anyone who
cared to look at it honestly. Inspired and instructed by the example
of Frederick Douglass's life and work, Du Bois began the task that
would occupy him the rest of his life when he issued his challenge to
Washington in the essay "Of Mr. Booker T. Washington and Others."

Thematically and stylistically, *Dusk of Dawn* is worlds apart from
Up from Slavery. Washington's self-portrait and his picture of the
world in which that autobiographical self asserts itself and conquers

all both reveal a naive and optimistic view of the self and of life. To what extent the Franklinesque vision of *Up from Slavery* reflects Washington's genuine beliefs is difficult to determine; like most autobiographers, Washington presents a carefully "edited" self for public inspection. His purpose, after all, is to further a particular view of African Americans' character and aspirations in relationship to their usefulness to the economic and social agendas of turn-of-the-century America. On the other hand, Washington's studied artlessness, a quality he also cultivated on the lecture platform, conceals a shrewd personality able to size up the values of its various audiences and capable of telling those audiences what they want to hear in ways they will find pleasing. No one can dispute what Washington achieved in and through Tuskegee, and *Up from Slavery* presents only one side of a personality more calculating and forceful than the autobiography hints at. Still, Washington's relatively uncomplicated understanding of human psychology seems genuine, not just a fabrication for his autobiography. His dealings with people were, by all accounts, consistent, as if he had arrived at a view of human nature that worked for him and remained true to it for life, despite mounting evidence that his programs were failing. If Washington secretly held a view of the white world and of black-white relationships other than the one he preached and lived, he did a remarkable job of concealing that view from everyone, perhaps even from himself. Despite the ever-worsening social and economic plight of African Americans during the height of his reign as the most powerful black man in America, Washington held on to his optimistic vision as long as he lived.

Written twenty-five years after *Up from Slavery*, years that saw the first World War and the rise of fascism, *Dusk of Dawn* presents a world view altogether more pessimistic than that proffered in the earlier book. Du Bois's training as a sociologist and his startlingly clear grasp of Freudian psychology, particularly of the power of the unconscious, color his self-understanding and his style. A comparison of a typical example of Du Boisian prose with one of Washington's will demonstrate the differences between the two men's understandings and manners of expression.

In both passages the authors describe their view of human nature. Du Bois writes:

The facts of the situation, however, as science today conceives it, are clear. The individual may act consciously and rationally and be responsible for what he does; but on the other hand many of his actions, and indeed, as we are coming to believe, most of his actions, are not rational and many of them arise from subconscious urges. It is our duty to assess and praise and blame for the rational and conscious acts of men, but to regard the vast area of the subconscious and the irrational and especially of habit and convention which also produce significant action, as an area where we must apply other remedies and judgments if we would get justice and right to prevail in the world. (*Dusk of Dawn* 171)

Stylistically, Du Bois's prose often sounds like a textbook: the sentences are long, and the concepts are dealt with in broadly general and abstract terms. Thematically, Du Bois here as in many other places expresses his awareness of the power of the unconscious and the challenge it presents to anyone who would seek to change society's basic assumptions and values.

A passage from *Up from Slavery* reveals Washington's willingness to speculate about motivating powers behind human behavior, but Washington is not comfortable with abstractions for long: each pronouncement of a general truth receives concrete illustration. Problems also receive solutions much simpler than any Du Bois could have accepted:

My experience is that there is something in human nature which always makes an individual recognize and reward merit, no matter under what colour of skin merit is found. I have found, too, that it is the visible, the tangible, that goes a long way in softening prejudices. The actual sight of a first-class house that a negro has built is ten times more potent than pages of discussion about a house that he ought to build, or perhaps could build.

The individual who can do something that the world wants done will, in the end, make his way regardless of his race. One man may go into a community prepared to supply the people there with an analysis of Greek sentences. The community may not at that time be prepared for, or feel the need of, Greek analysis, but it may feel its need of bricks and houses and wagons. If the man can supply the need for those, it will lead eventually to a demand for the first product, and with the demand will come the ability to appreciate it and to profit by it.[21]

In these passages with their short sentences and vivid illustration of each point, we find a style more accessible than Du Bois's; *Up from Slavery* resembles spoken English much more than does *Dusk of Dawn* with its scholarly meditations.

Washington's assumptions about human motivation, so easy to comprehend, must indeed have exasperated Du Bois, whose vision was altogether darker and more complex. *Dusk of Dawn* reflects that vision through its denser, tentative style, its presentation of an "I" less dominant and self-confident than Washington's, and its unwillingness to prescribe glib solutions to the problems it raises. It is no wonder that Du Bois's early charges against Washington and his policies were met with such widespread criticism: by giving America "solutions" to some of its deepest problems, Washington had soothed many consciences. Du Bois dared to say that all was not well in the nation; like a prophet, he delivered an unpopular message. By the time he wrote *Dusk of Dawn*, his early words had proven true, but the answers to his questions had not yet been found. Black Americans still lived in bondage to many of the prejudices directly against them, and in Europe, Hitler was demonstrating how the unconscious powers of a nation could be harnessed and directed against another minority, with horrifying results. Du Bois's understanding of the difficulty of dealing with a world largely governed by irrational powers and his admission of the relative powerlessness of the individual proved to reflect more accurately the reality of the cruel twentieth century than did Washington's optimistic naïveté.

4: Runaway Son: Richard Wright

In 1951, the Department of Justice indicted W.E.B. Du Bois and other officers of the Peace Information Center for "failure to register as agent[s] of a foreign principal," the unnamed "foreign principal" being the Soviet Union. Thus did Du Bois become embroiled in the anti-Communist hysteria of the McCarthy era. Although Du Bois was cleared of the charges against him, he was refused a passport until 1958; additionally, he was subjected to harassment and vilification.[1] When he was again free to travel, he visited the Soviet Union and China, where he was warmly welcomed. Finally, in 1961, Du Bois took two steps to formalize impulses that had apparently long been growing within him: he joined the Communist Party of the United States, and he took up residence in Ghana at the invitation of Kwame Nkrumah. In 1963, shortly before his death, Du Bois became a Ghanian citizen. All three actions signaled Du Bois's rejection of America—a rejection rooted in a lifetime of frustrated effort to change a racist and repressive society. Being tried, at the age of eighty-three, for so-called crimes against the state must have seemed like the final insult; this was how the nation Du Bois had sought to serve repaid him, one of the foremost thinkers, writers, and leaders of his day.

Du Bois's actions during the last two years of his life may have been more symbolic than born of absolute psychological need. Du Bois was ninety-three years old in 1961; he knew he would neither assume a leadership role in the Communist Party nor live long in his adopted African home. On the other hand, Du Bois's long postponement of joining the party and of expatriating himself may have resulted from practical lessons he had learned from observing a younger generation of black writers who had years earlier found racism within the Communist Party and discovered that flight from America did not magically confer "freedom." Claude McKay and Richard Wright had both abandoned Communism after bitter experiences; Wright and James Baldwin had both left America to live in

Europe, where overt racism was less evident, but where their personal problems persisted. As Wright and Baldwin came to learn, one can run away from home, but one cannot escape oneself.

If Du Bois's eleventh-hour attachment to the Communist Party and move to Ghana finally formalized his rejection of and exile from the mainstream of American life, those decisions merely gave outward expression to what had been facts of Du Bois's inner life for many years. As noted in Chapter Three, Du Bois had long felt himself isolated from the dominant white world and, by virtue of his extraordinary intelligence and education, also from the masses of black Americans. In a real sense, Du Bois had been expatriated most of his adult life, for *expatriated* means, in its root form, "out of, away from, one's homeland"—*ex patria*. The white world had first expatriated the black race by taking it from Africa, its genuine *patria*, then by putting it into internal exile in America, thus sentencing African Americans to a double expatriation. For Du Bois, the irony was to live *in* America physically, but *out of* America psychologically, and that not by his own choice.

Du Bois certainly felt displaced, yet postponed the choices the younger generation had already made. Was he more committed than they to staying in America? Was he constitutionally more hesitant to make dramatic changes, or had he learned too much from observing the experiences of men like McKay, Wright, and Baldwin to believe that the white worlds of Communism and of Europe were viable solutions for the African Americans? When Du Bois finally acted, he opted for change on his own terms. He joined the American Communist Party, it is true, but immediately removed himself physically from America. His choice of a new homeland was a young, socialist, *black* African nation, not any place in Europe or Asia. Du Bois's expatriation was as "black" as he could make it, as if at the end of his life he could finally reject the white world that had so long rejected him.

Although Du Bois was not the first among the autobiographers studied in this book to expatriate himself physically from America (Wright moved to France permanently in 1947, Baldwin in 1948), he is the first *born* among them to be unable to resolve for himself the issue of psychological expatriation. Both Frederick Douglass and Booker T. Washington overcame the deprived circumstances of their early years and attained positions of national prominence in America. Du Bois, whose childhood circumstances, although meager, were not nearly as harrowing as Douglass's or Washington's, also rose to leadership among black Americans and recognition among white Americans, but he never attained the apparent sense of belonging in

America that Douglass and Washington did. It is true that Douglass fought all his life for the cause of freedom, and Washington, the most popular black man of his era, still felt personally the sting of racism throughout his life; however, the overwhelming feeling of unresolvable psychic displacement that afflicted later black autobiographers is a phenomenon that begins with Du Bois. Frederick Douglass's body rests in Rochester, New York; Washington's grave is marked by a massive stone not far from the impressive Booker T. Washington memorial sculpture on the campus of Tuskegee Institute. But W.E.B. Du Bois's ashes lie in Accra, Ghana, and attempts to have them brought back to the United States have not met with great enthusiasm in this country. Richard Wright is buried in Paris's Pere Lachaise Cemetery, and James Baldwin is also buried in France. The graves of these three men, far from their places of birth in America, symbolize their fate; unable to "rest" in America during their lives, they now lie outside the country of their birth—eternally expatriated.

As we have noted, *expatriate* derives from *ex patria*. *Patria* is a feminine noun in Latin, from the same root as the masculine noun for "father." In a study of the Oedipal conflict among several generations of black writers, some of whom ended up exiled from the fatherland, the term *expatriated* inevitably suggests a double meaning: separation not only from the father*land*, but also from the father himself, be that father a biological or literary parent. (Regardless of its Latin gender, *patria* does not require one to think of one's nation strictly in feminine terms, although Wright does, as we shall see in his nightmare visions after being beaten nearly to death for almost burning down his house. Actually, many people's image of their homeland seems to combine both masculine and feminine traits.) All three of the writers whom we have studied thus far experienced expatriation in this second sense: Douglass and Washington never knew their fathers, and Du Bois grew up without the father who deserted his family when Du Bois was a child. Washington came to terms with Douglass, his "father" in the black autobiographical line; the two men were on cordial terms at the time of Douglass's death in 1895, and any resentment toward or threat from Douglass that Washington experienced was surely unknown to Douglass and was probably largely unconscious in Washington as well.

With Du Bois, expatriation in the sense of separation from the father figure becomes reality for the first time in this black autobiographical line. Du Bois was never reconciled to Washington; indeed, he identified Washington and the Tuskegee Machine as collaborators with the dominant, paternalistic white world he so hated. In Du Bois's view, Washington had betrayed the black race, over which he loomed as father figure for twenty years; Du Bois saw himself as just one of thousands who had felt the effects of that betrayal.

Du Bois, then, experienced a double expatriation: first an unresolved conflict with Washington, the paternal figure from whom he and his generation sought to wrest leadership and power; second a sense of exile from America itself. Curiously, the absence of Du Bois's own father seems not to have been a significant factor in Du Bois's life, perhaps because his father's disappearance did not dramatically affect the circumstances of his youth. However, when we come to Richard Wright, whose autobiography was published only five years after *Dusk of Dawn* even though Wright was forty years younger than Du Bois, we encounter a black autobiographer expatriated in every sense of the word. Like Douglass, Washington, and Du Bois, Wright was separated from his biological father, but Nathaniel Wright's desertion of his family left permanent emotional scars on his son. Wright ran first from the South and then from all of America, expatriating himself for the last thirteen years of his life. He was also a man at odds with his predecessors in the black autobiographical tradition because the hellish vision of black life in America with which he filled his own writing offended them and caused them to worry over the impression his work would make on the white world. Like Du Bois, who was separated from most other blacks by his naturally reticent personality as well as by his training and education, Wright also felt isolated from the masses. He was one of Du Bois's "Talented Tenth," an individual who, by virtue of his innate gifts, was supposedly destined to rise to a place of leadership among African Americans. Ironically, as Du Bois should have realized from his own experience, extraordinary gifts, while perhaps fitting individuals for leadership, can also prevent them from forming relationships with the very people they are "born" to lead. Separation, division, alienation, isolation—all are constant themes in the life and works of Richard Wright, the writer who presents what is, to my mind, the most terrifying portrait of the African American experience that we have.

In 1901, seven years before the birth of Richard Wright, William Dean Howells wrote his review of *Up from Slavery*. In it he praises Washington's "conservative" temper of mind, his "unfailing sense of humor," and his "cool patience." Howells detects similar qualities in other black leaders like Paul Laurence Dunbar, Charles Waddell Chesnutt, and even Frederick Douglass.[2] Douglass's refusal to join John Brown's raid at Harper's Ferry is cited as evidence of his ability to keep a "judicial mind" and "not lose his head" despite the appeals of a man whom he loved and respected. Commenting on this frame of mind, which he wants to believe is present in the majority of blacks, Howells continues:

This calm is apparently characteristic of the best of the race, and in certain aspects it is of the highest and most consoling promise. It enables them to use reason and the nimbler weapons of irony, and saves them from bitterness. By virtue of it Washington, and Dunbar and Chesnutt enjoy the negro's ludicrous side as the white observer enjoys it, and Douglass could see the fun of the zealots whose friend and fellow-fighter he was. The fact is of all sorts of interesting implications; but I will draw from it, for the present, the sole suggestion that the problem of the colored race may be more complex than we have thought it. What if upon some large scale they should be subtler than we have supposed? What if their amiability should veil a sense of *our* absurdities, and there should be in our polite inferiors the potentiality of something like contempt for us? The notion is awful; but we may be sure they will be too kind, too wise, ever to do more than let us guess at the truth, if it is the truth. (*Papers* 6, 195–96)

One hopes that Howells intends irony in these lines, for if not, his words express willful ignorance and wishful thinking. He is much closer to the truth than he dares admit when he speaks of blacks' ability to feel contempt for whites, if not something worse. But he is dead wrong in his stated certainty that black Americans would forever be "too kind, too wise" to let white Americans guess at their true feelings. If African Americans long hesitated to voice their genuine emotions about their oppression, their motive was grounded more on fear than on innate kindness. It took time before one black man gathered his courage and wrote the truth that existed for many of his race—a truth too long concealed from the white world. Richard Wright might well have responded to Howells's naive words with bitter laughter; then he might have handed him copies of his two books—a novel and an autobiography—that forever changed the way America thought about its black citizens.

*   *   *

Native Son may not be the greatest novel yet written by an African American—many would reserve that honor for *Invisible Man*—but no novel by a black writer has caused such a stir at the time of its publication. Harper and Brothers, the book's publisher, announced in the newspapers that the public had "stampeded" the bookstores to buy copies of the novel. *Native Son* sold out of Manhattan bookstores within three hours of its appearance; the Book-of-the-Month-Club selected it for its readers. The critics praised it, and Wright quickly earned more than $20,000 from sales.[3] *Native Son* showed America facets of black life and of the black personality it had not previously acknowledged, and in Bigger Thomas the world met a character who personified the alienation and pent-up rage in many black men and women, Richard Wright among them.

Native Son is divided into three books: "Fear," "Flight," and "Fate." In Book I, fear causes Bigger to commit the crime that costs him his life: so afraid is he of being found in Mary Dalton's bedroom and of having her mother believe he has raped the drunken girl that he inadvertently smothers Mary in his efforts to prevent her answering when the blind woman calls out to her. Bigger burns Mary's body in a furnace to cover his crime, having first beheaded her to fit her body into it. When the charred remains are found, he must flee; in his flight, he murders his girlfriend to keep her from betraying him. Bigger's futile attempt to evade the police occurs in Book II, "Flight." Apprehended, Bigger is tried, found guilty, and condemned to death: this is Book III, "Fate." Just as Wright makes it clear that Bigger kills out of fear, so does he emphasize the hopelessness of his flight and the inevitability of his punishment.

In this three-part structure of *Native Son*, we observe a version of the bondage/flight/freedom motif of the slave narratives as perfected by Douglass and reshaped by Washington and Du Bois. Wright links fear and bondage by showing that fear is a kind of slavery that drastically restricts his protagonist's choices (he makes the same connection in *Black Boy*); he also gives the old pattern a terrible twist when he changes the third part, "freedom," to "fate" and has Bigger's quest end in the electric chair where he finally finds freedom—and death. Before Bigger dies, he tells his lawyer that he has figured out a meaning for his life and for his actions, but such an assertion is questionable. Faced with death, Bigger *must* discover something to salvage from his wasted life, but his anguished cry, "What I killed for must've been good!" convinces neither Max nor the reader.[4] The ending of *Native Son* is perhaps the grimmest in any African American novel, for Bigger's realizations about himself, imperfect at best, come too late in his life to make much difference.[5]

Just at the time *Native Son* was receiving its enormous critical and popular acclaim, Paul R. Reynolds, Jr., Wright's agent, proposed that Wright consider writing his autobiography.[6] Wright was put off by the idea—he felt he was still too young to be able to articulate the meaning of his life—but he was attracted, too. He took no immediate action on Reynolds's suggestion; not until 1942 did he begin writing his autobiography. In that interval, Wright's personal life was eventful. During an extended vacation in Mexico in the summer of 1940, he became disenchanted with his wife, Dhima Meadman, and left her behind when he returned to the United States. Taking a train from Mexico, Wright traveled in the South for the first time in twelve years. He visited Jackson and Memphis before going on to Chicago and New York, which he reached by August. There he made the final break with his wife; in March of the following year, he married Ellen Poplar, whom he had met through his association with the Communist Party. Their daughter, Julia, was born in April, 1942; shortly after her birth, Wright began the autobiography. A year later, he was half finished with it; he sent the completed work to Paul Reynolds on December 17, 1943. Published in 1945 as *Black Boy*, the book was an abridgement by about one-third of Wright's original manuscript, which traced his life through his Chicago years and his involvement with the Communists. *Black Boy* omits all the Chicago material, ending with Wright on his way to that city. (The second part of the work, published in 1977 as *American Hunger*, will be treated later in this chapter.) By March of 1945, *Black Boy* had sold 400,000 copies and was at the top of all the New York papers' best-seller lists.[7]

Constance Webb notes that Wright's decision about the tone of his autobiography was determined during his train trip from Mexico to Chicago in the summer of 1940. As soon as the train crossed the Texas border, the passengers, who had so far traveled together regardless of race, were separated; Wright then had to use the Jim Crow car. At the border, his bags were inspected. The customs inspector was suspicious of Wright's typewriter and of the books he was carrying. He had difficulty grasping that Wright was a writer; he apparently could not imagine any black person except a preacher or teacher having any use for books or a typing machine. That incident was Wright's reintroduction to a South where he was again called "boy" and where he had to use segregated public facilities. Once more, Wright was at the mercy of whites who saw him only as a "nigger," not a famous author. His old fears associated with his childhood came flooding back during the train trip and his stops in Mississippi and Tennessee. Once again he saw the degraded lives his family and other blacks led. Wright's feelings of repulsion, yoked with his own fear of being attacked for being a black man, found their way into the autobiography, although its writing was still two years away.

With pervasive fear the key to its tone, *Black Boy* in its full-length version, which includes the *American Hunger* material, bears remarkable similarity to *Native Son*, for it also uses the novel's variation of the three-part structure of the slave narratives and other, earlier black autobiographies. As he did in *Native Son*, Wright here connects bondage and fear; he also changes freedom to punishment. (*Black Boy* ends on a seemingly positive note, but when the entire work is read as originally conceived, the hero ends up alone—ostracized for daring to assert intellectual and artistic freedom.) Wright's bleak vision of the entrapment of blacks within American culture thus shapes both his fiction and his view of his own life.

*   *   *

The fear/flight/punishment pattern in *Black Boy* is brilliantly set forth in the work's opening episode, as are some of its major themes.[8] When Richard is four years old, he is kept inside all of one long, cold day because his grandmother is ill. Wright's mother commands him and his younger brother to keep quiet lest they disturb the sick woman. Bored and frustrated, the young Richard seeks some way to amuse himself. He begins plucking straws from a broom and throwing them into the fire in the fireplace, watching them smoke, blaze up, and finally burn completely. Tired of this game, Richard wonders how the fluffy white curtains at the window would look if they were set ablaze. Despite his brother's protests, Richard ignites the curtains; they burn, setting the wall and ceiling afire. Soon half the room is burning. Richard runs outside and hides himself under the house, driven by fear of punishment. Overhead, he can hear the panicky movements of the adults as they remove his grandmother from the blazing house; then he hears his parents outside frantically calling for him. Finally, Wright's father looks under the house, sights his son, and despite the boy's attempt to evade him, succeeds in pulling him out from under the house. Richard tries to run, but he is caught before he can escape. His mother then whips him so severely that he loses consciousness, becomes delirious, and has to be forcibly kept in bed. During the illness that results from his beating, he has persistent hallucinations, which recede only with time.

A bare retelling of the events of the house-burning episode reveals the same pattern Wright uses in *Native Son*: young Richard experiences intense fear, which prompts him to try to run away, but there is no escape; the wrong-doer is hunted down and brutally punished. In the same way, Bigger's fear leads him accidentally to kill Mary Dalton, hide her body, and feign innocence; when the crime is detected, fear makes him flee, but he is quickly caught and turned over for execution. Wright often uses this pattern in *Black Boy*. He repeats it, for instance, in the account of how Richard tells his Granny to kiss his backside after she has washed him there. Outraged, Granny descends upon Richard like an avenging angel. He runs from her, ending outside, naked; he then dodges his mother and returns to the house, cowering first in a corner and then hiding under a bed, refusing to come out. He remains there far into the night, but when hunger and thirst drive him from cover, his mother is waiting, and the promised beating is administered. Incidents like this one recur in Richard's life, and the elements of the pattern reoccur. Richard is accused of wrong-doing; sometimes he does not even know what his trespass is, as in the incident with his Uncle Tom. Feeling threatened, he succumbs to terror, which causes him to fight back, to meet threats to his safety with aggression. Ultimately, this fear of breaking unwritten laws and suffering brutal retaliation drives Richard Wright out of the South. In the sentence that originally ended the first part of his autobiography, Wright summarizes his life to that point: "This was the terror from which I fled."[9]

Throughout *Black Boy*, Wright connects his theme of fear with the bondage motif of the slave narratives. In the opening scene, after Richard sets the curtains on fire, he stands looking at the blaze. He recalls, "I was terrified; I wanted to scream but was afraid" (11). A short while later, as he hides under the house, his mother peers down, looking for him. Again Richard says nothing; fear prevents him from speaking. Wright often thus expresses his characters' bondage through their inability to speak: in many situations, Richard is presented as being literally too frightened to say a word. After killing the kitten, Richard is forced by his mother to say a prayer of contrition. He repeats her phrases until she intones, "And while I sleep tonight, do not snatch the breath of life from me." Wright recalls, "I opened my mouth but no words came. My mind was frozen with horror" (20). Later, when Richard is taken to an orphanage to leave his mother free to work, he becomes the director's pet. She tries to make him into an office helper, but he is so intimidated by her that he cannot follow her simplest instructions. She asks him to blot some envelopes; Richard stands and stares, unmoving. Not even her repeated commands can spur the boy to action. As he grows older, Richard has similar experiences each time he enters a new school. Although a bright boy, he is so painfully shy, by his own account, that in a new school he can hardly recall his own name or answer the most rudimentary questions. Even as a young adult, when placed in an uncomfortable situation, particularly when confronted by white people, Richard retreats into silence. About his dealings with whites, Wright notes, "in the past I had always said too much, now I found that it was difficult to say anything at all" (215).

Uncertain about how to respond to the white world and fearful of saying the wrong thing, Richard again and again loses his voice in *Black Boy*. In the same way, millions of African Americans for years said nothing, masking their true feelings in silence or by the smiling faces whites liked to see. Du Bois's description of blacks' "double consciousness" in *The Souls of Black Folk* comes to mind here, raising the question of black identity. Forced to wear a public face so much of the time, the black woman or man could easily suffer psychic splintering from trying to keep a genuine self alive and separate from the facade demanded by the white world. Richard finally cannot cope with the double life demanded of him; unlike Shorty, the elevator operator who invites whites to belittle him in exchange for their quarters, Richard will not surrender his dignity and flees north to save his self-respect and his sanity.

Richard is not the only paralyzed character in *Black Boy*; his mother suffers a series of physically debilitating strokes during the course of his youth. The first one leaves her temporarily unable to speak. She recovers her voice after a time, but gradually becomes more and more a prisoner in her own body, a victim of an uncontrollable sickness. In a similar way, Richard is a prisoner in the South, a prisoner in his own black skin. Wright draws the connection between his mother's illness and his own experience this way:

My mother's suffering grew into a symbol in my mind, gathering to itself all the poverty, the ignorance, the helplessness; the painful, baffling, hunger-ridden days and hours; the restless moving, the futile seeking, the uncertainty, the fear, the dread; the meaningless pain and the endless suffering. Her life set the emotional tone of my life, colored the men and women I was to meet in the future, conditioned my relation to events that had not yet happened, determined my attitude to situations and circumstances I had yet to face. (111)

Growing up, Wright was closer to his mother than to any other person; she alone seems to have felt genuine sympathy for him. No wonder that her protracted illness affected him deeply and that he saw in her paralysis a symbol for his own suffering and for the suffering of black women and men in general. Although his mother's illness caused Richard's family much distress and accounted in part for their poverty, their rootless wandering from one place to another, and their uncertainty about their future, in a more basic way, her paralysis was the *result* of such things; Ella Wright became sick because of the intolerable physical and emotional burdens inflicted on her. Up against the impossible odds the white, racist world offers, she, like many African Americans, retreats into silent paralysis, afraid of retribution for saying or doing the wrong thing. Ella Wright's agony is later epitomized in Richard's inability to act or to speak in front of those who have power over him. Fear causes his paralysis; fear creates—or is—his bondage.

Wright quickly demonstrates that he blames the white world for the bondage in which he and his family lived. This motif is explicitly worked out and expanded through virtually every contact with white people described in *Black Boy*. But Wright hints at this theme already in the autobiography's opening episode. Richard sets fire to the curtains because he is bored. He wants to go out of doors, but his grandmother's image fills his mind and makes him afraid: an "old, *white*, wrinkled, grim face, framed by a halo of tumbling black hair" (9; emphasis added). Margaret Bolden Wilson *was* virtually a white woman, but the trace of black blood in her veins consigned her first to the slavery into which she was born and then, after Emancipation, to the black world.[10] She looked white, a fact that troubled young Richard when he tried to sort out the differences between the races; more importantly, Granny, as she is called in *Black Boy*, behaves like a white person. Her attitude toward Richard is as scornful as any white person's he encounters; her brutal physical treatment of the young boy seems to symbolize Richard's emotional brutalization at the hands of whites. He is not often physically assaulted by white people, but the "white" member of his own family supplies the tangible form of the psychological abuse the white world deals out.

Having to be quiet and stay indoors because of the sickness of his white-skinned grandmother leads Richard to experiment with the broom straws and then with the curtains. And what color are they? White, of course. The moment Richard comes into contact with anything white and makes one wrong move, things go up in flames—figuratively, usually, but this time literally.

These details about whiteness might easily be overlooked in Wright's retelling of how he burned down the house were it not for his description of the hallucinations he suffered after his mother beats him. Wright remembers:

Whenever I tried to sleep I would see huge wobbly white bags, like the full udders of cows, suspended from the ceiling above me. Later, as I grew worse, I could see the bags in the daytime with my eyes open and I was gripped by the fear that they were going to fall and drench me with some horrible liquid. (13)

The shapes that torment the child in his delirium are two gigantic white breasts, filled not with wholesome mother's milk but with "some horrible liquid." The black child finds no consolation, no nourishment, at the breast of his white motherland, but rightly recoils in terror from its impending threat; the breasts of his *dura mater* have no milk for him, only some horrible liquid to scald or drown him. Even in his earliest youth, the child is expatriated, for he is *ex patria*, separated from the motherland. His real mother and grandmother cannot nourish him, nor can his "mother race" sustain him. Wright ends his recollection of this episode by specifically linking the terrifying white breasts, his mother, and death: "Time finally bore me away from the dangerous bags and I got well. But for a long time I was chastened whenever I remembered that my mother had come close to killing me" (13). The significance of this cluster of images becomes increasingly clear as the reader proceeds with *Black Boy*. The white bags/breasts are a maternal symbol; two women, one of them "white," figure in the first scene. Granny is the indirect cause of the fire and of Richard's punishment, which is delivered by the other female figure, Richard's mother. As the bags Richard sees contain no milk, so the two prominent women in Richard's young life, themselves symbols of the two races, are unable to nourish him. Not only is white-skinned Granny devoid of the milk of human kindness, but her religious fanaticism and material poverty keep decent, sustaining food from the table while Richard is growing up. Granny also impoverishes the boy's spirit, for her distorted faith tries to ban literature ("lies," to her) from her house, thereby starving Richard's mind.

Richard's mother, who wants to provide better for her son, is helpless to fill his belly or feed his mind because of her progressive physical deterioration. When the boy looks to the maternal breast for sustenance, he finds either the "horrible liquid" of his grandmother's cruelty or the shriveled vessel of his stricken mother. Whether the breast contains poison or is empty, the child cannot drink; the result is hunger, perhaps the major theme of the autobiography. Hunger—physical, emotional, and spiritual—is soon specifically introduced, but here again, in *Black Boy*'s opening sequence, an essential theme makes an early, subtle appearance. The empty breasts of America produce the peculiar hunger that Richard Wright feels so keenly. No wonder that his original title for his two-part autobiography was *American Hunger*.

*   *   *

The opening scene of *Black Boy*, then, lays down the work's major themes and overall structure in a few brutal strokes. A literal-minded critic of autobiography might, however, feel uncomfortable with the house-burning episode, despite its genius. Is it not a little *too* perfect? Is the gathering together of so many images and themes not too convenient? Wright is free, of course, to begin his life story with whatever event he chooses. A tragedy like the burning of the house can be externally verified; no one suggests that the fire did not occur or that young Richard did not start it and was not punished. With the huge, wobbly white bags in his hallucinations, however, we enter the subjective world of Richard Wright's mind. No one can say if he actually saw such things in his nightmares, nor can anyone know if Wright accurately remembers the substance of his visions. An adult can vividly recall events from his childhood, particularly traumatic events like the burning of a house, so Wright could accurately remember the details of his sickness. But the white bags seem too good to be true. What if they are fabrications, deliberate creations of Richard Wright, the adult writing his autobiography and seeking appropriate images for the opening scene of his life story? Such a suggestion may well disturb some readers who have a particular notion of autobiographical "truth."

Today we know that Richard Wright intentionally fictionalized parts of *Black Boy*. That he should have done so comes as no surprise, for every retelling is in some sense a fictionalization, and autobiographers have been consciously (and unconsciously) employing fictional techniques since Saint Augustine.[11]

Recall Frederick Douglass's account of his fight with Covey: the retelling of that incident is clearly more polished, more "literary" in Douglass's second autobiography than it is in the first; it had settled into a tidier form through constant reiteration in Douglass's numerous public lectures during the years that separate *My Bondage and My Freedom* from *Narrative of the Life of Frederick Douglass*.[12] Remember also the episode in *Up from Slavery* in which Washington is on shipboard reading from Douglass's autobiography how Douglass was mistreated aboard a transatlantic vessel years before. Washington puts down that book to be greeted by white passengers who invite him to address the whole ship that evening. Granted, the event may have happened as Washington narrates it, in which case it is a wondrous coincidence, but the scene has the marks of "improvement" on it, if not invention. Yet "true" or not, it serves Washington's purpose by making a thematic point, the progress of African Americans. If Wright did no more in *Black Boy* than Douglass does in the *Narrative* or Washington in *Up from Slavery*, few critical eyebrows would be raised. But we know that at least one episode in *Black Boy* never occurred at all—to Richard Wright, at least. The incident of Richard's Uncle Hoskins's driving his carriage into the Mississippi River, thus terrifying his young nephew, is fabricated by Wright from a similar incident told to him by Ralph Ellison. The tale suits Wright's thematic purpose—to show young Richard's pervasive fear and his distrust of adults—so he includes it without comment as true.[13] In fact, not only does he not qualify in any way the literal truthfulness of the episode but he also *realizes* it as vividly as any scene in the book.

Other students of Richard Wright's life have detected a second fictional technique employed throughout *Black Boy*—the "fiction of omission." Charles T. Davis notes in detail what Wright leaves out of his autobiography: missing are references to friendships with peers and to the Walls family, white people who employed Richard for two years and who treated him generously and fairly.[14] Constance Webb describes Richard's youthful friendships and tells how he was the leader of a closely knit club of boys who named themselves the "Dick Wright Klan" after their acknowledged leader.[15] Edward Margolies notes other significant omissions, particularly Wright's friendship with the sons of a college president in Jackson and the fact that several members of his family taught school.[16] As Davis asserts, Wright consistently omits such elements in his life in order to highlight his isolation as a child and to intensify the brutality and degradation of his environment.[17]

Wright, of course, is neither the first nor the only black autobiographer to employ this technique of omission. As William Andrews points out, Frederick Douglass omits in his *Narrative* many details of his early life, particularly of the security and love he felt in the home of his grandmother, Betsey Bailey.[18] Du Bois, as we have noted, omits a great deal of information about his personal life, choosing to focus instead on those aspects of his life that further his understanding of race and its connections with the unconscious and how that maturation process leads him into a life as propagandist in the battle for African Americans' rights.

Faced with the manipulations of fact in *Black Boy*, Wright's critics have evinced a variety of responses. All understand the artistic motivation behind Wright's fictionalizing strategies, but some are more comfortable with them than others. Charles Davis and Edward Margolies both believe the trade-off of absolute adherence to fact for artistic effect to be worth it; Davis calls *Black Boy* Wright's "supreme artistic achievement," and Margolies also considers the book an "artistic triumph."[19] George E. Kent, on the other hand, although hailing *Black Boy* as a "great social document," believes that the work could have been greater had Wright remained truer to the facts of his life.[20] Kent is troubled by the unrelieved bleakness of Wright's description of his childhood, finding it unbelievable and apt to make the reflective reader ask how Wright could have survived such an upbringing. Kent further believes that if Wright had given greater indication of the "cultural supports" present in his environment and the ways his mother (who taught school) *did* feed his imaginative and emotional life, the reader could better understand the genesis of his own creative gift, which later flowered in his fiction and autobiography.[21] But what Kent seems not to realize is that this is precisely what Wright wishes *not* to do. On the contrary, Wright employs fictionalizing techniques in *Black Boy* to make an undeniably grim childhood and youth even grimmer, for this makes the miracle of his survival and the growth of his self-as-artist all the more wondrous. Wright is not as interested in making *Black Boy* an accurate social document as he is in forging it into the heroic myth of Richard Wright.

No critic seems to realize this as clearly as does David Littlejohn, who finds in Wright's work the creation of a heroic self set in a mythic landscape of race war.[22] For those who accept the brutal clash of the races as an inevitable fact of life, as Wright does, life assumes a certain clarity. One always knows, for instance, who are one's enemies and who are one's friends. In Westerns, heroes wear white hats and villains black ones; in the world of the black race-war myth, the good have black skin and the evil, white. In this world, that the more powerful white race victimizes blacks is always a foregone conclusion: there will be, as Littlejohn expresses it, "lynching, murder, fire, beating, castration, psychotic sex combats, police brutality, race riots, pure hate against pure hate."[23] Wright's black characters, although belonging to the "good" tribe, are by no means always attractive; no one could claim that Bigger Thomas is lovable or noble. But if Wright's black characters commit crimes, even the most brutal (Bigger smothers Mary Dalton, cuts off her head, and places her body in a furnace; later he smashes Bessie's skull with a brick and throws her body down an airshaft), their motives are understandable because they have themselves been victimized and brutalized by white society. This is the essence of Max's defense of Bigger in *Native Son*: he tries to persuade the white jury that Bigger is their creation. If he has killed, they must bear the blame, for even Bigger's horrifying crimes pale compared to the sins the white world has perpetrated against him and millions of other black people.

Richard Wright lived in a nightmare world similar to that which he describes in his fiction, essays, and autobiography; furthermore, his vision—admittedly shaped in part by selection, exaggeration, and omission—nevertheless often painfully evokes the world that the African American really experienced during the first decades of this century.[24] This vision is limited and limiting, of course, but it is nevertheless powerful and, as Littlejohn reminds us, *necessary*.

*   *   *

It is one thing to fashion a fictional oeuvre in which a consistent world view is carried from novel to short story and back again over the course of a creative lifetime; it is something else again when the writer of fiction casts his or her autobiography within the boundaries of his or her fictional vision. Yet Wright does just that in *Black Boy*; partially fictionalized though it is, one comes away from it, having also read Wright's fiction, with the disturbing realization that the world of both his fiction and his autobiography *is* the world as Wright saw and felt it. And in this world of race war and race hatred, he himself, Richard Wright, is his greatest hero.

We have seen how Frederick Douglass's *Narrative*, embodying, as it does, so many of the elements of the monomyth of the hero, gains greatly in suggestive power. It touches us at unconscious levels and gathers to itself meanings of which Douglass himself was unaware. We have also seen how Booker T. Washington's attempt to cast his life into mythic form falls flat because his essential view of himself is domestic, rising lower-class. Washington may have become something of a legend, but he is no mythic hero. Du Bois does not attempt to cast his autobiography or himself in mythic terms; he is more comfortable in his role of scientific observer who occasionally discards his detached point of view to speak passionately on behalf of his people. Not until Wright do we again come to a black autobiographer with a strong enough sense of his own heroism and sufficient literary skill successfully to shape his life story as heroic myth. *Black Boy* derives its greatness precisely from Wright's narrow, concentrated vision of himself and of his world; were it more literally "true," it would not be nearly so powerful.

Littlejohn has this to say about the heroic aspect of *Black Boy*:

> *Black Boy* . . . reveals its author-hero (never was author more heroic) as a man governed by the most absolute, unreflective, and uncritical certitude of his own virtue. He has had, it would seem, no mean or ignoble motives, no mixed motives even. Any "faults" that appear in the boy Richard are the result of others' moral blindness. He possessed, from infancy nearly, a humorless ethical monumentality; the world is a moral arena for the young Prince Arthur-Wright. Every episode is seen as another fierce combat in the career of this militant young atheist martyr.[25]

Littlejohn's characterization of Richard is somewhat exaggerated. His youthful motives and actions *are* sometimes portrayed as consciously wrong. Richard knows, for example, that he should not hang the kitten even though his father has told him to kill it or to do anything to keep it quiet. The child understands that his father has not intended his words literally but uses a literal interpretation as his excuse to get back at his father, whose restrictions about making noise during the day he resents. This young hero, smaller and weaker than the adult villain he cannot conquer in open physical combat, wages psychological war instead, turning the adult's words against him: "You told me to kill it," Richard can say to his father, knowing that the man cannot justifiably punish him for following his orders to the letter. The hapless kitten becomes the victim in this strife between the ogre-father and hero-son. As *Black Boy* proceeds, we frequently see similar interactions. Richard wrongly threatens to slash his Uncle Tom with razors, but his aggressiveness results from Uncle Tom's unwarranted decision to whip him. Richard's ignoble acts, whatever they are, are always *reactions* to mistreatment. If others would leave him alone or treat him decently, this young hero would be free to perform great deeds.

And great deeds performed in the face of overwhelming odds are the substance of *Black Boy*. The mythic hero descends into an underworld peopled with frightening monsters; from this underworld he wrests a priceless boon. He then escapes to the upper world, returns to his own people, bestows on them the benefits of the prize he has won, and often assumes among them an elevated role of king, warrior, or saint. Frederick Douglass, although born into slavery, did not make his descent into the "underworld" until he was six years old. Before that time, his childhood had been relatively secure and carefree. Only after being separated from his grandmother did Douglass come to experience the horrors of slavery. Richard Wright, on the other hand, was born directly into an underworld of unrelieved brutality. His earliest recorded memory is of the house fire and how his mother nearly killed him when he was four years old. By the time he was six, Wright had lived through his father's desertion, hunger, physical and psychological abuse, gang violence, and drunkenness resulting from frequenting a bar where patrons bought him drinks. Physical survival alone would have been a victory, but Wright is more interested in chronicling a different battle fought and won: his youthful struggle to discover an imaginative world beyond the barren externals of his life—in short, the process of learning how to read and then getting his hands on books to feed his mind.

The uphill battle toward literacy is one of the primary motifs in African American literature, beginning with the slave narratives. As such, it assumes mythic proportions in that literature. Knowledge of reading and writing was denied slaves, for their white owners understood perfectly, as Douglass makes clear, that literacy would quicken their discontent. Consequently, it was illegal in many places to teach a slave to read or write. Such prohibitions made the knowledge of letters a forbidden fruit all the more to be desired, for such knowledge opened the world of ideas to the slave and often helped aid his or her escape. Frederick Douglass, for instance, was able to forge passes in his first, abortive escape attempt. He could not have begun such a plan without his ability to read and write. But Douglass and many other slave narrators trace the history of how they came to read not simply for the utilitarian benefits of such knowledge. Literacy opens the realm of ideas; it enables a "thing" to become a person. Literacy marks intelligence and culture. The slave, by proving he or she can read and write, asserts her or his humanity. No wonder the acquisition of literacy figures so vitally in slave narratives.

Robert B. Stepto, then, correctly recognizes a strong connection between Wright's account of how he discovered the world of literature and Frederick Douglass's account in his *Narrative*.[26] In both works, the authors tell how they gained rudimentary knowledge of words from children on the street. In both, there is a "primal" scene of interrupted instruction. In the *Narrative*, Douglass recalls how his mistress, Sophia Auld, begins to teach him to read and write. This process continues until Hugh Auld discovers it. He strictly forbids his wife to continue, but young Frederick resolves to learn despite his master's prohibition; he realizes that something so strongly forbidden must be for his good.

Wright recalls a similar scene. Ella, a young school teacher who boards with Richard's family, begins to tell him the story of Bluebeard.[27] Wright recalls: "My sense of life deepened and the feel of things was different, somehow. Enchanted and enthralled, I stopped her constantly to ask for details. My imagination blazed. The sensations the story aroused in me were never to leave me" (47).

Here the artist is born, but here, too, an enemy appears to stifle him at birth. Just as the story of Bluebeard reaches its climax, Granny breaks in on Ella and the boy. Upon discovering that the teacher is telling Richard "lies," Granny forbids further contact between the two, and soon afterward, Ella is forced to find other lodging. As in Douglass's *Narrative*, a white person (for that is how Granny is portrayed) tries to stop the hero's attempt to become literate, and as in the *Narrative*, the taboo is imposed too late: once knowledge is tasted, the desire for it is unstoppable. Richard defies all the odds against him to further his knowledge. Despite a record of spotty school attendance, he learns to read well. He even aspires to become a writer, and actually has a short story (the wonderfully titled "The Voodoo of Hell's Half-Acre") published when he is in the eighth grade. Later, when Richard moves to Memphis, he obtains books from the white-only library through the ruse of a library card borrowed from a sympathetic Northern white man and a cleverly forged note: "Dear Madam: Will you please let this nigger boy have some books by H. L. Mencken?" Note by note and book by book, Wright acquaints himself with Mencken, Sinclair Lewis, Theodore Dreiser, and others, mostly of the realist-naturalist school of writing. In the face of almost universal opposition, the hero-as-artist equips himself for his life's task. His fanatical grandmother, who believes all fiction to be lies from the devil, cannot stop him; the whites who want to keep him in ignorance by forcing him to attend inferior schools and excluding him from public libraries cannot prevent him. As in the myth, where no powers of the underworld can keep the hero from attaining his prize, so the entire world of the American South in the 1920s cannot prevent this one determined young man from entering the secret world of ideas in books and from wanting all that those books promise him. Richard Wright's achievement is remarkable, given the circumstances of his early years; his fictionalization of those circumstances to the point that they resemble a mythic hell serves to heighten his triumph. Despite its manipulation of literal truth, or perhaps because of it, *Black Boy* is the most powerful autobiography by a black man since Douglass's *Narrative*.

The growth of the artist through literacy is, then, another of the principal themes of *Black Boy*. As Robert Stepto reminds us, this quest for literacy has long been a basic motif in black autobiography: we have already seen the similarity between the "instruction scenes" in *Black Boy* and Douglass's *Narrative*. *Up from Slavery* also treats Washington's search for an education; recall how he tells his reader that he wanted to learn to read and write so that he could study Frederick Douglass's books for himself. Desire to learn also prompts him to walk from his home in West Virginia to Hampton; there his persistence wins him a place at the school. When his sweeping of the classroom to Miss Mackie's exacting standards wins him acceptance, Washington recalls that he was "one of the happiest souls on earth"; of all the exams he ever passed, he considers that one to be the hardest. Education was the vital factor in Washington's rise from slavery, and he made education of a certain kind the cornerstone upon which his life's work was founded. W.E.B. Du Bois also underscores the importance of his education; he acquires his with less difficulty than did Douglass or Washington, but his achievement—European study and a Ph.D. from Harvard—was, in its way, as remarkable as his predecessors'.

✳   ✳   ✳

All the autobiographies we have examined stress education, and *Black Boy* seems to fit into the tradition. But is this simply coincidence, or does Wright consciously employ elements of the autobiographical tradition in his own life story? Some uncertainty arises here, and at least one critic is uneasy with too simple an answer.

In her biography of Wright, Constance Webb notes that Wright was asked by Hollywood in 1940 to write a screenplay of *Up from Slavery*, but that he had never read it (186). She remarks:

> Wright was almost ashamed to admit that he had never read *Up From Slavery*. He had escaped being educated in Negro institutions and never got around to reading those books which everyone was supposed to read. He did know that the greatest split among educated Negroes of a generation or so ago was over Washington's proposals.[28]

Wright's ignorance in 1940 of the important texts in the black literary tradition *may* be true; if so, the similarity between the fear/flight/fate pattern in *Native Son* and the bondage/flight/freedom motif in black autobiographies is difficult to explain. Wright may also have become familiar with *Up from Slavery* and other, older autobiographies in the years between 1940 and the time he began his own autobiography. George E. Kent has difficulty believing in Wright's unfamiliarity with his predecessors. Of Webb's claim that Wright was ignorant of *Up from Slavery* and other texts, he writes:

> Miss Webb is valiant, but the explanation is lame. That very boyhood which Wright was attempting to understand in *Black Boy* depends, for proper dimension, upon an intimate knowledge of Booker T. Washington and W.E.B. Du Bois and of the issues with which they grappled. . . . [I]t would hardly seem that a person as obsessed with black problems as Wright was would require an education in negro institutions to put him in touch with the major figures in his history.[29]

Although Kent admits he would like to know more about Wright's reading, especially works by other black men, he obviously doubts the truthfulness of Wright's claims not to have read books such as *Up from Slavery*. Knowing, as we do, of Wright's insatiable desire for reading and, more importantly, of the striking similarity between the instruction scenes in *Black Boy* and Douglass's *Narrative*, Kent's doubts seem reasonable. Robert Stepto goes further: he asserts that in the 1940s Wright *had* read "most of the corpus of Afro-American literature" and that tradition *did* guide him; in fact, having read his forebears, Wright was compelled to write his own life story.[30] It also seems consistent with Wright's independent character that he would claim a certain freedom from other writers, black writers in particular. If Wright had still not read Douglass or Washington by 1942, the year he began his autobiography, the similarities between his work and his predecessors' are the more startling. On the other hand, it is not unreasonable that Wright, for his own reasons, would deny having read the earlier works, particularly if he wished to further the mythic aspects of his life and of his literary achievement. To have sprung, like Athena, fully armed literarily from a hostile environment makes better drama than to acknowledge one's debt to earlier writers.

From the information available, I suspect that Richard Wright, despite his protestations, did in fact know in 1942 the literary tradition in which *Black Boy* stands. The similarities between its structure, its themes, and some of its scenes to those of the black autobiographical tradition are too numerous for them all to be sheer coincidence. Whether Wright *chose* to use certain elements from the tradition or was somehow *compelled* to employ them is not altogether clear; Robert Stepto goes so far as to suggest that Wright *had* to write his autobiography after reading the earlier texts because it was the only way he could "authenticate" the "extraordinarily articulate self" that lies behind two of his own earlier texts, *Native Son* and "How Bigger Was Born."[31] Although I do not always follow Stepto's reasoning, I believe his claim about some kind of inner necessity operating in Wright points in the right direction. The decision to tell one's own life story, particularly after one has read his or her strong predecessors' stories, seems related to Harold Bloom's contention that the artist must clear his or her own imaginative space. To do so, he or she often uses inherited forms but must somehow alter those forms or pour new content into them to assert his or her individuality. Richard Wright does this to a remarkable degree, as the following passages from his work demonstrate.

When Richard Wright was in his early teens, his mother joined the Methodist Church. Accompanying her, Richard encountered what for him was a "new world":

prim, brown puritanical girls who taught in the public school; black college students who tried to conceal their plantation origin, black boys and girls emerging self-consciously from adolescence; wobbly-bosomed black and yellow church matrons; black janitors and porters who sang proudly in the choir; subdued redcaps who served as deacons; meek, blank-eyed black and yellow washerwomen who shouted and moaned and danced when hymns were sung; jovial, potbellied black bishops; skinny old maids who were constantly giving rallies to raise money; snobbery, clannishness, gossip, intrigue, petty class rivalry, and conspicuous displays of cheap clothing. (166)

This unkind, satiric, and undoubtedly accurate description sounds a new note in African American autobiography. Admittedly, Booker

Washington told jokes about ignorant blacks as part of his talks on the lecture circuit; Du Bois writes less than flatteringly of the foibles of blacks in "The Colored World Within" in *Dusk of Dawn*; even Douglass, whose distance from the black masses has sometimes been commented upon, notes the ignorance and superstitions of other slaves. But none of these earlier men writes so caustically about the pettiness and pretentiousness in black society as does Wright. Nor had any earlier writer described so bluntly African Americans' ability to be cruel to their own people.

Regardless of the unattractiveness of the world of the black Methodist church, a world in some ways a step up from what he knew in his youngest years, Richard still finds it attractive: "I liked it and I did not like it; I longed to be among them, yet when with them I looked at them as if I were a million miles away" (166). Thus Wright sums up his relationship with the black world of his youth: he wants to belong because he needs human contact, yet the petty concerns of a defeated people repel him. As he portrays himself, Wright is already, at a young age, too sensitive, too *aware* to fit docilely into this stultifying black society. Because of his particularly harsh childhood, he trusts scarcely anyone, black or white. In fact, every close relationship he describes in *Black Boy* is marked by conflict, even violence. Richard remains outside even his own family, which characterizes him as a troublemaker destined for the gallows, if not for hell. But although Richard tries to assert his independence from other people, he still longs to belong somewhere.

In another, more famous passage, Wright remarks on his race in general terms, not just upon the world of the black Protestant church he encountered when he was a teenager. He writes:

(After I had outlived the shocks of childhood, after the habit of reflection had been born in me, I used to mull over the strange absence of real kindness in Negroes, how unstable was our tenderness, how lacking in genuine passion we were, how void of great hope, how timid our joy, how bare our traditions, how hollow our memories, how lacking we were in those intangible sentiments that bind man to man, and how shallow was even our despair. After I had learned other ways of life I used to brood upon the unconscious irony of those who felt that Negroes led so passional an existence. I saw that what had been taken for our emotional strength was our negative confusions, our flights, our fears, our frenzy under pressure.

(Whenever I thought of the essential bleakness of black life in America, I knew that Negroes had never been allowed to catch the full spirit of Western civilization, that they lived somehow in it but not of it. And when I brooded upon the cultural barrenness of black life, I wondered if clean, positive tenderness, love, honor, loyalty, and the capacity to remember were native to man. . . .) (45)

This passage, which has aroused much controversy, presents a view of African American culture diametrically opposed to that of other important black writers like James Weldon Johnson and Zora Neale Hurston, who celebrate the richness and vitality of black life and credit their black heritage with nourishing their artistic gifts. Wright's assessment of his cultural inheritance, although singled out by some for blame because of its unrelieved pessimism, is nevertheless not unique within the autobiographical line under consideration in this book. In his *Narrative*, Douglass hardly praises slave culture but stresses the ignorance and superstition pervasive among slaves. Even Sandy Jenkins's gift to Frederick of the root charm as a protection from further beatings, a talisman seen by some as a symbol of the strength of African folkways to encourage an oppressed people, is ultimately *not* credited by Frederick as a decisive force in his victory over Covey. The power to resist comes from some unknown source within Frederick himself. Later, after Frederick has learned to read and write, he teaches the ignorant slaves lacking his skills; he is also the ringleader of some fearful, hesitant blacks in his first escape attempt and does not hesitate to state that he believes the plot was foiled by another slave's betrayal.

In *Up from Slavery*, Washington recalls the ignorance of many of the students who come to Tuskegee; these young blacks sometimes need to be taught about regular bathing, about tooth brushing, even how to make beds. Some become discouraged by the Spartan conditions at Tuskegee in the early years and rebel against the demands of the physical labor to be done. Washington also was wont to tell racist jokes in many of his speeches to white audiences; this practice, while revealing the shrewdness of the man in dealing with potentially unfriendly listeners, also seems to indicate an ambivalent attitude toward his own race. (One cannot imagine any black leader today publicly telling jokes at blacks' expense.)

Criticism of other blacks is also present in the works of Du Bois and Malcolm X. Du Bois, certainly a champion of his people's rights, includes a satiric picture of black people themselves bemoaning the character failings of other blacks in a passage at the beginning of his chapter "The Colored World Within" in *Dusk of Dawn*. Fictionalized as it is, it shows how Du Bois felt about at least some others of his own race. In his autobiography, Malcolm X deplores the lack of racial pride and the misplaced values of the black world; note, for example, his criticism of blacks who try to model themselves after whites, imitating white society and even straightening their hair.

My point is this: in the autobiographical line beginning with Douglass and moving forward to Malcolm X—a line that does *not* include writers like Johnson and Hurston—we find repeatedly a low estimate of African American culture. Wright's is the most vitriolic and therefore has received harshest criticism, but similar opinions are expressed by all the other writers. These men certainly experienced first-hand some of the degraded values and practices they condemn in their work and so rightly mention them, but they *emphasize* the negative facets of black culture in order better to separate themselves and their achievements from the masses. Each of these autobiographers envisions himself in heroic terms, and each sees himself as a leader and educator of his people. But leaders and educators need people who require both leading and educating, hence the devaluation of popular culture. If that culture were portrayed as rich and sustaining, what need would it have of the heroic selves portrayed in these works? In the case of Richard Wright, the bleak description of the black world is linked thematically to his portrait of his father, which appears just two pages earlier in the text: his father epitomizes the sterile culture that has created him and from which his son has fled (45). Richard finally faces and overcomes the father who years earlier had abandoned his family; *Black Boy* as a whole records Richard's victory over the entire black world with which his father is so strongly identified.

Richard Wright's relationship with the black America of his youth—alienation partially tempered by a desire and need to belong—also figures in his attitude toward the black autobiographical tradition. His desire to be a part of that tradition shows itself in the ways he uses the forms; he employs the bondage/flight/freedom motif, and he uses the time-honored theme of the acquisition of literacy. But if the forms are familiar, the content is sometimes startlingly new, and nowhere is it more jarring than in the critical descriptions of black culture and character epitomized by the two passages already mentioned; similar ones appear throughout *Black Boy* to paint a bleaker picture of African American life than any other appearing earlier.[32] Wright asserts his individuality by denying he has even read the texts of the tradition. This hero-as-artist emerges from the underworld by his own powers, yet he has paid a great price for his self-acquired knowledge and freedom: when Richard Wright makes his break for the North, he is alienated not only from the white world that has always been his deadly enemy but also from the black world as well.

Wright's success in "clearing imaginative space" for himself in African American letters is well illustrated by W.E.B. Du Bois's reaction to *Black Boy*. Writing in the New York *Herald Tribune* (March 4, 1945), Du Bois criticizes the autobiography precisely for the characterization of black life that is its new note. Du Bois takes exception to Wright's portrayal of himself as a youth and, as Dan McCall notes, seems to doubt that the work is altogether true.[33] Du Bois writes: "the hero whom Wright draws, and maybe it is himself, is in his childhood a loathsome brat, foul-mouthed, and 'a drunkard.'" Du Bois also objects that Wright portrays no black person who is "ambitious, successful, or really intelligent." Du Bois, of course, knew that such black people existed in large numbers, and he surely saw himself as one example. As McCall notes, Du Bois must have felt that *Black Boy*, by presenting blacks in such bad light to a white audience, could only hurt the causes to which he himself had devoted his life.[34]

W.E.B. Du Bois was, in 1945, probably the recognized leader of African Americans, the greatest scholarly authority on their sociology, their most ardent defender, and himself the author of a recent autobiography, one that linked him with the black autobiographical line going back to Frederick Douglass. Did he feel his authority under attack by Wright's work? Du Bois probably knew that the portrait of the youthful Richard in *Black Boy* could feed anti-black sentiment, even become grist for the racist propaganda mill. Although Du Bois was not himself averse to tracing the rise of a black person from relatively humble beginnings to a place of prestige—he had drawn such a self-portrait in *Dusk of Dawn*—the level of degradation Wright depicts in *Black Boy* surely offended him. In writing of black culture and of his own grim childhood as graphically as he did, Wright must have seemed to be revealing "family" secrets; Du Bois must have felt both chagrin and annoyance when one of his "Talented Tenth" dared to expose a dark underside of African American life for purposes of self-aggrandizement. That Du Bois, who had come to represent the best in black accomplishment, should take offense at *Black Boy* shows that Wright had managed to clear space for himself by speaking with a voice that compelled notice.

*   *   *

Most of *Black Boy* fits the "bondage" element of the three-part structure prevalent in this line of African American autobiographies. Wright characterizes his youth as marked by fear that sometimes renders him paralyzed, literally unable to speak or move; that sometimes makes him want to run away, to stop living; and that sometimes causes him to lash out hysterically at those he perceives as his enemies. The white world keeps him in psychological bondage, but it has also so perverted black culture that it too becomes hostile to the young Richard. Under relentless attack from two alien cultures, Richard feels that he must flee the South or stay and risk madness or death. He determines to run.

The "flight" element of *Black Boy* is first expressed in the opening episode as Richard seeks to escape his mother's punishment for setting fire to the house and is repeated in each of his later attempts to evade his tormenters. Flight as a structural device in the autobiography appears in Chapter 11 with Richard's arrival in Memphis. Here he hopes to make a new life for himself, but he encounters more blacks who do not comprehend him and more whites who persecute him. In Memphis, Richard works for an optical company; after a while, his white co-workers concoct a scheme to put him at odds with another black man who works in a nearby office. White men tell each of the two black youths that the other has threatened to hurt him. They hope to cause violence between the black men to satisfy their own lust for blood sport. Worn down by relentless pressure, Richard and Harrison, the other black man, finally agree to box, although they have no reason to hate one another. Once in the ring, they first try to feign a genuine match, but soon, egged on by their white audience, they fall prey to the violence inherent in the situation and try with all their might to beat one another. The money they are paid to thus entertain their white spectators in no way compensates for their shame. Richard realizes he has been goaded into violence by cynical whites who actually care nothing for him.[35] He comes to Memphis to escape the racism of the Deep South, but finds the racism of Memphis just as ingrained.

This fight scene illustrates the many ways the white world traditionally sought to cause division among blacks. Douglass recalls how some slaves were elevated to overseer-deputy positions and given power to beat other blacks. On a deeper level, Richard's fight against another black man might symbolize once again the inner division he and other blacks have sometimes experienced; as Malcolm X points out in his autobiography, African Americans have been so taught to devalue their blackness and value all things white that they may come to hate themselves simply for being born black. Malcolm suspected that he was a favorite of his parents because, of all the children in the Little family, he had the lightest skin. Later, as part of his reaction against the white world, Malcolm claimed to hate every drop of white blood in him, thus giving another example of the blacks' estrangement from themselves because of confusion with their racial identity.

Memphis does offer Richard one opportunity: with the borrowed library card and his forged notes, he greatly expands his reading. Mencken, Dreiser, Edgar Lee Masters, Sherwood Anderson, and Sinclair Lewis fire his imagination and make him realize how greatly restricting is the world of Southern blacks. Wright notes: "I could endure the hunger. I had learned to live with hate. But to feel that there were feelings denied me, that the very breath of life itself was beyond my reach, that more than anything else hurt, wounded me. I had a new hunger" (274). To satisfy that hunger, Richard finally determines to leave the South for good. *Black Boy* ends with Richard on a northbound train, heading for Chicago—and, he hopes, freedom.

As it stands today, *Black Boy* concludes with a brief section in which Wright sums up the experience of his youth and speaks with guarded optimism about his dreams for a better future in the North. Disappointed by human contacts white and black, Richard finds solace, strength, and inspiration from his books from which, more than from any other source, he "had gotten the idea that life could be different, could be lived in a fuller and richer manner" (281). He admits that in going north he is running away more *from* something—the terror of the South—than *to* something, for the North is an unknown. But he must go; the South has branded him "nigger," has denied him his personhood, and has kept him from learning who he really is. *Black Boy* ends on a cautious, poetic note that holds out some hope for a freer future:

> With ever watchful eyes and bearing scars, visible and invisible, I headed North, full of a hazy notion that life could be lived with dignity, that the personalities of others should not be violated, that men should be able to confront other men without fear or shame, and that if men were lucky in their living on earth they might win some redeeming meaning for their having struggled and suffered here beneath the stars. (285)

With this ending to *Black Boy*, readers disturbed by the bleakness of almost all that has gone before may take some slight comfort. Wright seems to say, "Freedom is there, and I will attain it if I can." In one way, such an ending seems jarring at the end of a book as pessimistic as *Black Boy*, almost a "happy-ever-after" conclusion to a *grand guignol*. On the other hand, young Richard is above all a survivor. We believe that, if anyone can, he will make it in the North. The daring-to-hope ending puts *Black Boy* into the autobiographical line we are examining, for we can see Richard taking his place with Douglass, Washington, and Du Bois as a black man who overcomes great odds and succeeds. *Black Boy* would thus seem to allow Richard

Wright to have it both ways, for not only does he clear his own imaginative space with his generally acknowledged exaggerations about the poverty of African American culture, but he also gets his work into the line of black autobiographies stretching back to Douglass. *Black Boy* could almost be read as the standard success story with a slight variation at the end: it only hints at a successful future, but the reader is expected to know that Wright did, after all, make good. The very book that the reader is holding is tangible evidence of its author's success in the North.

This scenario threatens to collapse, however, as soon as one remembers that *Black Boy*, in its original form, comprises only part of the autobiography Wright submitted to his agent in 1943. The original manuscript also included what was published three decades later as *American Hunger*, an account of Wright's experiences in the North, the land of "freedom." What we read today as the cautiously optimistic close of *Black Boy* was written by Wright as an ending to the work when he realized in 1944 that Harper's had decided to publish only the first part of it.

Although Constance Webb mentions Wright's initial suspicion about Harper's reasons for wishing to publish only the first part of the autobiography, both Michel Fabre and John Reilly stress his willingness to have *Black Boy* published alone.[36] Wright apparently felt sure that the *American Hunger* portion of the work would appear soon afterward. His supposed notion that someone was trying to censor his work because of its references to the Communist Party is countered by the fact that much of the material in *American Hunger* had already appeared in print in other places before 1945, and another portion appeared in *Mademoiselle* shortly after *Black Boy* was published. The suggestion of a conspiracy to keep *American Hunger* out of print does not stand up before these facts.[37] As it turned out, *American Hunger* was not published in its entirety until 1977, but almost all of it existed in print for years before that date, and Constance Webb had had the entire manuscript privately printed and circulated in 1946.[38] Accordingly, although the general public did not become aware of the second portion of the autobiography until thirty years after the publication of the first section, *American Hunger* did not come as a revelation to those who had followed Wright's work carefully.

Read together with *Black Boy* as Wright's complete autobiography in the form the author originally intended, *American Hunger*, does, nevertheless, somewhat change the reader's view of the first part of the work. If we read it as Wright originally wrote it, we must omit the last pages of *Black Boy*, those that offer a guarded, hopeful vision of the future. Instead, we end the first part of the work at the words,

"This was the culture from which I sprang. This was the terror from which I fled." Richard's bondage has been described and his flight noted. There is no "freedom" section; that will come in *American Hunger*. The second part of the work begins, "My glimpse of the flat black stretches of Chicago depressed and dismayed me, mocked all my fantasies." From that first sentence, we know that what Richard finds in the North is not really freedom, but something as bad as what he fled, if not worse. When the tacked-on ending of *Black Boy* gives way to this rapid "this-is-what-I-fled-and-this-is-what-I-found" transition, the reader suspects that the relentless tensions of *Black Boy* will continue in *American Hunger*.[39]

*   *   *

American Hunger itself divides into two parts. Chapters 1–3 recount Richard Wright's efforts to make a new life for himself and his family in Chicago. His various jobs are noted—all of them subsistence level and all meaningless to a young man aspiring to be a writer. Chapters 4–6 recount his experiences with the Communist Party in Chicago and re-emphasize a prominent theme from *Black Boy*— Richard's ongoing alienation because of his determination to have an intellectual and emotional life of his own.

As a place of refuge and opportunity, the North first took on mythic dimensions in the slave narratives. Because of its association with freedom, it was sometimes identified with the Promised Land sung about in so many black spirituals. The realistic slave realized, however, that the North guaranteed no paradise for the successful escapee from the South. The black man or woman who could get out of the South before or after Emancipation was likely to find new, different hardships in a strange environment. Douglass did, and so did millions of others, Richard Wright among them.

Wright's description of Chicago in the first paragraph of *American Hunger* alerts us to how its reality mocked its promise. Instead of streets paved with gold, Chicago (which Wright explicitly calls "mythic") is more a hellscape: "An unreal city whose mythical houses were built on slabs of black coal wreathed in palls of grey smoke, houses whose foundations were sinking slowly into the dank prairie."[40] Missing is the overt racism of Mississippi and Memphis; an indifference worse than active hatred replaces it. Richard finds that he does not know how to behave. In the South, he at least knew the unwritten rules of Jim Crow, but in Chicago, he must deal with uncertainty. He is as unsettled by the way most whites ignore him as he is by the kindness of others like the Hoffmans, for whom he works for a brief time. When a white waitress at the restaurant where he works as a dishwasher asks Richard to tie her apron, he hardly knows what to do; for a white woman in the South to invite such closeness from a black man would be unheard of. Wright characterizes himself in Chicago as a baby having to learn things from the beginning.

From the start of his stay in Chicago, Wright describes his life as one of continuous loneliness. Although he comes to Chicago with his Aunt Maggie, lives for a while with another aunt, and later brings his mother and brother north, his family ceases to have a meaningful place in his life. They linger in the background for a time, act disappointed in Richard's efforts to find steady work, are baffled by his interest in Communism, and finally just disappear from the scene. With few exceptions, the people with and for whom Wright works are strangers to him and he to them. The white waitresses at the restaurant are portrayed as living the shallowest of lives, with "their tawdry dreams, their simple hopes, their home lives, their fear of feeling anything deeply, their sex problems, their husbands" (12). They cannot understand any person, particularly a black, who wants to have an interior life. Having never felt deeply, they cannot grasp what Wright has experienced, marked as he has been from childhood by emotional trauma. Even the young woman with whom Richard has sex as payment for premiums on her burial insurance policy is a cipher. She can neither read nor write, has no ideas, and can relate to a man only through sex; all she wants from life is to go to the circus.

With his customary skill, Richard Wright epitomizes these early experiences in one fine, strategically placed scene. At the end of Chapter 3, Wright describes a fight between two of his black co-workers in one of Chicago's large hospitals. Richard has found work there as a janitor; among his jobs is the care and cleaning of laboratory animals and their cages in a basement lab deep inside the hospital.[41] During their lunch hour, Richard and his fellow workers eat in the room housing the animals; all around them are diseased rabbits, dogs, rats, mice, and guinea pigs, the subjects of assorted experiments perpetrated on them by the white doctors who treat the black janitors as if they too were mindless creatures. One day, Richard's co-workers, Brand and Cooke, get into a fight over some trivial matter. A knife is pulled, and soon the two enemies are engaged in serious combat. In their scuffle, they knock down some tiers of animals' cages. These fly open, animals escape, and some are injured or killed. The black men find themselves with a lab full of loose animals and little idea which go back into what cages. To protect their jobs, the janitors do their best to return the rabbits, mice, rats, and guinea pigs to what they hope are the right places. When the white doctors come in and begin asking for their specimens, the black men fear that their errors will be discovered, but no white doctor even notices that some animals are missing and others are in the wrong pens. They pay as little attention to the identity-less rodents on which they experiment as they do to the blacks who perform menial tasks for them. Wright detracts somewhat from the biting humor and horror of the situation with his rather too literal explanation:

The hospital kept us four negroes, as though we were close kin to the animals we tended, huddled together down in the underworld corridors of the hospital, separated by a vast psychological distance from the significant processes of the rest of the hospital—just as America had kept us locked in the dark underworld of American life for three hundred years—and we had made our own code of ethics, values, loyalty (59).

The sole compensation for the disappointment Richard finds in Chicago is his continuing opportunity to educate himself. His incessant reading helps him wall out reality and feed his hungry spirit. While living in a tiny, dirty two-room "apartment" with three other people, Richard reads Proust's *Remembrance of Things Past*. The incongruous image of an impoverished black dishwasher reading Proust seems the artist's defiant answer to Booker T. Washington, who recalls, in *Up from Slavery*, what he considers the sad spectacle of a poor black boy sitting in the weeds by his shack struggling to learn French grammar. Washington would probably have had as much trouble with a Chicago dishwasher reading Proust, but this is the point Wright wants to make: no one understands this artist—not his family, not those whose values center on material gain, and not the white world that sees him fit only to scrub floors and clean dung from the bottom of animals' cages. Although Chicago disappoints Richard, he survives in (and because of) his private world of thought and feeling fed by his books, not by human contact.

Richard's frustrating inability to form human relationships and to fit into a group is treated even more fully in the last three chapters of *American Hunger* than in the first three. The last half of the work details his association with the American Communist Party in Chicago and New York. Despite his work for the party over several years and his faithful adherence to Marxist doctrine (verified by his writing apart from *American Hunger*), Wright's picture of his association with the Communists in many ways reiterates his earlier, failed efforts to make friends. This time the problem is not race: Wright takes pains to show that his colleagues in the party are, for the most part, remarkably free from racial prejudices. The problem is ideology, and because Wright reserves the right to think for himself even after he has heard the official party line, he is always suspected of being an "intellectual," an enemy of the party he serves.

By the time he wrote *American Hunger*, Wright had severed his ties with the Communist Party and had written of it critically. His portrait of the organization in his autobiography depicts a paranoid, factionalized body embroiled in never-ending internecine strife of Byzantine complexity. No member knows when he might be charged with outlandish crimes such as "anti-leadership tendencies," "class collaborationist attitudes," or "ideological factionalism." One party member, a certain Ross, is tried for alleged crimes against the people; at his trial the prosecution spends hours detailing the oppression of the world's workers, the wrongs of their oppressors being ever narrowed until Ross's own "crimes" are recounted. By this time, he has been made to feel personally responsible for all the injustices dealt to all the world's workers. Unable to stand up against such an onslaught, he confesses to every charge leveled against him.

This is the Kafkaesque organization to which Richard attaches himself. He quickly rises in the ranks and finds himself elected to the position of executive secretary of the Chicago John Reed Club, a Communist organization for writers and artists. Just as quickly, Richard is entangled in political infighting. In trying to appease two warring factions in the club, he alienates both. Furthermore, he is suspect from the beginning because of his education; he remains an outsider, an "intellectual."

Looking for a place to belong, Richard instead finds renewed fear and isolation in his dealings with the Communist Party. Party officials try to cow him into submitting to the party line, but he maintains his intellectual integrity even at the cost of being ousted from the ranks. Although he still sympathizes with Communist ideology— in fact, he believes Communism to be the hope and the inevitable way of the future—he cannot fit into the party as it exists in actuality. Once again, Richard is an outsider, cast out from two outcast groups, the black race and the Communist Party, as well as from the white world, which oppresses them both. And once again, Wright manages to express his isolation in a memorable scene. *American Hunger* ends on May Day, 1936. Richard has dissociated himself from the party, but his union has decided to march in the May Day Workers' Parade. When Richard misses his union contingent, he is invited by a black Communist to march with his old colleagues from the party's South Side section. Richard finally falls in only to be accosted by two white South Side communists who physically remove him from the parade and throw him roughly to the pavement. His black friends from the party stand by and watch, helpless. This final scene of human interaction repeats and summarizes a pattern that has run throughout the entire autobiography: the black man (Richard) is forcibly ejected from the flow of American life (the parade) by his enemies (white men) while other blacks are powerless to help. *American Hunger* ends with Richard alone in his tiny room, meditating on the meaning of his life so far and its purpose in the future.

American Hunger traces Richard Wright's growing alienation from other people, indeed, from the mainstream of American life. As John Reilly remarks, this second part of Wright's autobiography shows that his existentialism predates by years that theme's overt appearance in *The Outsider* (1951–52), which another critic has called Wright's most autobiographical novel.[42] But *American Hunger* also tells of the growth of Richard Wright, young writer, and critics have cited its thematic resemblances to James Joyce's *A Portrait of the Artist as a Young Man*.[43] I have noted that Wright emphasizes how he greatly expanded his reading during his years in Chicago and how books were his lifeline during that time. Those years also saw his first successful attempts at writing: Wright published some poems in Communist periodicals and had his short story "Big Boy Leaves Home" accepted for an anthology. He was also beginning consciously to articulate his life's mission. When, as he recounts it in *American Hunger*, Richard's mother accidentally gets hold of some of his Communist literature, she is horrified by its crude and brutal political cartoons. This makes Richard examine more closely the written propaganda as well. Finding the writing to be out of touch with its intended audience's needs and capabilities, Richard realizes that *he* could act as mediator between the Communists and those they hoped to recruit:

In their efforts to recruit the masses, they had missed the meaning of the lives of the masses, had conceived of people in too abstract a manner. I would make voyages, discoveries, explorations with words and try to put some of that meaning back. I would address my words to two groups: I would tell Communists how common people felt, and I would tell common people of the self-sacrifice of Communists who strove for unity among them. (66)

Something of the priest inheres in Richard's articulation of his vocation: he will bring the needs of the people before the higher power; at the same time, he will explain Truth to the masses. But Richard is not prepared for the hostility his efforts awaken among the leaders of the Communist Party. When he decides to interview black Communists and write their life stories, he immediately falls under suspicion. The party, it turns out, cares more for pure doctrine than it does for the humanity of the individual. Richard the artist wants to tell the truths of the heart, but the party wants only to hear "truths" that accord with the official line.

Three times toward the end of his autobiography, Wright employs the image of the human heart to describe his calling, underlining, I believe, the religious implications of the artist's role. He writes, "I wanted to share people's feelings, awaken their hearts." Later he declares,

Politics was not my game; the human heart was my game, but it was only in the realm of politics that I could see the depths of the human heart. I had wanted to make others see what was in the Communist heart, what the Communists were after; but I was on trial by proxy, condemned by them (123).

On the last pages of the work, Wright mentions the heart twice, calling it the "least known factor of living" and, in the last sentence of the book, stating, "I would send other words to tell, to march, to fight, to create a sense of the hunger for life that gnaws in us all, that keeps alive in our heart a sense of the inexpressibly human" (135). Now the artist-priest becomes the artist-prophet, his work to recall humanity to an awareness of its almost-lost purpose and potential. It is not too extreme to suggest that Richard Wright saw himself as a kind of Old Testament composite figure, both the "Man of Sorrows" despised and rejected by others as well as the "voice crying in the wilderness." If this self-awareness were not enough, Wright adds to it the image of Prometheus, the god who brings fire (here, read *truth*) to humanity but pays the penalty of isolated suffering. Having been thrown out of the May Day parade and having returned home "really alone now," Wright muses, "Perhaps, I thought, out of my tortured feelings I could fling a spark into this darkness" (134). The spark is the written word, and the reader ends *American Hunger* sensing that the book itself is the priceless boon that its heroic priestly-prophetic-godlike author has wrested from the powers of darkness. The hero may languish in tortured isolation, but the world has, at the price of his suffering, been blessed.

When we read *Black Boy* by itself, we realize how it follows the slave narrative pattern in many ways. It presents bondage and flight, and hints at freedom in its final pages. But when *American Hunger* is read as the second part of the large work as Wright originally intended, we discover that the "freedom" section does not deliver the standard success-story ending. Instead, Wright tells of further oppression, further struggles, and further flight—this time not to any geographic place, but an interior flight into the world of books, into the self as he gradually discovers his true vocation. As a whole, then,

American Hunger, Wright's title for the entire two-part work, turns out to be his own "portrait of the artist-savior as a young man," utilizing elements of the slave narratives to help tell the tale. Wright employs the mythic aspects of the slave narrative to heighten the miraculous element in his survival and his emergence as an artist, for there is no reasonable explanation for how a young black man with such blighted origins could become a writer of stature. *American Hunger* owes a debt to Douglass's *Narrative*, for Wright effectively uses the mythic possibilities Douglass uncovered in the slave narrative. Additionally, Wright draws his autobiographical self-portrait along the lines Douglass employs in the *Narrative*. As William Andrews points out, the *Narrative* "pictured its protagonist in slavery as a heroic loner whose relationship to his environment was largely adversarial" (218). Wright's depiction of Richard is startlingly similar; Andrews goes so far as to call the characterization of Frederick at the turning point of *My Bondage and My Freedom* Promethean, precisely the image Wright uses of himself at the end of *American Hunger*: "Perhaps . . . I could fling a spark into this darkness." Those critics who have asserted Wright's familiarity with the African American literary tradition prior to his writing of his autobiography have here another fact with which to build their case: the alignment of Wright's self-portrait with Douglass's hardly seems coincidental, but an intentional revisioning of the heroic self established by Douglass.

While identifying himself with Douglass, Wright responds to and refutes *Up from Slavery*, which expresses pity for poor blacks who seek higher learning when what they really need, in Washington's opinion, is a way of putting food on the table. Richard Wright is part of Du Bois's "Talented Tenth," those from the race who will rise from humble beginnings to serve as the spokespersons and leaders of their people. In *American Hunger* Wright not only traces his own rise but also presents his work itself as tangible proof of his accomplishment. We may quibble with some of the means by which he clears his imaginative space, but in this case, knowing how the organism works in no way detracts from the wonder of its life.

5: Repeated Patterns: James Baldwin and Eldridge Cleaver

Richard Wright's father, Nathaniel Wright, deserted his wife and went to live with another woman when Richard was still a young child. In the first chapter of *Black Boy*, Wright recalls being taken by his mother to visit his father to ask for money. Nathaniel Wright flippantly tells his wife and son that he has only a nickel for them; Ella Wright proudly forbids her son to accept it. She and Richard leave Nathaniel Wright with his woman, and Richard does not see him again for twenty-five years.

Wright's understandable bitterness toward his father surfaces several times in the first chapter of *Black Boy*, particularly in the episode of the kitten. Richard takes literally his father's words to kill the kitten although he knows better. Dragged before his father, Richard has the pleasure of defiantly insisting to his father that hanging the kitten was a simple act of obedience. But deeper issues are involved, as Wright notes in his interpretation of the incident:

I had had my first triumph over my father. I had made him believe that I had taken his words literally. He could not punish me now without risking his authority. I was happy because I had at last found a way to throw my criticism of him into his face. I had made him feel that, if he whipped me for killing the kitten, I would never give serious weight to his words again. I had made him know that I felt he was cruel and I had done it without his punishing me.[1]

Father and son are at odds before the incident of the kitten; the son questions the father's authority and contrives to free himself from it. Soon freedom appears, but in an unexpected way: Nathaniel Wright deserts his wife and children and forever severs his relationship with them. Resentment at his father's restricting presence is replaced by resentment that his absence causes hunger, for with Nathaniel

Wright gone, there is not enough money for food. Wright recalls, "As the days slid past the image of my father became associated with my pangs of hunger, and whenever I felt hunger I thought of him with a deep biological bitterness" (22).

When he was a child, Richard Wright was unable to punish his father for leaving him; he could only refuse the cynically offered nickel. But the adult Richard Wright can settle the score, and he does so in the same way he triumphs over his father in the matter of the kitten—with words. As a child, Richard deliberately misconstrues his father's command. As an adult, Wright deals with his father for good in his description of him at their final meeting many years later.

During his trip through the South in 1940, Wright saw his father in Natchez. The older man had returned from Memphis, where he had failed. Once again he was sharecropping, having retreated to his birthplace at the end of his life to resume the work he had done years earlier. One can imagine the awkward meeting between this sad figure and his famous son, the author of a best-selling novel; the two men were strangers living in different worlds. Wright's description of his father at this reunion is a small masterpiece of characterization and *categorization*, for with a few strokes, Wright forever makes his father a type, a symbol of the black man of the earth whose life has been blighted by the racism of the South:

—he was standing against the sky, smiling toothlessly, his hair whitened, his body bent, his eyes glazed with dim recollection, his fearsome aspect of twenty-five years ago gone from him— . . . I stood before him, poised, my mind aching as it embraced the simple nakedness of his life, feeling how completely his soul was imprisoned by the slow flow of the seasons, by wind and rain and sun, how fastened were his memories to a crude and raw past, how chained were his actions and emotions to the direct, animalistic impulses of his withering body. . . .

From the white landowners above him there had not been handed to him a chance to learn the meaning of loyalty, of sentiment, of tradition. Joy was unknown to him as was despair. As a creature of the earth, he endured, hearty, whole, seemingly indestructible, with no regrets and no hope. . . . From far beyond the horizons that bound this bleak plantation there had come to me through my living the knowledge that my father was a black peasant who had gone to the city seeking life, but who had failed in the city; a black peasant whose life had been hopelessly snarled in the city, and who had at last fled the city—that same city which had lifted me in its burning arms and borne me toward alien and undreamed-of shores of knowing.[2]

A photograph of Nathaniel Wright taken at the time of Richard's visit shows a man dressed in overalls and denim jacket over an open-collared shirt; his large, veined hands suggest years of manual labor. The face is unremarkable except for the eyes fixed straight ahead; their blankness is disturbing. In their lifeless gaze one finds scant suggestion of intelligence or personality.[3] The portrait supports Richard Wright's assessment of his father as a harmless wreck, but Wright's verbal picture supposes far more. As his son presents him, Nathaniel Wright is little more than a creature, an elemental force, dumb and lasting as the earth itself. Richard Wright asserts that his father knew neither joy nor despair, was ignorant of loyalty, sentiment, or tradition, and had neither hopes nor regrets, labelling him "a black peasant." Although this description is delivered without overt rancor, it oozes malice: Wright can elicit sympathy for this ruin of a human being and can state "I forgave him and pitied him" while simultaneously relegating him forever to a blighted pastoral world. With this portrait, "Wright banishes his father from the remaining pages of both volumes of his autobiography."[4] He does more than that: he take his revenge on his father for his desertion of his family years earlier and asserts his own superiority and authority over the older man. After all, Wright implies that *he himself* partakes of the human values (loyalty, sentiment, tradition) and emotions (joy, despair) that are unknown to his father. He asserts "I am fully a man" while suggesting at the same time "my father was not." Nathaniel Wright, who once deserted his family, is now repaid: his son leaves *him* behind, literally and figuratively. Richard Wright, redeemed by the city, continues his life of intense feeling, his life of the mind, of books and ideas, his life in New York and Paris, while Nathaniel Wright stays in Natchez, "[a] sharecropper, clad in ragged overalls, holding a muddy hoe in his gnarled, veined hands" (42).

Each autobiographer treated thus far in this study has in some way struck out against the father figures in his life. Frederick Douglass did not know his biological father, but his *Narrative* is a blow against the white, paternalistic, slave-owning society under which he grew up and from which he escaped. Douglass makes his victory over Edward Covey emblematic of his clash with slave society: in defeating one white man, Douglass scores a victory over all his white masters and attains his own manhood. Booker T. Washington did not know his white father either and so knew of no blood relation whom he had symbolically to defeat to assert his own identity. But Frederick Douglass loomed in Washington's consciousness as the father figure of all black Americans who had to be relegated to an unthreatening position so that Washington could assume leadership over his race. W.E.B. Du Bois knew his father, but only slightly. He writes little of his father, and that without animosity, but Du Bois, too, had a potent father figure with whom to struggle: Booker T. Washington. The contest between the two took several years to play itself out, years during which both spent untold hours and reams of paper in the fight for the leadership of black Americans.

Richard Wright is the first of the autobiographers we have studied to have waged a battle against a father figure on two fronts: he had both to clear his own space in the black autobiographical line by imposing his vision over that of his predecessors, and he had also to defeat his biological father, whose desertion had caused him so much suffering. Wright proves equal to the task: in *Black Boy* he does make his voice heard and asserts himself as a force with which others must reckon, and he ruthlessly deals with his own father, making him a creature forever bound to the soil from which he sprang. Richard Wright surely realized, however, that any author who stakes his claim in literary territory is going to be challenged by others who want the space for themselves: Wright did it to Booker Washington and (to a lesser degree) to W.E.B. Du Bois; eventually James Baldwin would do it to him.

*   *   *

James Baldwin did not write a full-length autobiography, but several of his essays are autobiographical, and he produced one fairly long piece, *No Name in the Street*, which is built of autobiographical fragments. In these essays, Baldwin writes about the two father figures who decisively influenced his life: his stepfather, whom he confronts in the significantly titled essay "Notes of a Native Son," and his literary father, Richard Wright, whose authority he challenges in "Everybody's Protest Novel." In a later essay, "Alas, Poor Richard," Baldwin deals with Wright much as Wright deals with *his* father in *Black Boy*: he makes his peace with his "father" while simultaneously robbing that father of his power and consigning him forever to a lost past. Because of his own autobiographical works and because of his tangled relationship with Richard Wright, James Baldwin merits a place in this study. Furthermore, we shall see that Baldwin falls prey to the same patricide that he inflicts upon Wright: he is "slain" by Eldridge Cleaver in a particularly acrimonious essay, "Notes on a Native Son" (note again the title), part of *Soul on Ice*, Cleaver's own declaration of independent manhood.

James Baldwin first met Richard Wright in 1945. Wright was famous and respected, the author of two best-sellers; Baldwin was an unknown twenty year old with literary aspirations. Both had grown up in deprived households, but Baldwin was a child of the urban North, as much a product of Harlem as Wright was a child of Mississippi. Both had managed to educate themselves, and both knew from an early age that they wanted to be writers. Wright was Baldwin's ideal, as Baldwin acknowledges in "Alas, Poor Richard":

I had made my pilgrimage to meet him because he was the greatest black writer in the world for me. In *Uncle Tom's Children*, in *Native Son*, and above all, in *Black Boy*, I found expressed, for the first time in my life, the sorrow, the rage, and the murderous bitterness which was eating up my life and the lives of those around me. His work was an immense liberation and revelation for me.[5]

Wright spent an evening with Baldwin, questioned him about the novel he was writing, and agreed to read the sixty or seventy pages Baldwin had completed. Wright praised what he read and recommended Baldwin for the Eugene F. Saxton fellowship, which Baldwin won.[6] The money from the fellowship permitted Baldwin to continue work on the novel, which ended up an unpublished failure. Feeling ashamed and blaming himself for that failure, Baldwin faced Wright again in 1946, just before Wright left for France. Baldwin sensed that both he and Wright had come to an end point: he had abandoned his novel and had no literary projects promising success; Wright, although highly successful, had grown weary of the pressures of life in the United States and was fleeing to Europe. A note of envy sounds in Baldwin's description of the meeting, as well as a hint of a feeling of abandonment—both of which may help account for what happened between the two men later. Baldwin writes:

he had done what he could for me, and it had not worked out, and now he was going away. It seemed to me that he was sailing into the most splendid of futures, for he was going, of all places! to France, and he had been invited there by the French government. ("Alas, Poor Richard" 276)

The two men did not meet again until 1948, when Baldwin, following Wright's lead, also went to France, intending never to return to the United States. On the very day of his arrival in Paris, he ran into Wright at the Deux Magots and was warmly received. He also met the editors of *Zero* magazine, who would, the following year, publish "Everybody's Protest Novel," the essay that challenged Wright's authority as leading black writer of his day and that also effectively ended Baldwin and Wright's friendship.

The substance of Baldwin's attack on Wright can be briefly summarized. Most of "Everybody's Protest Novel" critiques Harriet Beecher Stowe's *Uncle Tom's Cabin*. Baldwin argues that the novel fails because its stereotyped characters have no life of their own but serve as pawns in Stowe's propagandistic scheme, which is her primary purpose. The value of *Uncle Tom's Cabin* as protest novel is offset by Stowe's disservice to her characters in making them one-dimensional figures whose destinies are completely determined by their assigned positions in the framework of the novel.

Baldwin faults the protest novel for replacing complex human characters with symbols or types who derive their life solely from their place within the novel's deterministic social plan. He mentions *Native Son* as a novel guilty of the same faults as those in *Uncle Tom's Cabin* and sees in Bigger Thomas a character completely constrained by his external circumstances, his life controlled by his hatred and fear. Bigger is as much a stereotype as Uncle Tom; in fact, he is his exact opposite, but just as much a type. According to Baldwin, *Native Son* thus continues the harmful tradition of *Uncle Tom's Cabin*, for Bigger confirms in the minds of white readers the image of black men as brutal and subhuman just as Uncle Tom symbolized another favorite stereotype of whites, the black man completely cowed, endlessly patient, somehow less than a man. Both stereotypes—all stereotypes—render disservice. Baldwin ends his essay by claiming:

The failure of the protest novel lies in its rejection of life, the human being, the denial of his beauty, dread, power, in its insistence that it is his categorization alone which is real and which cannot be transcended. ("Everybody's Protest Novel" 33)[7]

Wright's response to "Everybody's Protest Novel" was swift, strong, and predictable. He accused Baldwin of betraying him and all African Americans by attacking protest literature, which had, after all, helped the cause of black rights over the years. Baldwin seemed to have ignored the enormous impact of *Uncle Tom's Cabin* and its part in bringing the slavery issue to a head. Wright accosted Baldwin shortly after the essay appeared in *Zero*; Baldwin writes, "I will never forget the interview, but I doubt that I will ever be able to recreate it" ("Alas, Poor Richard" 277). Baldwin, ostensibly, was taken by surprise at the vehemence of Wright's reaction; he somehow imagined that he would be "patted on the head" for taking an original point of view. Admittedly, Baldwin's comments about *Native Son* seem almost an afterthought, grafted somehow into the end of an essay essentially about *Uncle Tom's Cabin*; granted, too, that Baldwin was just twenty-four when his essay appeared—perhaps he didn't realize its potential to hurt and anger Wright. At least one critic, however, suspects Baldwin's ingenuousness: Maurice Charney, noting Baldwin's admiration for Wright as a writer and his affection for him as a man, sees his attack on *Native Son* as "deeply premeditated and deliberate; he [Baldwin] uses it to define his own position as a novelist and critic, which is opposed to the values of naturalism and naturalist view of reality" (69). Michel Fabre persuasively argues that Baldwin's struggle to complete his first novel, *Go Tell It on the Mountain,* depended on the resolution of his conflict with his stepfather and with Wright; Fabre thus agrees with Charney's position and describes the conflict in strikingly "Bloomian" terms. He claims that Baldwin could not complete his novel because the American literary establishment was pushing him to become another Richard Wright—a "pugnacious, militant black writer." But that was not Baldwin's sense of himself, nor did he want to compose Wright's brand of fiction. To remove Wright as "a sort of blocking obstacle across his natural path," Baldwin wrote "Everybody's Protest Novel" "against the notion of the militant writer which Wright embodied, so that he could claim his right not to be such a writer."[8] (Ironically, as Fabre also points out, Baldwin *did* become the militant spokesman for African Americans in the 1960s, taking upon himself the role of Richard Wright *after* Wright himself was dead.) The reward for Baldwin's declaration of artistic independence was the successful completion of *Go Tell It on the Mountain* in 1957; the cost was Baldwin's friendship with Wright—the loss of the father/helper he so desperately wanted.

Richard Wright and James Baldwin continued their personal and professional association for several years, but their relationship never overcame the effects of Baldwin's attack. They could not agree on the nature and value of protest literature, although they discussed it on several occasions. Baldwin wrote "Many Thousand Gone" in 1951; that essay, while praising Wright's powerful and honest expression of what it means to be a black man in America, expands the brief critique of *Native Son* first made in his earlier essay, reiterating that the character of Bigger Thomas serves primarily to reinforce the harmful stereotype of the black man as vicious killer.[9] In "Alas, Poor Richard," Baldwin remembers how he long hoped that Wright would someday understand his point of view, that the two men could re-engage in "a great and valuable dialogue." It never happened. Unable to reach a meeting of the minds, the two men drifted apart, and their chance for reconciliation was ended by Wright's death in 1960. In 1961, Baldwin published "Alas, Poor Richard," a memoir of his relationship with Wright.

In "Alas, Poor Richard," Baldwin openly acknowledges that Richard Wright was a father figure for him. He writes, "He became my ally and my witness, and alas! my father." But Wright was more: he was Baldwin's idol, and idols, as Baldwin notes, "are created in order to be destroyed." Baldwin is candid about his purposes in writing "Everybody's Protest Novel"; he can afford to be honest (and even penitent) because his father/idol is dead. Grief often involves a confession of sins committed against the deceased and the cry, "If only I had done things differently while he was alive!" In 1961, Baldwin could look back and admit his motives of 1949; what is unclear, however, is whether or not Baldwin knew in "Everybody's Protest Novel" that he was out to slay his father. A decade of thought and the removal of the threatening father figure finally free Baldwin to own up to his true motives:

Richard was right to be hurt, I was wrong to have hurt him. He saw clearly enough, far more clearly than I had dared to allow myself to see, what I had done: I had used his work as a kind of springboard into my own. His work was a road-block in my road, the sphinx, really, whose riddles I had to answer before I could become myself. ("Alas, Poor Richard" 277)

Any doubt about the Oedipal aspect of the relationship between Wright and Baldwin disappears when Baldwin himself calls Wright the sphinx whose riddles he, like Oedipus, had to answer before he could proceed on his road to authority. We also recall the fate of the sphinx: deprived of its power over those who passed by its dwelling, it dashed itself on the rocks and died. Richard Wright did not, of course, commit literary suicide after the publication of Baldwin's essays; as far as Baldwin was concerned, he didn't have to because Baldwin was quite capable of disposing of Wright in his own way. This he does in the last section of "Alas, Poor Richard." The portrait of Wright in the essay is indeed peculiar in a piece intended as a tribute, for Wright emerges as a kind of paranoid egomaniac, incapable of tolerating anyone who dared question his opinion on any subject about which he felt himself an authority.

Baldwin mentions several of the charges leveled at Wright by acquaintances—that he had been away from America too long, that he had "[c]ut himself off from his roots," even that he thought he was a white man. Baldwin denies that *he* thought these assertions true, but still he repeats them. His final view of Wright shows the man surrounded by sycophants, "an indescribably cacophonous parade of mediocrities," a man out of touch with his homeland, divided from the French existentialists, frequenting the Parisian cafes visited by writers and intellectuals but no longer one of them. We last see Wright playing the pinball machines, ignored "spitefully and deliberately" by the younger generation of black American writers. Baldwin summarizes:

The American Negroes had discovered that Richard did not really know much about the present dimensions and complexity of the Negro problem here, and profoundly, did not want to know. And one of the reasons that he did not want to know was that his real impulse toward American Negroes, individually, was to despise them. They, therefore, dismissed his rage and his public pronouncements as an unmanly reflex; as for the Africans, at least the younger ones, they knew he did not know them and did not want to know them, and they despised *him*. It must have been extremely hard to bear, and was certainly very frightening to watch. I could not help feeling: *Be careful. Time is passing for you, too, and this may be happening to you one day.* ("Alas, Poor Richard" 285–86)[10]

Baldwin does a thorough job on Wright, including in his closing shots nearly every charge designed to belittle a black writer: he hates his own race; his pronouncements against racial oppression are "reflexes" and "unmanly," to boot; he is out of touch with his homeland and with the concerns of the rising generation. Baldwin even suggests that Richard Wright's comfortable life in France is purchased at the cost of his deliberate turning away from the problems of African Americans.

Many readers will recognize Baldwin's description of Richard Wright's last years in Paris as an exaggeration, a caricature. Wright *was* in some ways a lonely, frustrated man, but his last years were nevertheless filled with travel, writing projects, and future plans. Constance Webb's picture of Wright's last years differs in tone from Baldwin's short study. She portrays him as a man plagued by recurrent illness who nevertheless kept a lively interest in the world and his work. Others have defended Wright against Baldwin's charges, as well. Nick Aaron Ford notes that Baldwin fails to mention certain facts beyond Wright's control that probably help account for his occasional testiness: his continual harassment by the American Secret Service (for his alleged ties with the Communists), the unwillingness of publishers to bring out his new works, the "unexplained cooling of the ardor of white friends," and ongoing financial problems.[11] Addison Gayle, who has documented at length the C.I.A. and F.B.I.'s surveillance of Wright, also defends him: he claims that Wright's estrangement from the black expatriate community was not simply the result of his inflated sense of self-importance but that some did indeed openly attack him whenever opportunity presented itself, calling *him* "expatriate" as if it were a dirty word and even suggesting that Wright himself was an agent of the C.I.A. and F.B.I.[12] Wright appears as much a victim of his isolation as he was an instigator of it.

Several critics have recognized Baldwin's strategy in his three essays on Richard Wright and his work. How could they not, since

Baldwin himself offers so many hints about his motives and attitude in "Alas, Poor Richard"? Maurice Charney summarizes the dynamic: "Baldwin's relation to Wright was complicated by Baldwin's own sense of the older writer as his mentor and spiritual father, from whom he needed to revolt in order to prove his own manhood and integrity and skill."[13] Michel Fabre argues that Baldwin, rejected by his stepfather, "set up a new myth by projecting on Wright the image of a spiritual and fraternal father who would recognize his value."[14] Calvin Hernton probes to discover *why* James Baldwin so wanted Richard Wright as a father. Hernton suggests that Baldwin went to Paris in search of a father (his own had died in 1943) and that his meeting with Wright in 1948 was the "crisis of this desire" to find someone to replace his own father.[15] But Wright did not respond as he had hoped; he treated the young man with what seemed "closer to denial or indifference than to love."[16] As Fabre reminds us, Wright, after all, never asked Baldwin to place him in the paternal role.[17] Baldwin hints at his feelings about Wright's reaction to him when he writes, "I don't think that Richard ever thought of me as one of his responsibilities—*bien au contraire!*—but he certainly seemed, often enough, to wonder just what he had done to deserve me" ("Alas, Poor Richard" 280). Hernton suggests that "Everybody's Protest Novel" is Baldwin's way of chastising Wright for not paying him more attention. When Wright reacted so violently to Baldwin's remarks about *Native Son*, the younger man, who had hoped to "have his head patted," retaliated. Hernton notes: "Rebuffed and angered, Baldwin took up his pen and, with hydrochloric pathos, dealt an avenging blow to perhaps the only black man he ever really loved. 'Many Thousand Gone' and 'Alas, Poor Richard' resolved (or dissolved), for the time being, the mean affair with Richard Wright in Europe."[18]

*   *   *

"Everybody's Protest Novel" destroyed Baldwin's vain hope that Richard Wright would somehow replace his father. But to understand Baldwin's need for a surrogate father, we must examine how he characterizes his relationship with his own stepfather. Once again, Baldwin himself supplies the information, for he writes about his relationship with his "father" in three of his autobiographical essays, "Notes of a Native Son," "The Fire Next Time," and "No Name in the Street." In all three, Baldwin sounds the same theme—his estrangement from a man he hated. In most of his autobiographical writing, Baldwin refers to David Baldwin as his father, although David Baldwin was apparently James's stepfather, marrying Baldwin's mother, Emma Berdis Jones, when James was three years old. Fabre writes of this family situation without comment as early as 1970. In a recent biography of Baldwin, W. J. Weatherby takes up the question of Baldwin's paternity; he gives evidence that Baldwin knew in his teens that he was illegitimate but did not know his biological father's identity. Weatherby cites Baldwin's ambivalent feelings toward David Baldwin; he quotes Baldwin: "No matter that he was not my biological father. He claimed me as his son. He gave me myself. I may not always like that self, have many quarrels with it—yet, here it is, and here I am, and I would not be here had it not been for him." But Weatherby immediately adds, "It was from his relationship with David Baldwin that he [James] developed his obsession about rebelling against father figures that was to make his relations with such older celebrities as Richard Wright and Elia Kazan so difficult." Weatherby also notes that his attempts to obtain information about Baldwin's paternity from Baldwin's mother and sister met with their refusal to discuss the matter.[19]

Baldwin begins "Notes of a Native Son" by recalling four events that occurred on the same day, July 29, 1943: his father's death, his youngest sister's birth, his own nineteenth birthday, and a Harlem race riot. The riot, Baldwin admits, seems to him chastisement devised by God and his father to punish his pride, for he has refused to believe his father's apocalyptic vision of the future; now black Harlemites provide something that will pass for an apocalypse until the real thing occurs. It may also feel like a reprimand for James's relief that his father is dead; the older man's tyrannic, paranoid reign over his family had been enough to drive James from home when he was eighteen. Baldwin is also sensitive enough to be relieved that his father's suffering is over. His father was indeed afflicted with clinically diagnosed paranoia and had also contracted tuberculosis. He ends in a state hospital on Long Island where James visits him on the last day of his life. The young man is shocked to see how the once robust and handsome man now lies in bed "all shriveled and still, like a little black monkey," tied by tubes to machines that seemed like instruments of torture ("Notes of a Native Son" 138).

Baldwin characterizes his father's life as a bitter one. Raised in New Orleans, the older man fled the South for New York City partly, Baldwin claims, because he was habitually incapable of establishing genuine contact with other people. A man who could not easily touch others' lives or be touched by theirs, the older Baldwin chose a profession for which he was eminently unsuited—the ministry. His career was marked by demotions to ever smaller churches; finally, having driven away all his friends, he ends up alone.

Like many other African Americans, James Baldwin's father sought refuge in his religion from the oppression of the white world.[20] In "The Fire Next Time," Baldwin traces his own conversion to "religion." He chooses—albeit unconsciously—to give his life to the church, for the alternatives are frighteningly clear. Other young men his age are already becoming corrupted by the sex, drugs, and violence of Harlem street life. During his fourteenth summer, James accompanies a friend to church (not his father's) and there meets its pastor. When this imposing, proud, and handsome woman asks him, "Whose little boy are you?" the lonely young man replies in his heart, "Why, yours." Later that summer, during a service in which the same woman is preaching, James falls into a religious ecstasy lasting some hours, at the end of which he knows himself "saved." Soon after, he becomes a junior preacher in that church and embarks on a career lasting three years.

By the time he is finishing high school, James has discovered doubt from his reading (Dostoevsky) and from his friends (agnostic Jews). The simplistic worldview of the church cannot stand up to the questions Baldwin is asking, and he gradually drifts away from it. Looking back, Baldwin realizes that the church as he knew it did not offer the haven or salvation he sought. In fact, he comes to believe that the black church is governed by the same principles that applied in the white church—Blindness, Loneliness, and Terror, "the first principle necessarily and actively cultivated in order to deny the other two" ("The Fire Next Time" 345). Baldwin also confesses that his motives in becoming saved and in becoming a boy preacher are not wholly pure: to punish his father, he does not preach for his father's denomination, but for another church; additionally, his role as preacher is a way of escaping his father's domination. He quickly becomes a more popular preacher than his father, and his demand for private time for prayer and sermon preparation helps keep his father from constantly interfering in his life. The standoff between the two men ends when James is in high school: a Jewish friend comes to his house. After he has gone, James's father asks, "Is he a Christian?" When James coldly replies, "No. He's Jewish," his father strikes him across the face, and Baldwin recalls, "everything flooded back—all the hatred and all the fear, and the depth of a merciless resolve to kill my father rather than allow my father to kill me—and I knew that all those sermons and tears and all that repentance and rejoicing had changed nothing" ("The Fire Next Time" 347). His conversion, which has been both a plea for his father's love and an act of rebellion, has not changed the antagonism at the root of the relationship.

About a year later, James leaves home, and a year after that, his father is dead.

These few details of Baldwin's relationship with his father help explain his relationship with Richard Wright. Clearly, Baldwin misses paternal affection growing up. In a bid for recognition and acceptance, he becomes a junior version of his father. Yet this is also an act of assertion; after all, he gets saved in an alien church and ends up competing with the older man. Finally, seeing that rapprochement is impossible, Baldwin leaves home, and after his father's death writes "Notes of a Native Son," an essay in some measure a eulogy (in fact, it closes with a description of the funeral oration delivered over his father) but also an attack on "the most bitter man I have ever met." This man, who could and should have been something, is eaten away by his bitterness against the world until he retreats into paranoia. Baldwin writes, "In my mind's eye I could see him, sitting at the window, locked up in his terrors," and "by the time he died none of his friends had come to see him for a long time." The similarities between Baldwin's relationships with his father and with Wright are now startlingly clear. Having been denied acceptance from his stepfather, Baldwin looks to Wright; he ventures into Wright's territory, receives early encouragement, but when further help is not forthcoming, turns his literary skill against the "father" who has let him down, just as he has turned his preaching skills against David Baldwin. After Wright is dead, Baldwin "makes peace" with him just as he has with his own father—both times in essays that express sorrow at the loss of the father while at the same time they kick the corpse. The portraits of Baldwin's father and of Wright in their last years are even alike—two men alone, deserted by friends, wrapped up in their private, unreal worlds. In his attempt to break away from a destructive father-son dynamic, Baldwin manages to involve himself in its recreation in his relationship with Richard Wright, with all the attendant disappointment, anger, and need for revenge.

*   *   *

In the first part of "The Fire Next Time," Baldwin recounts his conversion and its failure to reconcile him with his preacher father. He continues by tracing his gradual falling away from Christianity and ends with a meditation on the ways that Christianity has failed African Americans, noting especially the arrogance of white European Christians in their approach to black Africa, where evangelism and colonization occurred simultaneously—both to the whites' advantage. He concludes by asserting:

whoever wishes to become a truly moral human being . . . must first divorce himself from all the prohibitions, crimes, and hypocrisies of the Christian church. If the concept of God has any validity or any use, it can only be to make us larger, freer, and more loving. If God cannot do this, then it is time we got rid of Him. ("The Fire Next Time" 352)

Baldwin the father-slayer who has taken on his earthly fathers here challenges the ultimate paternal power, the white Father-God of Christianity. He, too, has let James Baldwin down: He has failed to keep His part of the bargain that James struck with Him when he became a preacher. The Jesus who would never fail James is permitted to know all the secrets of his heart, but has pledged never to allow James himself to find out those secrets. But, as Baldwin admits, "He failed His bargain. He was a much better Man than I took Him for" ("The Fire Next Time" 346). James apparently wants to exchange his commitment to God for protection from painful self-knowledge, knowledge that he does not explicitly state, but that may have had something to do with his homosexuality, his ongoing hatred of his stepfather, and his ambivalence about white people, black people, and himself—all interrelated issues in his life. Furthermore, James discovers that his Christianity is no answer to life's hard questions; to the contrary, the church seems to avoid such questions because it has no answers. So Baldwin turns away from Christianity and its Father-God, just as he has turned away from his own father, who represents all the worst aspects of the faith.

If Baldwin can dispose of these father figures human and divine, he nevertheless continues to seek them out. In the second part of "The Fire Next Time," Baldwin recounts his meeting with Elijah Muhammad, leader of the Black Muslims. He is invited to dinner at Muhammad's South Chicago mansion. When Muhammad enters the room, James notices that he teases the women "like a father." When Muhammad turns to him, James remembers his encounter with the pastor who asked him, years earlier, "Whose little boy are you?" Elijah Muhammad makes James feel like that young boy again, the young boy seeking a place to belong, although he cannot answer Muhammad as his heart had answered before "because there are some things (not many, alas!) that one cannot do twice." Muhammad *feels* like a father to him, a father able to take the burdens from his shoulders. Baldwin notes, "He made me think of my father and me as we might have been if we had been friends" (360). But Elijah Muhammad cannot be a spiritual father to James, however attractive his personality or however appealing his gospel of black racial superiority. The Black Muslims' teachings of racial pride and the rejection of the

white man's religion, attractive in themselves, are based upon a doctrine of the origin of the races so bizarre that James cannot accept it.
Muhammad offers a faith that has a strong emotional appeal but that
oversimplifies human relationships. If the white man is the devil,
what is Baldwin to make of his own friendships with whites? He
knows a few white people to whom he would entrust his life, and isn't
love more important than race? James can feel the appeal of Elijah
Muhammad and his religion, but he cannot give himself to it. He
rejects the white God of Christianity, as do the Muslims, but finds no
father in Allah. His quest for the one who can be his father must
continue.

   Baldwin's life, finding frequent expression in his essays and (at
least) in his first novel, the autobiographical *Go Tell It on the Mountain,*
shows absorption in a cluster of related issues centering on unresolved feelings for his various fathers.[21] Like Richard Wright, he tries
to dispose of his biological father, and like several of his predecessors
in the black autobiographical tradition, he battles against his literary
forebears. But no other black autobiographer enters into the struggle
with Baldwin's intensity. Furthermore, no earlier writer, not even
Wright, has so many father figures of such power arrayed against
him. Baldwin's stepfather is a stronger figure than Nathaniel Wright
is; therefore, he is more difficult to overcome. Wright's rage against
the white world that dominates the black world in so many paternalistic ways is powerfully expressed in *Native Son* and *Black Boy,* but
Baldwin's work goes farther by expressing the frustration and fear of
a black man who is also a homosexual as he faces the white world that
hates him not only for his color but also for his sexual preference
("Here Be Dragons" 678ff).[22] Up against such odds, it is little wonder
that Baldwin was not altogether successful in freeing himself from
these various paternal influences, a fact he himself recognized.

   In "Notes of a Native Son," Baldwin writes of his father's bitterness, a bitterness directed against the white world for its brutal oppression of blacks. On the way to his father's burial, passing through
Harlem streets ruined by the race riot on the day of his father's
death, Baldwin feels frightened "to see how powerful and overflowing this bitterness could be and to realize *that this bitterness now was
mine*" (129; emphasis added). (An echo of these words appears in *Go
Tell It on the Mountain,* in which John, in a dream-vision, hears the
word, "You got everything your daddy got"—not a reassuring message considering John's bitter hatred of his father and determination
not to duplicate his father's life.)[23] Baldwin fears inheriting his
father's bitterness because he senses its destructive power; the
smashed windows and looted stores of Lenox Avenue are just two of

its manifestations. If bitterness has killed his father, it can also kill him. "Notes of a Native Son" ends with Baldwin's description of the tension that characterizes the lives of so many black people: they must struggle against the hatred that leads to spiritual death but must simultaneously fight with all their might against the injustices that foster hatred. Acceptance of life as it is and the vow to fight life's wrongs are the seemingly contradictory charges laid on the heart of every black person. James Baldwin's father shows him by negative example the consequences of bitterness; now James must strive to free himself from repeating his father's fatal errors.

Baldwin was aware of the legacy of bitterness he inherited from his father, a bitterness resulting in alienation from others and from oneself, and he strove during his life to overcome it. In many places in his essays he expresses his hope for integration—not only of the races but of the warring parts of the individual personality. The endings of two of his essays written more than twenty years apart show his preoccupation with this theme of unity. At the end of "The Fire Next Time" (1962–63) he writes:

If we—and now I mean the relatively conscious whites and the relatively conscious blacks, who must, like lovers, insist on, or create, the consciousness of others—do not falter in our duty now, we may be able, handful that we are, to end the racial nightmare, and achieve our country, and change the history of the world. (379)

In "Here Be Dragons" (1985), which treats the issue of androgyny of all individuals and which also discusses his own hetero- and homosexual involvements, Baldwin asserts that there is always "male in female, female in male, white in black and black in white. We are part of each other" (690). This truth, that we must accept the reality of things, has already been shown as one of Baldwin's themes; yet how we handle that reality makes all the difference. When reality leads to bitterness, spiritual disaster results, as it has in the case of Baldwin's father. When differences are accepted and when people work together despite those differences, a new world can be forged. An individual may not like having to deal with the warring elements in his own personality or the racial differences in his own neighborhood, but those heterogeneous elements exist, like it or not. Baldwin asserts: "We are part of each other. Many of my countrymen appear to find this fact exceedingly inconvenient and even unfair, and so, very often, do I. But none of us can do anything about it" (690). The implication is "make the best of it, and perhaps something better can be created." On the other hand, Baldwin does not hesitate to predict disaster if individual lives are not reintegrated and if American culture does not accept its racial diversity. His father's death from bitterness of spirit somehow relates to the Harlem race riot that also resulted from unresolved hatred and frustration. Richard Wright, in Baldwin's judgment, ends up alone and out of touch because he refuses to continue facing the racial problems of America. The whole thing may well blow up in everyone's face if the nation as whole does not act: Baldwin ends "The Fire Next Time" with a quote from the Negro spiritual that gives him the title for the piece: "God gave Noah the rainbow sign, No more water, the fire next time!" Baldwin's ongoing preoccupation with these issues shows that they remain unresolved for him, or at least that he realizes the ever-present possibility of giving in to bitterness and of allowing his troubled personality to break into warring elements. Being aware of the issues is a step toward solving them, and writing about them is another act of asserting one's control. The years have seen progress in race relationships, but the years have also brought setbacks and sorrows—the deaths of King, Malcolm X, and others, about which Baldwin writes at length in "No Name in the Street." The apocalypse prefigured by the Harlem race riot on July 29, 1943, the day of David Baldwin's death, has not yet materialized; but it may still appear, and James Baldwin's writing is a cry of warning that unless Americans reintegrate their lives and their culture, destruction may yet follow. Far from escaping his fathers' legacy, Baldwin shouldered their burden and struggled with the same issues that tormented his own father and Richard Wright, his literary father. He tried to lay both men to rest, but because the conditions that troubled their lives always existed in Baldwin's life, the dead again and again rose up to compel him to wrestle against the bitterness and the anger that marred their lives.

*   *   *

In writing of his literary relationship with Richard Wright, James Baldwin admits that he used Wright's work as a springboard into his own. He adds, "this was the greatest tribute I could have paid him." And then, prophetically, he states, "But it is not an easy tribute to bear and I do not know how I will take it when my time comes" ("Alas, Poor Richard" 277). Baldwin had occasion to find out how he would take it when, in 1968, Eldridge Cleaver published *Soul on Ice*. That book, a collection of essays and letters with many autobiographical elements, includes a piece on Baldwin—"Notes on a Native Son." In it, Cleaver does to Baldwin what Baldwin did to Wright: he acknowledges his importance and praises his achievement, but then takes away with the other hand twice as much as he gives with the first. In fact, Cleaver's "notes on" James Baldwin are a sustained attack altogether more vitriolic than anything Baldwin writes about Richard Wright. Yet if one reads Cleaver's chapter on Baldwin within the context of the rest of *Soul on Ice*, the attack becomes understandable, even inevitable.

Soul on Ice, together with *The Autobiography of Malcolm X*, published four years earlier, marks a new militancy in African American autobiography. Earlier writers had written passionately of the wrongs inflicted on African Americans and of their smoldering resentments, but Cleaver and Malcolm X sound some new notes. Gone is an expressed desire that African Americans be allowed to take their place in an integrated society; black exclusivism and black nationalism replace integration as goals. Gone are the pleas for white America to abandon its oppressive policies; the promise of coming revolution and judgment blots out appeals to the oppressor's conscience. Malcolm X's stridency mellows toward the end of his autobiography, after his pilgrimage to Mecca gives him a new vision of the possibility of the brother- and sisterhood of all people, but *Soul on Ice*, which appears to have been written in a black heat, stands as a direct challenge and threat to white America.

To describe the black man's predicament in America, *Soul on Ice* creates an elaborate myth of interrelated racial and sexual conflicts in three of its sections: "Lazarus, Come Forth," "The Allegory of the Black Eunuchs," and "The Primeval Mitosis." The villain in the tale is the white man, usually referred to as the "Omnipotent Administrator." This figure, who controls the nation's wealth and power, has developed his mind at the expense of his body and is consequently physically weak and effeminate. His greatest crime has been perpetrated against his primary victim, the black male, or "Supermasculine Menial." This black male has been robbed of his mind by the Omnipotent Administrator and has been left with only his body, which he has developed to a high degree. The Supermasculine Menial is the raw muscle power that carries out the designs of the weak-bodied white male. But the white man has taken more than the black man's mind: he has stripped him of his masculine power by depriving him of his penis.

To keep him in his place, the Omnipotent Administrator has castrated the black man by laying claim to black women as his sexual prerogative along with white women. The black man is left to watch, helpless, as the white man rapes his black women. The black woman, or "Amazon," in her turn loses respect for the black man, who cannot protect her. Since her man has been deprived of his mind, she must do the thinking for them both. She must become hard and strong in order to survive, so she ends up losing her femininity and her appeal to the black man. Thus, the sexual relationship between the black man and the black woman is unsatisfying. The black male has access to black women but finds them a threat, so he turns his desire elsewhere. The black woman, for her part, often ends up desiring the white male because she admires his power and his brains. This desire may take on a religious form, manifesting itself in emotional Christianity. The black woman may betray her sexual passion for the white Christ by calling on Him at the moment of her orgasm: "Oh, Jesus, I'm coming!"

The white woman, or the "Ultrafeminine," is the final component in this tortured dynamic. Her white consort secretly despises her because of the ultrafemininity that she has developed to make his effeminacy less noticeable. To hide his aversion, he puts her on a pedestal and makes her an idol. The white woman, treated as an icon and so locked in femininity that she loses touch with her body, constantly runs the risk of frigidity. Her effeminate white partner cannot satisfy her, so she develops a secret yearning for the physical potency of the black male. The Supermasculine Menial desires her in return, for she is the forbidden fruit. Could he possess her, the black man could retain his lost phallus and his lost masculinity. But contact between the black man and the white woman is the ultimate taboo, punishable, for the black man at least, by death. Yet the black man cannot quench his desire for the white woman; desire for her is a sickness in his blood, a cancer. She is the symbol of freedom, while the black Amazon represents slavery. To be free, to assert his manhood, the black man will risk the consequences of sex with the white woman, even at the cost of his life.[24]

All the players in this tangled nexus face the frustration of their natural desires. The solution, from the black man's perspective, lies in his regaining his forfeited mind and penis; he will then be able to provide for his woman and protect her from the white man. The black woman will then respect her man and desire him, and he will begin to desire her. United at last, the black couple can begin to rebuild the world, recreating it as a kind of African Eden, as described in the last section of *Soul on Ice*, "To All Black Women, From All Black Men." The fate of the Omnipotent Administrator and his Ultrafeminine consort is not commented on; perhaps they are left to try to re-establish their broken relationship in a world outside Black Paradise.

For Cleaver, then, the predicament of the black American male is intimately tied to his sexuality, or lack of it. Images of castration appear throughout his book; the black man is impotent, a eunuch, and, in his most horrible manifestation, a hanged body, its sexual organs ripped away from a bloody socket. To be desexed is Cleaver's metaphor for the black man's place in America; it is his equivalent of the "bondage" motif in the three-part pattern of bondage, flight, and freedom. Actually, *Soul on Ice* contains the bondage motif explicitly: Cleaver writes from Folsom prison, where he is serving a sentence for rape. The inmates feel themselves castrated because their incarceration prevents their having access to women. Cleaver, like many of the other prisoners, posts a pinup picture of a white woman in his cell; a guard removes it and destroys it, affronted that a black man should have a white woman's picture. The guard informs Cleaver that he can have a *black* pinup, but not a white one. This incident reinforces Cleaver's sense of impotence, but it also reveals to him the shocking truth that he actually prefers white women to black ones; he has been infected with the sickness of desire for the unattainable white goddess.

Cleaver leaves no doubt in his reader's mind that the imprisoned, castrated black man has but one option if he is to free himself: he must fight. *Flight* as a possible way to freedom is not even considered; there is nowhere to run, for the white man has invaded every dark-skinned nation. Cleaver himself has ended up in the white man's prison for asserting his manhood. His rapes have a specific meaning:

Rape was an insurrectionary act. It delighted me that I was defying and trampling upon the white man's law, upon his system of values, and that I was defiling his women—and this point, I believe, was the most satisfying to me because I was very resentful over the historical fact of how the white man has used the black woman. I felt I was getting revenge. (14)

Cleaver deliberately mentions these rapes as a way of shocking and threatening his white readers; he seems to want to confirm what white men supposedly harbor as their greatest racial fear—that black men actually do desire nothing more than to have sexual intercourse with white women. To assert his manhood, Cleaver defiantly waves his black phallus in the face of the white man and warns, "Watch out; your worst fears can become reality."

The "fight" motif in black autobiography appears in *Soul on Ice* in the image of the boxing ring as well as in the threat of rape. In the section "Lazarus, Come Forth," Cleaver uses the Floyd Patterson-Muhammad Ali fight to illustrate the black man's necessity to fight and to show the white man's fear of his self-assertion. In keeping with his overall theme of the relationship between the races and between the sexes, Cleaver points out how white men, the Omnipotent Administrators, admire black athletes, allowing them to be champions in the arena as long as they are submissive outside it. The black man may use his brawn in sport but may not assert his manhood in the world. Thus, Floyd Patterson can be a world champion as long as he submits to racism: a cross was burned on his doorstep when he tried to integrate a white neighborhood; he moved soon afterward.

In the Patterson-Ali fight, whites back Patterson because he is tractable; they hate and fear Ali because he is the first "free" black champion ever to confront America. Ali does not subscribe to the white man's values or to his religion. His victory means so much to blacks because they sense in him a man not chained to the white world. The white man likes to think of his black boxers as trained animals, apes who box:

But when the ape breaks away from the leash, beats deadly fists upon his massive chest and starts talking to boot, proclaiming himself to be the greatest, spouting poetry, and annihilating every gunbearer the white hunter sics on him (the white hunter not being disposed to crawl into the ring himself), a very serious slippage takes place in the white man's self-image—*because that by which he defined himself no longer has a recognizable identity*. "If that black ape is a man," the white hunter asks himself, "then what am I?" (94)

The voice calling the black man in America, the Lazarus too long in his tomb, is that of Elijah Muhammad, exhorting the black man to reject the white God, to reject the white world, and to create his own black world in its place. The white world will find it hard to accept the black man who knows he is a man, especially when he is also a Black Muslim and the world heavyweight champion. But accept him it must: "Swallow it—or throw the whole bit up, and hope in the convulsions of your guts, America, you can vomit out the poisons of hate which have led you to a dead end in this valley of the shadow of death" (96).

If the white world finds Muhammad Ali a bitter pill to swallow, how much more will it hate and fear Malcolm X, the spokesman for the Black Muslims, a man who combines in himself the assertive masculinity of Ali with a creative, rebellious intelligence? Cleaver includes a chapter describing his reactions to the death of Malcolm X. He expresses the outrage felt by millions of African Americans at the death of such a strong figure and acknowledges the satisfaction that his removal will surely bring to whites and to many blacks ("the bootlickers, Uncle Toms, lackeys, and stooges") who play up to the white power structure. Cleaver quotes from Ossie Davis's eulogy for Malcolm: "Malcolm was our manhood, our living, black manhood!" Malcolm is held up as a symbol of the fight for black freedom, as is Muhammad

Ali. Malcolm may be dead, but what he symbolizes lives, and others will take up the fight. Cleaver closes his meditation on Malcolm X with another threat: "We shall have our manhood. We shall have it or the earth will be leveled by our attempts to gain it" (61). This warning is repeated in explicit detail further on in *Soul on Ice*, where a friend of Cleaver's, presumably a man who shares his imprisonment, declares, "the day is here when I will march into the Mississippi legislature with a blazing machine gun in my hands and a pocketful of grenades. Since I will be going to die, I definitely will be going to kill" (174–75). This hostility toward whites may not be completely new in black male writers, but Cleaver's way of relishing the prospect of violence (the same character who fantasizes about executing the Mississippi legislature also has a desire to drink deeply from the white man's blood) *is* new, joined as it is to the black man's avowed willingness to die even as he brings whites down with him. *Soul on Ice* asserts, "I will fight—*and* die" in a voice stronger than any we have yet heard among black autobiographers.

Although *Soul on Ice* spends most of its force decrying the plight of the bound and castrated black male and threatening the bloody havoc he will wreak when he finally claims his freedom and his manhood, Cleaver is able to imagine another world, which he describes in his final chapter. He leaves it to us to puzzle out how the black man will fight his revolution, how he will reclaim his missing parts, and how he will reforge the ties that bind him to his black woman. But by a leap of imagination, his and ours, Cleaver sets us down in a new paradise where the restored black man greets his woman, whom he hails as "Queen—Mother—My Eternal Love." He is the Lazarus returned from the dead, no longer impotent, very much repossessed of his Balls (as he puts it), ready at last to protect his woman, to look her in the eyes, to be her lover. His exhortation to her ends, "But put on your crown, my Queen, and we will build a New City on these ruins" (210). Curiously, this last chapter seems overblown and trivial compared to the weight of what has preceded it; Cleaver powerfully conveys the black man's torment and his hatred, and he can deliver his threats as powerfully as any writer, but his inability or disinclination to describe seriously *how freedom can be obtained* (will there be any world left after the bloodbath he envisions, or any black men left to love in it?) makes his dream of endless love with his black goddess sound too easily won.

*   *   *

When we realize that the potency of the black male is, for Cleaver, the lost commodity that must be reclaimed if the black man is to win his freedom, Cleaver's antipathy for James Baldwin becomes understandable. In "Notes on a Native Son" Cleaver berates Baldwin for criticizing Richard Wright, for hating blacks, and for loving whites, but lying beneath these criticisms is Baldwin's "sin" that Cleaver cannot forgive—his homosexuality.

Because James Baldwin offers a less-than-flattering opinion of the Conference of Negro-African Writers and Artists (Paris, 1956) in his essay "Princes and Powers" and because he writes in another place, "I despised blacks because they didn't produce a Rembrandt," Eldridge Cleaver concludes that Baldwin harbors a deep, intense hatred for his race *and* a concomitant adoration of whites:

There is in James Baldwin's work the most grueling, agonizing, total hatred of the blacks, particularly of himself, and the most shameful, fanatical, fawning, sycophantic love of the whites that one can find in writing of any black American writer of note in our time. (99)[25]

This opinion, which can be reached only by a rigorous misreading of Baldwin's work as a whole and which one critic dismisses out of hand as so absurd as to warrant no serious discussion, is nevertheless congruent with Cleaver's world view.[26] His militant, pro-black racism compels him to glorify all things black, to vilify those who dare to criticize anything and anyone black, and to suspect any expression of liking, let alone of loving, anyone white. James Baldwin, whose artistic vision is far more complex than Cleaver's, both feels and expresses the tensions he experiences as a black man in white America; he could not agree with the Black Muslims' opinion that all whites are devils because he has loved some white people who have loved him and have treated him in undevilish ways. Baldwin also can express his frustration at the ways blacks sometimes behave and at their racial failings. Cleaver, however, to establish his own political and artistic space, makes a break with the "militant" line in black autobiography in which Baldwin stands, one "trained and rooted in a tradition of ideas and maintaining a reasonable tension between moral complexity and political imperative."[27] But in so doing, he traps himself in a world view so constricting that it leads him to utter some of the absurdities we find in *Soul on Ice*. As Jervis Anderson notes, "His vision is so narrow and racially determined that it is incapable of accommodating the tragic sense or of displaying any interest in what we are used to calling the sadness and ambiguity of the human condition."[28] James Baldwin *can* express both the sadness and the ambiguity at the heart of the American racial situation, and for that, Cleaver excoriates him; as we shall see, however, Cleaver himself is also involved in such ambiguities but seems blind to them.

According to Eldridge Cleaver, James Baldwin's crimes do not stop with hating blacks and loving whites. He is also guilty of betraying and killing Richard Wright. Although Baldwin believes his disagreement with Wright is over literary matters, Cleaver claims to have discovered the true cause of the quarrel: Baldwin, the homosexual, hates and fears Wright's masculinity, which Wright also pours into his characters. To escape the threat he feels from the strongly heterosexual Wright, Baldwin strikes at him in a weak moment, calling into question the older writer's artistic vision in order to disguise his true goal of revenging himself on Wright for being a real man. Once again, Cleaver's simplistic world view, this time manifest in his insistence that sexuality is the single, underlying force behind all human activity and interaction, leads him into a critical position that, while it probably touches on one aspect of the Wright-Baldwin relationship, doggedly ignores other, more important dynamics.

A similar, equally willful interpretive approach appears when Cleaver discusses Baldwin's work. Although Cleaver never asserts it in so many words, he appears to claim that James Baldwin's characters invariably express the personality and desires of their creator. In comparing Baldwin's *Another Country* and Wright's *Native Son*, Cleaver asks of Baldwin,

> isn't it true that Rufus Scott, the weak, craven-hearted ghost of *Another Country*, bears the same relation to Bigger Thomas of *Native Son*, the black rebel of the ghetto and a man, as you yourself bore to the fallen giant, Richard Wright, a rebel and a man? (*Soul on Ice* 106)

By calling Bigger Thomas and Richard Wright "rebels" and "men," Cleaver connects the two; he thereby also suggests that Rufus Scott and James Baldwin stand in the same kind of relationship. Later, he quotes Baldwin's words to his nephew concerning white people in the introduction to "The Fire Next Time": "you must accept them and accept them with love. For these innocent people have no other hope." Immediately thereafter Cleaver turns to Rufus Scott, the hero of *Another Country*, describing his relationship with whites, as if Scott represents Baldwin's belief about *how* the black man's love for the white man should be expressed. Rufus Scott, in his sexual confusion and self-hatred, allows a white man to perform anal intercourse on him. Cleaver suggests that Baldwin loves white men by permitting them to use him as Scott's white lover uses Scott.

Here we arrive at the center of Cleaver's aversion for Baldwin: for Cleaver, the identity and power of the black man are rooted in his sexuality, in possessing a penis and using it on other people, ideally on the black woman. The black phallus means freedom, racial pride, and self-assertion. The antithesis of the heterosexual black male is the homosexual black male who, instead of giving his penis to a woman, receives the penis of a white man, thereby humiliating himself both as a black and as a man. Because James Baldwin admits to being a homosexual, acknowledges that he loves whites, and peoples his novels with characters who supposedly reflect his own problems, he is, in Cleaver's opinion, unfit to be a spokesman for the black race. To Cleaver, homosexuality is a sickness, "just as are baby-rape or wanting to become the head of General Motors" (*Soul on Ice* 110). Unless the black race can cast off this sickness and re-establish its true racial identity symbolized by the potent, heterosexual male, its oppression will continue and worsen. To prevent that, James Baldwin and what he represents must be cleared away.

Just as Baldwin tries to tame Richard Wright, the powerful father figure standing in the way of his self-assertion, so Eldridge Cleaver deals with Baldwin in "Notes on a Native Son." Baldwin is no father figure to Cleaver, for he is made to represent all that the dominant masculine figure is not. Yet he still threatens Cleaver's world view, just as homosexuals threaten a particular class of supermasculine men. The homosexual male complicates a narrow view of relationships that cannot tolerate or acknowledge the complexity of human needs and desires, which find expression in many ways. To the homophobic Cleaver, Baldwin is doubly damned for revealing breaks in the walls of both male and black solidarity. For his crimes, he is punished just as homosexuals have long been punished: he is hunted down and beaten up by a gang of macho heterosexuals on the prowl. This time, the "gang" is Eldridge Cleaver, and his weapons are not fists but words; Cleaver's attack on Baldwin is even more unfair than Baldwin's attack on Wright, for the punches are almost all below the belt. Cleaver's interpretive techniques are flawed, his arguments *ad hominem*, and his assumptions erroneous, but "punk hunting," as he calls it, has never been fair. Cleaver lives up to the tradition.

Soul on Ice expresses myths of race and human sexuality in which black writers like James Baldwin can only be seen as aberrations; consequently, they must be demeaned and silenced if racial and sexual justice are to be reestablished. Ironically, though, Eldridge Cleaver cannot see that his book itself exposes him as a more complex figure than his mythic identity as supermasculine black male would suggest.

We have seen that the final chapter of *Soul on Ice*, "To All Black Women, From All Black Men," describes a black paradise in which the black man and the black woman will come together in mutual love and respect. Yet human relationships are more complicated than this edenic vision suggests: Cleaver's own life illustrates this very point. The same book that ends with a panegyric on the love between the black man and the black woman also contains an exchange of love letters between Cleaver and his lawyer, Beverly Axelrod, who, according to my research, is white, although Cleaver never says so. The book's dedication, in fact, reads "To Beverly, with whom I share the ultimate of love." Were they to discover Beverly Axelrod's race, "All Black Women" would have to wonder what he is doing pouring out his love to this woman, who, although she is herself a radical, on the side of blacks, and dedicated to revolution and liberation, is, nevertheless, *white*. Baldwin is faulted for loving whites; how does Cleaver account for his devotion to Axelrod? He acknowledges that all prisoners feel a high regard for their lawyers, who represent their cause and fight for their freedom. Not all prisoners, however, have women lawyers as Cleaver does; so most do not have to distinguish between regard and love. Cleaver claims, however, that what he feels is more than gratitude: he *is in love*. The ways of the heart remain mysterious, all the same; two years after his exchange of letters with Beverly Axelrod, in which he writes, "Ours is one for the books, for the poets to draw new inspiration from, one to silence the cynics, and one to humble us by reminding us of how little we know about human beings" (149), Eldridge Cleaver married Kathleen Neal, a black woman. Perhaps he thereby fulfilled the ideal of "To All Black Women, from All Black Men," but readers of *Soul on Ice* will always be reminded that Eldridge Cleaver, for a while at least, was prone to more complications of the heart than even he could comprehend.

It is easy to be hard on Eldridge Cleaver, to bash him as thoroughly as he bashes James Baldwin in *Soul on Ice*. We might mention his hypocrisy in condemning Baldwin's "sin" of homosexuality while himself serving a prison term for what he describes as rape-on-principle, or we might deplore the rhetorical excesses of his writing— the unsubtle use of vulgarity for shock effect, the threats, the almost embarrassing flights of "poetry" in the letters to Beverly Axelrod and in the final section, "To All Black Women." Twenty years after the publication of *Soul on Ice*, we can look at the later career of this avowed "full-time revolutionary" devoted at one time to the Black Panther Party and to the teachings of Malcolm X and see his conversion to Christianity (written about at length in *Soul on Fire*, a sequel to *Soul on Ice*, altogether less interesting than the first book) and then, more recently, his arrest for possession of drugs. Inconsistencies seem to abound in this man's life; which of his various selves is the true one? Cleaver's severest critics have ample evidence for charges of his instability, if not opportunism; the more charitable might find in Cleaver's career, as in Malcolm X's, an ongoing quest for the self through a series of startling metamorphoses.

Regardless how one reacts to the Cleaver of *Soul on Ice*, a figure difficult to contemplate apart from the Cleaver so well known as a controversial public figure in 1960's, the critic of African American studies and of autobiography must see in his work an attempt both to define and to give voice to a self both different from and similar to the autobiographical selves that precede it.

The Eldridge of *Soul on Ice* has clear affinities both with the Frederick of *My Bondage and My Freedom* and with Richard in *Black Boy*. As William L. Andrews notes, Douglass, in describing his conflict with Covey in his second autobiography, stresses the devilish aspects of his character, consciously associating himself with Satan, the original rebel.[29] He makes this connection, Andrews states, "only when all his gods and fathers fail and he must become his own self-authorizing presence in a world bereft of legitimate structure or sanction" (229). The rebellious energy Frederick discovers in his satanic role will be used in the fight for liberation for other blacks; like Prometheus, whom the Romantics associated with Satan in anti-authoritarianism if not in self-service, Frederick devotes himself to bringing light into darkness. If this deed must be accomplished at the cost of hatred of those who see in Frederick's "devilishness" only destructive power, then Douglass is willing to pay that price.

On the whole, Douglass portrays Frederick as virtuous, condoning his self's "law-breaking" in escaping slavery as really no crime at all since the laws that keep slaves in bondage are themselves evil. Richard Wright, who like Douglass has an interest in presenting his autobiographical self in a heroic mold, follows Douglass's strategy in revealing a dark side to Richard's character, but for a different reason. Douglass shows Frederick capable of rebellion rooted in some "devil within" because the slave needs to be cognizant of an inner source of self-assertion, an assertion intentionally stifled by slave-owning society, if he or she is ever to seize freedom. Wright shows the personality problems in Richard—the unreasoning fear, the hostility, the potential for cruelty as inculcations into the soul of an innocent victim in the grasp of the corrupt white world. But whereas Douglass shows Frederick capable of turning his rebellion against whites, Wright shows Richard lashing out at other blacks, for he is too terrified of the power of the white world to challenge it directly.

Only later in his life, when Wright is relatively safe from retaliation, does he attack the white world with all the bitterness in him, and that through the very autobiographies that trace how the white world twisted his personality.

In the Eldridge of *Soul on Ice*, Cleaver combines the autobiographical strategies of both Douglass and Wright, for he makes no bones about the sins of his self, admitting that he has raped white women—the most heinous crime a black man can commit, according to the value system of the white world Cleaver outlines in "The Primeval Mitosis." Like Frederick, who, inspired by the "devil" inside him, commits the greatest crime the white world of *his* day could imagine—running away, thereby performing a revolutionary act—Eldridge shows himself capable and willing to create a terrible mischief against the white oppressors of *his* time, rape of white women. As Wright does in *Black Boy*, Cleaver portrays his autobiographical self as victim, infected with cancerous attitudes and desires, epitomized by his desire for the forbidden white woman, imposed on him by the corrupt white world in which he is forced to exist. The new thing that Cleaver accomplishes in *Soul on Ice* centers in his willingness to express openly both the threat Eldridge presents to white society and also the depth of his self's degradation, the degradation making possible, even probable, the revolutionary acts *Soul on Ice* threatens. It can be argued that Cleaver anticipates, even welcomes, the revulsion many readers have felt toward Eldridge, for in revealing to the reader a self unwilling to play by the rules of society, a self become its own standard of right and wrong, Cleaver means to confront the white world with its own creation, a kind of monster that now threatens to rise up against its makers and destroy them. Here Cleaver turns the Prometheus myth on its head: Douglass portrays himself as a kind of self-centered Satan/Prometheus, emphasizing the life-giving, selfless aspect of the character; Cleaver, like Mary Shelley, whose *Frankenstein* is subtitled "The New Prometheus," shows what happens when a person is not allowed to be self-created but is the realization of another's unholy powers. When the self-styled Prometheus meddles where he ought not, the creature of his making turns against him; like the monster who kills Frankenstein's wife, the black man also—albeit somehow against his will—rises to claim the forbidden fruit, the white bride of the Omnipotent Administrator.

Twenty years ago, when *Soul on Ice* was first published, the views it expressed were taken as a serious threat to the status quo. The Black Panthers, whom Cleaver served as minister of information, were regarded with both alarm and hostility by the authorities, and the numerous bloody encounters between the Panthers and the

police remain as testimony to the seriousness with which both sides
enacted their stated positions. As a follower of Malcolm X, Cleaver
was also associated with the other best known radical black organization of the sixties, the Nation of Islam, which also came under intense
governmental scrutiny for several years. Cleaver thus stood at the
forefront of the black revolution, and *Soul on Ice* is, in some ways, his
manifesto of that revolutionary self. Just as *Black Boy* had twenty
years earlier jolted America with a vision of the black world unknown
to many, so did *Soul on Ice* cry anew black hatred and alienation. But
whereas Richard's strategy is first to retreat to a haven of safety and
then fight with words, Eldridge Cleaver predicts, even espouses, the
coming to reality of the race war Wright only imagined, replete with
its "lynching, murder, fire, beating, castration, psychotic sex combats,
police brutality, race riots, pure hate against pure hate."[30] What's
more, as Cleaver sees it, it is blacks who will both begin and win this
racial Armageddon.

Cleaver must hate James Baldwin and any black who pleads for
understanding, patience, and any kind of accommodation with the
white world; he must hate Baldwin not primarily for his homosexuality, but for being a complex thinker capable of seeing more than
one side of the issue; such complex thinkers stand in the way of the
brutal action *Soul on Ice* demands. Not surprisingly, Cleaver also despises Booker T. Washington, whom he sees as a tool used by the
white world to help clamp the doctrine of segregation onto the backs
of blacks (*Soul on Ice* 124). The rebellious self Cleaver creates stands
in the autobiographical line originating with Douglass, a self taking
its place in the struggle among those other selves, echoing and mir-
roring the heroic Frederick and Richard, despising and seeking to
obliterate any other black selves that do not measure up to its demands. The stridency and vulgarity of this autobiographical "I" alienate some readers, as Cleaver intends; this I's threats at one time
frightened others, as they were also clearly intended to do, but most
of all, this self demanded—and still demands—to be heard in all its
rage, frustration, and emerging power. If *Black Boy* pointed the way
in 1945 to the possibility for new self-realization and self-actualization
for blacks both in their autobiographies and in their lives, then *Soul
on Ice* represents both a fruition of the seeds Wright planted and, at
the same time, another beginning in black consciousness, one rooted
in the revolutionary character of Frederick Douglass, but given new
and powerful expression.

6: Out from the Shadow: Malcolm X

Like the works that precede it, *The Autobiography of Malcolm X* records a struggle for freedom. Originally conceived as a conventional conversion story, the *Autobiography*, even in its final form, can be viewed as the chronicle of a sinful soul's flight from the bondage of sin to the freedom of true faith through spiritual rebirth. Additionally, Malcolm traces his struggle to free himself from the dominance of a powerful father figure, thereby repeating the Oedipal theme already noted in earlier writers. First intended as a paean to Elijah Muhammad, Malcolm's "savior," *The Autobiography of Malcolm X* in its final form records Malcolm's fight for intellectual and emotional independence—his quest to think for himself and to *be* himself. Bondage, flight, and freedom may be the most pervasive *pattern* in one line of black men's autobiography, but the creation of a free self, a self unconstrained by the likes of a white master, a domineering father, a strong predecessor in the literary tradition, or a charismatic spiritual leader, is doubtless the most important *theme* in African American men's autobiography. Black men's autobiography is a revolutionary act; it asserts the author's ego against all "others" in the world. As such, it exemplifies in a striking way a central theme in *all* autobiography, the creation of a free, autobiographical "I" that is identified with, yet distinct from, the writer.

Black men's autobiography illustrates the establishment of the free "I" as a dominant theme in autobiography through motifs of bondage, flight, and freedom to describe the journey of individuation that every man and woman is challenged to undertake. *The Autobiography of Malcolm X* is unique, however, for it reveals the way in which that autobiographical "I" is conceived and how it changes as the autobiographer writes his story. Alex Haley, Malcolm's collaborator, furnishes an illuminating account of the genesis of the work and of the changes both in Malcolm X and in his autobiographical "I" as the work was written. Haley's epilogue to the work is integral to it; as such, it offers something missing in other autobiographies—a third-party perspective on the process through which an autobiographer constructs her or his autobiographical self. Of course, Haley is hardly a disinterested spectator, for he had a hand in the creation of the Malcolm of the *Autobiography*; nevertheless, his ultimately distinct viewpoint allows us to see a changing Malcolm X revise both the stated purpose of his life story and the character of its protagonist. Additionally, Haley's epilogue, written after Malcolm's assassination, gives the *Autobiography* a sense of closure on a life—a feeling missing in other autobiographies, which must, by their nature, end before their writers' deaths. For all these reasons, *The Autobiography of Malcolm X* fittingly concludes this study.

A publisher who had read Alex Haley's interview with Malcolm X before it appeared in the May, 1963 issue of *Playboy* first had the idea for an autobiography of the outspoken leader of the Nation of Islam, popularly known as the Black Muslims. Taken with the idea, Haley proposed it to Malcolm early in 1963, and after Elijah Muhammad gave his approval, Malcolm and Haley began the series of conversations that eventually produced the autobiography. As Paul John Eakin notes, Malcolm originally conceived the work as a standard conversion story, relating how he, a sinner, was saved and given new life by Elijah Muhammad, the man who became his mentor and spiritual father.[1] The *Autobiography* was thus to stand in the "exemplary life" genre, pointing the way for other lost souls to find salvation. As such, it was to take a two-part pattern: the first detailing Malcolm's downward descent into ever-greater degradation, the second tracing his ascent through his acceptance of Muhammad's doctrine.[2] Both the original purpose and the pattern of the autobiography are implied in its first dedication, which Malcolm X handed to Haley the day the contract for the work was signed. This dedication, later discarded, seems to have been Malcolm's way of letting Haley know from the outset that the active agent in the autobiography would be Elijah Muhammad; Malcolm (and, by extension, all African Americans who followed his example) would be the passive recipient of Muhammad's bounty. That dedication reads:

This book I dedicate to the Honorable Elijah Muhammad, who found me here in America in the muck and mire of the filthiest civilization and society on this earth, and pulled me out, cleaned me up, and stood me on my feet, and made me the man that I am today.[3]

In crediting Elijah Muhammad with saving him and remaking his personality into what he at the time considered its preordained, final form, Malcolm was unconsciously thwarting the true purpose of every autobiographer—to create a self *through* the act of autobiography. A popularly held notion supposes that the autobiographer must first discover the shape of his or her life and then write that life on the basis of that discovery; the living of the life precedes the writing of it.[4] At first, Malcolm held to this misconception that his life had already reached its ultimate form, not through his own doing, but through the ministrations of Elijah Muhammad. Malcolm thus sought both to abdicate responsibility for having shaped his life through the living of it and to relinquish the privilege of creating a life through the writing of it. All the credit was to go to Elijah Muhammad, who had somehow taken both that burden and that power into himself.

It is little wonder, then, that the composing of the *Autobiography* got off to a poor start. In his epilogue, Haley mentions Malcolm's distrust, grounded in the suspicion that Haley was working for the F.B.I. More to the point, however, was Malcolm's determination to make the work a piece of Black Muslim propaganda. Haley recalls, "He would bristle when I tried to urge him that the proposed book was *his* life" (394); that, of course, was what Malcolm did not want the book to be. It was to be the story of how another man, Elijah Muhammad, had fashioned a life *for* him.

By comparing the writing of the autobiography to the process of psychoanalysis, Eugene V. Wolfenstein offers another explanation for the difficulties Malcolm and Haley initially experienced.[5] Wolfenstein sees Haley in the role of analyst whose purpose it was to help Malcolm break through an unquestioning devotion to Elijah Muhammad so that his "true" self could surface. Eakin suggests something similar by calling Haley the "lure" that brought the suppressed "counterrevolutionary" Malcolm into the open.[6] To extend the metaphor, we might say that the early difficulties of writing the autobiography were the result of the patient's distrust of and lack of rapport with his analyst. Wolfenstein compares Malcolm to the patient who consciously agrees to psychoanalysis but then resists free association of any ideas that she or he finds morally unacceptable.[7] More will be said about the relationship between Haley and Malcolm and that relationship's importance in the shaping of the *Autobiography*; first we will discuss some of the circumstances that broke the two men's initial impasse.

* * *

Malcolm's dedication of the *Autobiography* lauded Elijah Muhammad for virtually saving his life, and Malcolm's first sessions with Alex

Haley were, as Haley notes, "Almost nothing but Black Muslim philosophy, praise of Mr. Muhammad, and the 'evils' of 'the white devil' " (393). Although Malcolm presented a front of unswerving loyalty to Muhammad in those early meetings with Haley, causing Haley to despair of ever getting any material that would make a readable book, events had already been working before 1963 to breach Malcolm's defenses and allow a different self to emerge.

The break between Elijah Muhammad and Malcolm X was probably inevitable, for reasons that appear obvious today. Muhammad gave Malcolm the wings to fly from a life of crime and despair to a position of influence and power. In gratitude, Malcolm long afterward proclaimed and lived the gospel of the Nation of Islam, seeking to minimize his own growing fame while trying to magnify the man whom he adored.[8] Yet no amount of abnegation could hide Malcolm's high visibility in the press and public eye; his oratorical gifts and electric personality made him a much more popular speaker than Elijah Muhammad. Envy arose within the Nation; like any powerful leader, Malcolm had enemies among those less highly favored. Finally, Muhammad himself seems to have become prey to jealousy; even the idea of Malcolm's autobiography may have pained the older man, although he had consented to it. After all, it was *Malcolm*, not Muhammad himself, who had been asked to tell his life story. Ironically, the work that was intended to praise Muhammad probably contributed to the break between him and Malcolm and, consequently, to Malcolm's reassessment of both Muhammad's character and his own.

Malcolm says in the autobiography that he first noted in 1961 criticism from other high-ranking members in the Nation of Islam (294). By 1962, he was being slighted in *Muhammad Speaks,* the Nation's official newspaper, and criticism increased the following year. Whatever tensions such treatment caused Malcolm X were exacerbated when he heard—from Muhammad himself—that persistent rumors of "the Prophet's" adulteries with various of his private secretaries were true. Malcolm received this confirmation from Muhammad in April, 1963; the news became public in July. Malcolm had lived according to Elijah Muhammad's strict laws of sexual purity; it stunned him to learn that the Prophet had not practiced his own teaching. Worse, Muhammad expressed no remorse but told Malcolm that, as the "reincarnation" of various Old Testament figures, he was bound to repeat their sinful deeds.

Peter Goldman, one of Malcolm's biographers, suggests that Malcolm's peers in the Nation of Islam generally underestimated the depth of his shock at hearing of Muhammad's sins. Malcolm had built his new life upon an unquestioning acceptance of Muhammad's message as divinely inspired; Malcolm himself said toward the end of his life that learning of Muhammad's sins was the beginning of the collapse of his own faith.[9]

As Malcolm's doubts grew, Muhammad and his inner circle in the Nation were at the same time actively looking for a way to oust him from power. Malcolm unwittingly gave his enemies the excuse they needed with one ill-considered remark. Speaking at a Muslim rally in New York City a week after John Kennedy's assassination, Malcolm called the President's death a case of "the chickens coming home to roost." The press quickly picked up on the statement, and it made national headlines. Muhammad immediately silenced Malcolm for a period of ninety days as an act of discipline and as a means of distancing the Nation of Islam from a negative sentiment voiced amidst national grief over the death of a popular leader.

Malcolm's silencing was the beginning of the end of his relationship with Elijah Muhammad and the Nation of Islam. Although Malcolm put on a brave public front, submitting humbly to his humiliation and confessing his bad judgment in the remark about Kennedy, he was inwardly furious.[10] Then, shortly afterward, he first heard that his death had been ordered, and as he expresses it in the *Autobiography*, "any death talk for me could have been approved of— if not actually initiated—by only one man" (307). Elijah Muhammad, once Malcolm's savior, was now an apparently mortal enemy.

Against these events of 1963, *The Autobiography of Malcolm X* took shape. Although Malcolm's conscious loyalty to Muhammad was still intact when he began working with Haley, the seeds of doubt had been sown. After Malcolm's silencing, it was clear that the original tone and direction of the autobiography had to be changed, but the breakthrough Haley had hoped for had already occurred some time earlier.

One night in early or mid-1963, Malcolm arrived at Haley's apartment exhausted and angry. After Malcolm had delivered a two-hour tirade against black leaders who criticized Elijah Muhammad, Haley calmly asked him to talk about his mother. The request broke through a wall that had stood between the two men, and all the rest of that evening, Malcolm poured out the story of his early life. His words formed the basis for the first two chapters of the autobiography.

What happened that night to shatter Malcolm's defenses? He had begun the autobiography determined to make it not his own story, but Elijah Muhammad's, yet when his faith in Muhammad was shaken, Malcolm was freed to face his own traumatic past. Haley speculates that Malcolm was so tired that night that "his defenses were vulnerable." He calls Malcolm's talking that night "stream-of-consciousness reminiscing." Wolfenstein offers a thoroughgoing psychoanalytic explanation of why a question about Malcolm's mother undammed the stream of personal recollection. Whatever the reason, the plan of the autobiography began to change that night; the events of the latter part of 1963 changed the direction even more than Malcolm or Haley could have predicted. What began as a tribute to a virtually omnipotent father figure ended up as genuine autobiography: the delineation of the development of a free self.

After Malcolm and Haley had their "breakthrough" evening, the autobiography began to emerge as *Malcolm's* story. His adulation of Elijah Muhammad was secure enough at first, however, that the accounts of his early years with the Nation of Islam sounded very much as Malcolm had originally intended them to. Even though his faith in Muhammad was gradually being eroded by what he was learning about the Prophet's private life, Malcolm dictated the autobiography as if he were still a completely loyal devotee of the man who had saved him. But as the rift between Muhammad and Malcolm widened, Haley began to worry lest Malcolm go back through the chapters of the autobiography and drastically edit them in the light of his new disillusionment. His fear was realized after Malcolm's return from Mecca in the late spring of 1964. Malcolm returned chapters of the autobiography Haley had sent him for approval extensively blue-penciled wherever he had discussed his close relationship with Muhammad (416). Malcolm had previously promised Haley that the chapters about his early relationship with Elijah Muhammad would stand as originally written, despite recent changes in his feelings. Reminding Malcolm of that promise, Haley recalls, "I stressed that if those chapters contained such telegraphing to readers of what would lie ahead, then the book would automatically be robbed of some of its building suspense and drama" (416). Although Malcolm first resented Haley's caveat, he soon agreed that the early chapters should stand pretty much as written. In final form, they do recount Malcolm's early devotion to Muhammad with only a few hints of his later disappointment.

Haley's journalistic savvy rescued *The Autobiography of Malcolm X* at two crucial points. First, Haley realized before Malcolm did that the autobiography had to be *his* story if it were to appeal to a mass audience. Haley's initial pushing to get Malcolm beyond the Nation of Islam rhetoric to personal reminiscence is explained by his understanding that most readers were not interested in a whole book devoted to nothing but Black Muslim propaganda. A deeper insight

into the nature of genuine autobiography seems to be revealed, however, in Haley's contention that it would ruin the autobiography if
Malcolm were to rewrite the story of his earlier life in light of his
later, changed feelings. Although he does not articulate it, Haley may
have sensed that the autobiographer, in creating the autobiographical
"I," must in a way pretend *not* to know all that he or she knows about
the self being created. Even though the autobiographer has the advantage of standing at an end point looking back over the journey
that has led to his or her present position, the knowledge of the shape
of his or her life *as a whole* must be suppressed in order to show how
the self being created gradually develops and changes. If Malcolm
had rewritten his life as a Black Muslim by including parenthetical
comments indicating his later knowledge of the flaws in Elijah Muhammad's character or by claiming that he had been deceived and
only later learned the truth, he would have robbed the narrative of
its suspense. Additionally, he would have bypassed a crucial stage in
the development of his autobiographical self. In order to tell the
truth about the growth of the autobiographical "I," the autobiographer *must* lie—pretending not to know at every point what will come
next in the narrative and how the subject will change. Fortunately,
The Autobiography of Malcolm X, which examines the formation and
abandonment of one self after another, is preserved by Haley's contention—and Malcolm X's concurrence—that later realizations had to
be withheld until the appropriate moment. If Haley had not alerted
us to this decision that he and Malcolm made together, we might still
detect how Malcolm, like all other true autobiographers, had to sup-
press the insights and emotions of his current self in order to reveal
his earlier selves in proper order. Haley's epilogue, however, gives us
an unparalleled insight into the decisions autobiographers must
make.

*   *   *

The Autobiography of Malcolm X successfully portrays the growth of
Malcolm, who is identified with and yet is distinct from the Malcolm
X who narrated his life story to Alex Haley. The two men's awareness
that they are tracing Malcolm through a series of identities that are
developed, lived in for a time, and then discarded as the self continues to metamorphose is shown in the titles for several of the autobiography's chapters. Malcolm is, by turns, "Homeboy," "Detroit
Red," "Satan," and "Minister Malcolm X." His genius lies in his ability
to leave an identity behind when it no longer fits his changing personality. Early in his life, for example, after his family has disinte-
grated and he has been placed in a school for troubled boys, Malcolm

enjoys great success as the only black student in an all-white junior high school. Talented in sports and academics, he soon becomes a leader and is elected class president. But Malcolm discards this "house nigger" identity when a teacher lets him know that despite his popularity in the white community, he can never aspire to anything more than carpentry—a trade "fit" for blacks. According to the teacher, his desire to be a lawyer is unrealistic. Some young men would have been content with the degree of comfort Malcolm had attained, but Malcolm will not be constrained by the restrictions of the white world. Soon he leaves Michigan for Boston and so undertakes his first act of self-assertion; the world has tried to keep him in an unthreatening position, but Malcolm will not be a kept man. He leaves Michigan and his identity as "Mascot," the token black in a white community, to find a new identity in a strange place.

The first part of the autobiography follows Malcolm as he assumes one identity after another. In Boston, he becomes known as "Homeboy" because of his unsophisticated clothing and hair style. Malcolm soon remakes himself, however, first adopting the straight hair considered attractive among young black men, then buying outlandish clothing to match his straightened hair, or "conk." He refashions his values, too, learning quickly how to get along through petty hustling—buying alcohol and condoms for his shoeshine customers at the Roseland Ballroom. When Malcolm moves to Harlem, "Homeboy" disappears and his place is taken by "Detroit Red," a more serious hustler who makes money pimping and running a numbers racket. Soon he adds burglary to his crimes. Malcolm is finally caught, tried for heading a robbery ring, and sentenced to ten years in prison, where he assumes yet another identity, "Satan," the hate-filled, blasphemous inmate. When Malcolm hits bottom, he is ready for another transformation—this time one to reverse the downward spiral that has characterized his previous lives. Hearing about Elijah Muhammad and the Nation of Islam from his brothers brings about the conversion Malcolm has needed and gives him a new life as a follower of Muhammad.

Malcolm's various identities in the first part of his autobiography share some interesting similarities. In many of them, we see contempt for authority mixed with a fascination for it. Malcolm's early experiences with whites lead him to distrust and dislike them, yet by conking his hair, he tries to make himself look more like a white man. His various hustles are acts of rebellion against the white-controlled power structure, but "Detroit Red" ironically applies the work ethic of the white world as he toils day and night to make a dishonest living. Without realizing it, Malcolm adopts the values and practices of the dominant culture he professes to despise.

Malcolm's identities are also characterized by the extreme degree to which he carries them: he conks as faithfully as any black man he knows, and his zoot suits are the most outrageous money can buy. When Malcolm, in his "Detroit Red" phase, devotes himself to crime, he works harder at his calling than any other hustler he knows; when he winds up in prison, as "Satan" he screams and curses more violently than any other prisoner.

Malcolm X looks back over his early identities and notes their emptiness. He seeks to be an individual, but he actually is not very different from many other young black men of the times whose lives were just as aimless as his. The conked and zoot-suited hipster is a type, as is the petty hustler; although each character comes to life in the *Autobiography*, we are meant to see how inauthentic, how un-individual each figure is. When Malcolm X began working with Alex Haley, he wanted to show Haley, the world, and himself that his real life began when he was converted to the Nation of Islam. His pre-conversion selves were, to him, necessary steps on his road to the moment of salvation, but not embodiments of Malcolm's "genuine" self. That true self was called into being, Malcolm X once believed, when Elijah Muhammad's message reached Malcolm/Satan in prison.

As we have noted, Malcolm X first imagined his autobiography in two parts, pre- and post-conversion, with the real Malcolm emerging when he embraces the faith of the Nation of Islam. When he was first approached by Haley with the idea for the work, Malcolm X was still living comfortably enough in the latest of his identities, "Minister Malcolm X," that he could portray himself as a faithful adherent to Elijah Muhammad. Early in 1963 he did not imagine that by the year's end he would be cut adrift from the Nation and from the identity in which he had lived for twelve years.

Of all the roles Malcolm X ever abandoned, that of Minister of the Nation of Islam was the most painful to leave behind, for in it he had found what he had lacked since the death of his father—a relationship of love and trust with another man. Critics have discussed at length the various dynamics at work in Malcolm X that led to his surrendering of his life to Muhammad and his teachings; Malcolm X himself describes the event in language common to many conversion narratives.[11] Although the Nation of Islam proclaimed Allah as its God, Elijah Muhammad became, at the least, a physical embodiment of Allah for Malcolm, and this is how the Malcolm of the autobiography responds to him.

When Malcolm embraces the teachings of Muhammad, he assumes a new identity that he believes is the authentic self he has been seeking. Still, this new self repeats patterns of behavior we have already encountered. To become a Black Muslim is to undertake an act of rejection of the white world and its values; through that act, Malcolm reasserts his own earlier rejection of such a world. Additionally, Malcolm embraces his new identity with the same dedication he has given to earlier selves: just as he had been the best two-bit hustler in Boston and the hardest working con man in New York, now he becomes the most self-disciplined and loyal Black Muslim ever to follow Elijah Muhammad. Despite the radical quality of Black Muslim rhetoric and its demands for strict separation from the corrupt white world, many of the Nation's teachings about personal morality, economic success, and social organization mirror the values of the white world.[12] By accepting the Muslims' social program, Malcolm repeats his earlier practice of mimicking the white culture he believes he is rejecting.

*   *   *

We cannot say for certain how *The Autobiography of Malcolm X* would have turned out had Malcolm not been ousted from the Nation of Islam. We can speculate, however, that the work would have followed the typical conversion form while expressing its author's naive assumptions about autobiography. Malcolm X would have seen his life as a series of false identities predestined to give way one after another until his true self emerged through the process of conversion. He would have told his life story from the perspective of an autobiographer who assumes he can write about his life coherently because that life has been lived and has reached its final form by the time of writing. If Malcolm X had still been safely positioned in his identity as Minister of the Nation of Islam, he could not have imagined that either he or his autobiographical self would undergo any further metamorphoses. Having attained his life's preordained goal, he could not—indeed, would have no need to—change further. This, I imagine, resembles the way Malcolm X thought when he and Haley first began working together. The dedication of the autobiography and his initial conversations with Haley substantiate this view of his life and autobiography. According to the plan of the standard conversion narrative, the saved sinner, having attained his life's goal, has nothing further to report. Malcolm X would therefore probably have ended his autobiography shortly after recounting his conversion and explaining fully the doctrines and demands of the Nation of Islam. Of Malcolm, there would be nothing more to tell, for that self would no longer exist independently but would be subsumed into the body of the Nation. If we cast this hypothetical autobiography into the three-part pattern, its narration of Malcolm's early years of degradation would correspond to the bondage section, his experience of conversion to flight, and his life as a Minister of the Nation to the blissful experience of freedom. But as we have noted, Malcolm's dismissal from the Nation ended the possibility that his autobiography could follow such a standard format, just as Haley's question about his mother had earlier broken down his determination that the work would not be his own story. *Two* visions for the autobiography had to be abandoned because of changes in Malcolm's own life during the time of its writing. Now the third and final form of the work could emerge.

Malcolm X believed for years that in Elijah Muhammad he had found not only his savior but also his freedom. He threw himself into his work as Minister Malcolm X with a zest and dedication that were characteristic of him. Muhammad's word was truth, and like a true believer, Malcolm X preached that word tirelessly and selflessly. Yet, as Peter Goldman notes, Malcolm X came to chafe under aspects of Muslim doctrine even before he learned of Muhammad's adulteries.[13] The Nation's bitter denunciations of the white world were not linked to any program of action to secure equality for blacks, but Malcolm longed to be involved in the struggle for civil rights, if not for integration. Additionally, Malcolm X became disillusioned with the changing mood within the Nation itself. Once the Nation had established itself economically, some of its leaders fell prey to the temptation to take advantage of the material comforts the Nation could provide them. In his dedication to an austere Islamic life style, Malcolm came to out-Muhammad Muhammad himself and deplored the lowering of the values upon which the Nation had been built.

Malcolm's break with the Prophet was in some ways yet another repetition of a pattern he had lived through before. As a teenager, he had for a time accepted the values of the white world and had achieved a measure of success within it; only when he realized that the culture of such a world would forever limit his opportunities did he break free from it. In the same way, Malcolm lived in the world of the Nation of Islam for years, but finally began to realize that both he and the Nation were changing in ways that might no longer permit him to live within its constraining boundaries. Although Malcolm was forced from the Nation, he might well have eventually left it of his own initiative and discovered another calling had not the necessity of such a change been thrust upon him.

The Autobiography of Malcolm X ends up recording not Malcolm's eternal union with the Black Muslims, but his separation from them—an event that took its authors and their work by surprise. What had been planned as a conversion story with a predictable outcome now had to be changed again because the autobiographer and the life he was shaping were both overtaken by unforeseen events during the act of writing. Consequently, when the reader reaches the chapter titled "Out," he realizes that Malcolm X's "conversion" autobiography is not really a typical example of that genre at all; the hints Malcolm X and Haley put into the text earlier prove to be accurate: the autobiography, which begins as a conversion narrative, takes a turn and ends up as the story of Malcolm's struggle to be free from the dominance of his godlike father figure, Elijah Muhammad.

At first, Malcolm regards Muhammad as the replacement of his own father, Earl Little, who had been killed by white racists when Malcolm was six. For more than a decade, Malcolm accepts Muhammad as the purveyor of divine truth, a man he worships and for whom he would gladly give his life. But when Muhammad's other side is revealed to Malcolm—the adulteries, the deceptions, the jealousy, and the determination to protect his self-interest—Malcolm's attitude must change if he is to save his own integrity. Acceptance of Muhammad's teachings gives way to questioning; trust turns to doubt, and adoration to disappointment. As Malcolm X expresses it: "after twelve years of never thinking for as much as five minutes about myself, I became able finally to muster the nerve, and the strength, to start facing the facts, to think for myself" (310). The Malcolm who has served Elijah Muhammad so faithfully has not, it turns out, really found his freedom in the Nation of Islam. By accepting the tenets of the faith, he has given up his freedom of thought; what is more, he has given up the right to his own life. Now he reclaims it.

Malcolm's words, "I became able . . . to think for myself," recall words W.E.B. Du Bois puts into the mouths of the "bumptious, irritated, young black intelligentsia" of his own day when their ideas collide with those of Booker T. Washington, the "official voice" of black America: "I don't care a damn what Booker Washington thinks! This is what I think, and *I have a right to think*."[14] The realization that one can and must think for oneself links the Malcolm of *The Autobiography of Malcolm X* not only with Du Bois and the African Americans seeking freedom from the stifling influence of Booker T. Washington but also with Frederick Douglass in his struggle to learn to read and write, skills that unlock the world of ideas. The ability to think for himself sets Richard, the protagonist of *Black Boy*, against both the white and black cultures in which he grows up and makes the book the story of his growth as a young artist. When James Baldwin understands that he can have his own artistic opinions, he attacks the literary values of Richard Wright; the same dynamic causes Eldridge Cleaver to reject Baldwin. Malcolm also begins to think for himself, and so joins the other autobiographical selves we have studied. Unlike Douglass and Wright, who are never at peace with their worlds until they find their freedom (and not altogether, even then), Malcolm lives comfortably for a time in his various worlds before his own growing awareness forces him to strike out for new territory. Malcolm enjoys a longer period of good relations with a father figure than does any other autobiographer in this line, but when the break with that father figure occurs, the trauma, as detailed in his autobiography, is an painful as any we have examined, even James Baldwin's break with Richard Wright.

About his break with Muhammad, Malcolm writes:

I was in a state of emotional shock. I was like someone who for twelve years had had an inseparable, beautiful marriage—and then suddenly one morning at breakfast the marriage partner had thrust across the table some divorce papers.

I felt as though something in *nature* had failed, like the sun, or the stars. (308–9)

The shock Malcolm feels at being cut off from the Nation of Islam sets the struggle with his father figure apart from the other father-son conflicts we have encountered. Other autobiographers write of themselves as instigators of the conflict: Douglass rebels against the paternalistic slave society by standing up to Covey and then by running away; Du Bois fights Washington with his books and then by organizing the Niagara Movement and the NAACP; Wright fights both black and white Southern culture and then flees to the North. These autobiographers are not surprised by their separation from paternal power because they have long hated that power and desired to be free of it. Even Baldwin, whose love for Richard Wright resembles Malcolm's devotion to Muhammad, comes to realize that *he* initiated the break with Wright and should not have been surprised by Wright's furious reaction to "Everybody's Protest Novel." Malcolm alone appears not to have been looking for a fight; it is little wonder that he feels the world falling apart when he learns, in quick succession, that he is "divorced" from his surrogate father and that this same father has probably ordered his death. Malcolm, who planned to live out his life in his identity as Minister Malcolm X, secure in his relationship as adopted son and heir to Muhammad, instead finds himself once more in a position of spiritual chaos similar to that which he had experienced in prison before he was first found by the Nation.

So after twelve years as Minister Malcolm X, Malcolm finds himself a spiritual orphan. Realizing his old self no longer exists, he undertakes a quest for a new identity and for a new father. At this point in the *Autobiography*, the true pattern of Malcolm's life finally becomes clear. Malcolm's journey to Mecca and his discoveries there reveal, at last, that his life is not the chronicle of a self trying out various avatars and discarding them until the "true" one is finally discovered, after which the fulfilled self can live contentedly ever after. Instead, *The Autobiography of Malcolm X* traces the open-ended journey of a changing self stopped only by death. Malcolm's life story cannot be cast into the standard conversion genre he originally believed to express the shape of his life, and so the autobiography finally reflects "[t]he vision of a man whose swiftly unfolding career has outstripped the possibilities of the traditional autobiography he had meant to write."[15] Malcolm's life, as he himself states, turns out to be above all one of changes.

Although Alex Haley notes in his epilogue that anger filled Malcolm X in the days after his ouster from the Black Muslims, Malcolm himself expresses little overt rage against Elijah Muhammad in the autobiography. His reaction is more one of bewilderment, hurt, and betrayal than of fury. Malcolm in no way glosses over Muhammad's sins, presenting the Prophet as a man capable of adultery, deceit, and execution, but personal hatred is absent. Strangely enough, Malcolm seems never to have lost his love for Muhammad, even when betrayed. Charles Kenyatta, Malcolm's friend and associate, claimed, "Malcolm loved Elijah Muhammad better than his own sons loved him. . . . He never wanted to move away. If Elijah had come up to him five minutes before he got shot, Malcolm would have gone back."[16] But there was no going back. In fairly short order, Malcolm realizes this fact, accepts it, and with characteristic resilience, moves on.

*   *   *

Malcolm X says little in his autobiography about his motives for wanting to make the pilgrimage to Mecca beyond stating that the hajj is a religious obligation for every Muslim at least once during his or her life. The timing of his journey, however—about four months after his dismissal from the Black Muslims—explains a great deal. Just as Malcolm was ready for a new life and identity when he was converted to Islam in prison, so he is now prepared for another self to emerge. Indeed, having been so brutally wrenched away from one identity, Malcolm *must* find a new center for his life.

According to his description, Malcolm's hajj strips away the remnants of an old identity and gives birth to a new one. Taken out of his normal surroundings, stripped of his customary clothing, garbed in the white diaper-like loincloth of the pilgrim, and deprived of his powers of communication because he does not speak Arabic, Malcolm resembles a newborn baby. He describes how he must learn the unfamiliar rituals of Muslim prayer and purification, much as a child must learn the appropriate practices of his culture. Malcolm also details the important relational breakthrough he experiences while in Saudi Arabia. Complications with his travel papers compel him to remain at the Jedda airport while authorities decide whether he will be allowed to proceed to Mecca. While awaiting such permission, Malcolm remembers the name of a prominent Saudi family given him by a friend in America. Once he contacts this family, they take him in hand, treat him like visiting royalty, and smooth the way for him to enjoy preferential treatment during the rest of his visit. Significantly, this family is white. For the first time in many years, Malcolm is put in a position in which he must trust whites. Impressed by their friendliness and unable to detect in them any trace of racism, Malcolm gives them his trust. Through this act and through witnessing Muslims from every race and nation worshiping in harmony at Mecca, Malcolm takes a great step in thinking for himself. He comes to see that all whites are not the "devils" Black Muslim rhetoric declares them to be; he realizes that race war and race separation are not the only alternatives for black and white Americans. At Mecca, Malcolm's new self begins to emerge; the fatherhood of Elijah Muhammad is replaced by the fatherhood of Allah, and the brotherhood of the Nation of Islam by the "Oneness of Man under One God." Just as Malcolm Little had changed his name to Malcolm X when a new self was born, so now Malcolm X gives way to El-Hajj Malik El-Shabazz, the new name identifying the new self.

Critics disagree about the extent of the revision in Malcolm X's thinking about racial issues after his return from Mecca, but they agree that some changes did occur. The Malcolm of the *Autobiography* expresses changes in his thought primarily through the imagery of expansion: he comes to see the solidarity of African Americans with black Africans, and he admits that there *are* some whites who want to help end racism. The new Malcolm is more inclined to look at each person individually and not to make blanket judgments as Minister Malcolm X had done. During the last months of his life, El-Hajj Malik El-Shabazz works to create the Organization of Afro-American Unity as a way, one suspects, to give substance to his new vision and as a means to provide himself with meaningful work. A sense of urgency pervades the post-Mecca chapters of the autobiography, for this last Malcolm, like the earlier ones, holds on to the conviction that he will die young. In the final chapter, he expresses in brief what might serve as a fitting summary of the lives that together form his life:

Anything I do today, I regard as urgent. No man is given but so much time to accomplish whatever is his life's work. My life in particular never has stayed fixed in one position for very long. You have seen how throughout my life, I have often known unexpected drastic changes. (384)

*   *   *

Malcolm X and Alex Haley completed the autobiography not long before Malcolm's assassination on February 21, 1965. Malcolm had given his approval for the drafts of the latter chapters, so the book as it stands bears his imprimatur. The main text ends with its author still alive and so possesses the openendedness of all incomplete lives. Additionally, as we have seen, Malcolm's autobiography demonstrates little of the naivete of certain other life writings that assume autobiographers can achieve final perspective on their lives; as such, his work is quite unlike standard conversion narratives. Paradoxically, though, *The Autobiography of Malcolm X* does possess a feeling of closure not present in any other work in the genre.

Alex Haley's epilogue today stands as an integral part of the *Autobiography*. When the work was begun, Malcolm gave Haley permission to write an afterword not subject to his approval. Haley did compose such a piece, although his freedom to include in it whatever he chose resulted more from Malcolm's death than from the two men's initial agreement. Had Malcolm not died, Haley would probably have written of his reactions to Malcolm's life and to the message of the Nation of Islam. Instead, Haley was given the opportunity to write about Malcolm's last days and his assassination and funeral and to summarize his life.

As we have noted, the Epilogue furnishes information about how the autobiography was actually composed. During many lengthy sessions, Malcolm would talk about his life, and Haley would take notes. Haley also got into the habit of leaving scraps of paper about the room so that Malcolm could scribble on them. Some of those dashed-off notes reveal feelings Malcolm could not articulate even to Haley. At the time of Malcolm's silencing, for example, Haley discovered two notes Malcolm had scrawled during one of their sessions: "You have not converted a man because you have silenced him. John Viscount Morley," and "I was going downhill until he [Elijah Muhammad] picked me up, but the more I think of it, we picked each other up" (409). Using his own notes and some of Malcolm's, Haley would compose chapters of the work, then submit them to Malcolm.

The collaborative effort between Malcolm and Haley that produced the *Autobiography* inevitably raises questions about Haley's role in the production of the work. Because, as we have noted, *all* autobiography unavoidably fictionalizes a life to a greater or lesser extent, we must ask to what extent Malcolm's story is fictionalized and what part Haley played in shaping the Malcolm who is the protagonist of the work.

I believe, first of all, that *The Autobiography of Malcolm X* is indeed more Malcolm's book than it is Haley's. Haley scrupulously allowed Malcolm to approve each chapter of the work. When it appeared that Malcolm would re-edit the sections dealing with his relationship to Elijah Muhammad, Haley questioned the decision. Malcolm retorted, "Whose book is this?" and Haley conceded, "yours, of course." Fortunately, Malcolm reversed his decision and allowed the chapters to stand as originally written, but one receives the impression that they *would* have been changed if Malcolm had so desired.

Granted that Malcolm had control over the autobiography, we must next ask to what extent the work is an accurate representation of his life. Since its publication, the autobiography has assumed a kind of canonical status, much like that afforded to *Up from Slavery* at the turn of the century. No biography of Malcolm X has appeared that has been accorded general recognition as the standard account of his life; the *Autobiography* seems, by its overwhelming aura of authority, to have prevented anyone from challenging its preeminence by attempting a definitive biography. Here, a comparison with the life of Martin Luther King, Jr. proves instructive. King has been the subject of numerous biographies since his death; it might be argued that he merits so many because his fame and influence were so great—even greater than Malcolm's. The absence of a King *autobiography*, however, might also account for the large number of biographies. A strong male autobiography, as we have seen, tends to cast its protagonist in the role of father figure to be overcome by later generations. It might be that Malcolm is still so intimidating (actually, he has become something of a cult figure since his death) that his image to this day daunts the would-be biographer who would seek to tell his life anew.

Although the definitive biography of Malcolm remains to be written, critics have investigated Malcolm's past. Peter Goldman looked into Malcolm's years as a Harlem hustler but was unable to establish contact with any of his former associates. He notes that the journalist Ted Poston had made a similar effort while Malcolm was still alive, with disappointing results.[17] Only one man remembered Malcolm, and he deflated Malcolm's claims to have been a fairly important criminal. Goldman concludes that while Malcolm may exaggerate his past a bit, portraying himself as worse than he was, the degradation he describes is genuine enough.[18] That Goldman believes the Malcolm of the *Autobiography* is an accurate representation of the man Malcolm X is also borne out by his frequent recourse to the work as a source in his own book, which itself is meticulously researched. Eugene Wolfenstein also finds the autobiography to be a faithful portrayal of Malcolm X's life, for several reasons. He notes:

Was Malcolm representing himself accurately? Was Alex Haley, his biographical amanuensis, representing him accurately? From a purely empirical standpoint, I believe the answer to both questions is generally affirmative. Throughout the *Autobiography* . . . there is clear and self-consciously drawn distinction between fact and opinion. Furthermore, both men had a passion for accuracy and order, as is evident in Haley's epilogue as well as in the body of the text. Finally, and I think most convincingly, the relationship of Haley and the process of self-reflection this involved were integral parts of Malcolm's personal evolution. By permitting him to develop a knowledge of himself as a distinct individual, they were instrumental in helping to free him from his unquestioning devotion to Elijah Muhammad. It is extremely unlikely that such a process of individuation could have been premised upon major falsification of the life-historical record.[19]

I agree with Goldman and Wolfenstein that *The Autobiography of Malcolm X* is, by and large, both factually and emotionally true to Malcolm's life and that, therefore, while the Malcolm of the work is to be distinguished from Malcolm X his creator, he nevertheless bears an extremely close resemblance to him. Haley's role in the writing of the autobiography was not, then, to help Malcolm misrepresent himself, nor did he act as an "agent of truth" who prevented Malcolm from extensively fictionalizing his life. Moreover, Haley did not consciously or unconsciously seek to impose his own voice over Malcolm's, but reproduces Malcolm's voice in the work so that the autobiographical self has his own authentic tone and personality.

How, then, *did* Haley figure into the production of the autobiography? He played a part more important than simply assuring or hindering its factual accuracy—not the most important issue in autobiography, anyway. Through instinctive awareness that the work had to be *Malcolm's* life story, Haley made the first crucial contribution by prompting Malcolm X to talk about himself, not about Muhammad and the Nation of Islam exclusively. Second, and perhaps even more important, Haley, by his very involvement with Malcolm's life during its tumultuous last two years, helped Malcolm move from dependence and unquestioning trust in Muhammad to a trust of himself and of other people. At the beginning of their acquaintance, Malcolm told Haley, "I don't *completely* trust anyone . . . not even myself. . . . Other people I trust from not at all to highly, like the Honorable Elijah Muhammad. . . . You I trust about twenty-five percent" (394). But after Haley got Malcolm talking about his past, Malcolm never again, according to Haley's account, hesitated to tell him "even the most intimate details of his personal life" (395). Malcolm's trust in Haley obviously grew during the months that followed, for later Haley was awakened in the night by a call from Malcolm with the terse pronouncement, "I trust you seventy percent." The relationship between Malcolm and Haley may be described according to the patient-therapist model, as Eakin and Wolfenstein suggest, or as a growth of mutual respect and friendship, as Haley writes of it in his Epilogue. However that relationship is characterized, though, it helped Malcolm to change during the difficult time of his ouster from the Nation of Islam, and it figures as the clearest example I know of an autobiographer's changing *because* he or she writes his or her life story.

The dedication of the *Autobiography* that replaces the original tribute to Elijah Muhammad perhaps best summarizes the transformation in Malcolm X between the time the work was first conceived and its final realization. The new wording reads: "This book I dedicate to my beloved wife Betty and our children whose understanding and whose sacrifices made it possible for me to do my work." Such an expression of affection for a woman and an acknowledgment of dependence on her is a far cry from the adulatory yet rather distant praise of Muhammad first prepared for the text. Malcolm here acknowledges his own family and thereby signifies that his relationship to his wife and children has replaced his sonship to Muhammad as the most important in his life. The Malcolm who appears at the end of the autobiography and the Malcolm X who rewrites its dedication are both warmer and more human than the guarded, dogmatic figure who was first approached by Haley. Haley helped create this more attractive man, not by applying his skill as a writer and editor to the manuscript of the book, but by being a friend. That Haley was touched by Malcolm is also apparent in the tone of the epilogue and is summarized in its closing paragraph:

After signing the contract for this book, Malcolm X looked at me hard. "A writer is what I want, not an interpreter." I tried to be a dispassionate chronicler. But he was the most electric personality I have ever met, and I still can't quite conceive him dead. It still feels to me as if he has just gone into some next chapter, to be written by historians. (452)

Haley's epilogue is the element that gives *The Autobiography of Malcolm X*, a radically open-ended work, its feeling of closure. Once the autobiographical voice of Malcolm is stilled at the end of the chapter titled "1965," Haley takes over as Malcolm's biographer, or rather as his thanatographer, for the Epilogue deals at length with Malcolm's assassination and funeral. Through it, we are shown the end of Malcolm's story—the increasingly tense final days and a Malcolm who seemed to have, at last, run out of ways to escape his doom. A friend of Malcolm's told Peter Goldman, "Malcolm *wanted* to die." Goldman reacts, "One could not easily imagine a man so alive embracing death. Yet the desperation of those days finally did seem to push him past caring, and if he did not want to die, he was too spent to run from death any longer."[20]

The evidence does suggest that Malcolm was reaching the end of his resources, but he had been at such a place before; had he not been gunned down, one can imagine him rising phoenix-like into still another identity. Of all the lives treated in this book, Malcolm's ended most prematurely. Douglass and Du Bois lived to ripe ages and enjoyed the satisfaction of seeing their work for freedom bear much fruit; Washington actually seems to have outlived his time—and the appreciation of his compatriots. Wright and Baldwin produced their best work early in their careers and were both in artistic decline at their deaths. Cleaver still lives, but has produced nothing remotely equal to *Soul on Ice* in the twenty years since its publication. Only Malcolm died with his promise unfulfilled, a fact that adds poignancy to the sense of finality that Haley's Epilogue stamps on the *Autobiography*. Yet the work as a whole does not end simply with Malcolm's death, for the Epilogue, which is a biographical summation of his life, is at the same time an *autobiographical* excerpt from the life of Alex Haley. As Haley pays tribute to Malcolm's influence on him, he shows how Malcolm, although dead, lives on. Ossie Davis's remarks about Malcolm, appended after the Epilogue, do the same thing. Death brings closure to the life of Malcolm X as lived by Malcolm X, but his autobiography, a work both open-ended and closed, ultimately concludes with life, for Malcolm and his ideas live in Haley and in thousands of others whose stories are not yet come to their end.

In the last twenty years, African American autobiographies have proliferated. The Civil Rights Movement reawakened interest in African American life and culture among both black and white Americans, and this renaissance sparked an interest in all kinds of writing by and about African Americans. Since the early 1960s, black autobiographies have fallen by and large into two categories: "success" stories by sports and entertainment figures intended for the mass market, and works by women and men involved in the equal rights struggle, designed to show that the fight for freedom is an unfinished one. Few of these recent autobiographies, however, equal *Black Boy*, *The Autobiography of Malcolm X*, or even *Soul on Ice*, although a strong case can be made for Maya Angelou's *I Know Why the Caged Bird Sings*. Some others possess exceptional interest. For example, Anne Moody's *Coming of Age in Mississippi*, the best of the civil rights autobiographies, captures the feeling of the divided South of the 1950s and 1960s and powerfully expresses the relentless fear and pressure felt by rank and file civil rights workers. Bobby Seale's *A Lonely Rage* portrays his troubled youth so vividly that the reader readily grasps how Seale and men like him came to create the Black Panther Party. James Farmer's *Lay Bare the Heart* recounts Farmer's deep involvement in the fight for equal rights from the earliest days of the struggle, furnishing first-hand recollection of the freedom rides and of the imprisonment of hundreds of the riders in Southern prisons. Yet for all their merits, these works and many others like them lack essential qualities that make great autobiography. Missing are Wright's intensity and narrative drive, Malcolm X's ability to record the growth of an autobiographical self—even Cleaver's originality of expression. This is not to say that productive study might not be done on such texts, but the critic will realize that they are by and large intrinsically less interesting than many earlier works in the black autobiographical tradition. For these reasons, this study of individual work ends with *The Autobiography of Malcolm X*.

Autobiographers produce works that reflect the cultures in which they are born and grow to maturity. Although American culture might be viewed as so multifarious as to defy characterization, a distinctively "American" autobiography is nevertheless identified.[21] African American culture, although by no means homogeneous, is more unified than American culture as a whole, and its influence upon black autobiography is more readily apparent than "American" culture's impact upon American autobiography. Despite black autobiographers' inevitable fictionalizing, occasional exaggerations, and even rarer deliberate untruths, the genre accurately reflects the African American life and culture that have helped shape it. In so doing, it exhibits one of the qualities of autobiography that makes it so fascinating: as one critic expresses it, "autobiography is always something other and more, something other and less than literature and it inevitably shows a tension between its straining on the one hand toward literature, on the other hand toward history."[22] As it reflects African American history and culture in America, black autobiography shows its supraliterary side, for so read it resembles both history and sociology.

The critic of black autobiography who reads the many texts in the genre soon discovers that similar events recur many times. Although the autobiographies produced among any people cannot be said to speak authoritatively of the entire group's experience, one suspects that repeatedly recurring incidents in those works probably represent a reality common to many within that group. This is true of African American autobiography, which for all of its variety creates a collective suprapersonal self that gathers the lives of numerous individuals into one life expressing truth even for those who have not themselves lived that truth in all its details. Among these key events in black autobiography, I note four that illustrate the bitter realities and personal imperatives of African American life over the course of many years.

The first of these events (or realizations, for each centers on a moment of awareness) concerns the discovery of racial identity. In *Black Boy* Richard Wright recalls a childhood train trip to Arkansas. As Richard notices the separate ticket windows and train cars for blacks and whites, there arises in him "[a] sense of the two races . . . that would never die until I died."[23] The black child's realization that she or he *is* black occurs at a pivotal moment in many autobiographies, often accompanied by the second key event, one also seen in Wright's reminiscence—the understanding that being black means relegation to second-class status in a white-dominated world. In *Lay Bare the Heart*, James Farmer recalls that he first grasped his blackness as a child during a trip to town with his mother. James becomes thirsty and asks for a Coca Cola. Although she has the nickel to buy him a drink, his mother cannot, for no place in town will serve blacks. When James sees a white child drinking a soft drink in a store he cannot enter, he begins to realize the unfairness of his situation.

Related to the black child's awareness that his or her race automatically deprives him or her of respect as a person is the realization that whites, by and large, have easier and better lives than blacks simply because they are white. Anne Moody recalls her mother's dragging her from the whites-only lobby of a movie theater and forcing her into the blacks-only balcony. Later, as she plays with her white friends, young Anne sees them in a new way:

Now all of a sudden they were white, and their whiteness made them better than me. I now realized that not only were they better than me because they were white, but everything they owned and everything connected with them was better than what was available to me. I hadn't realized before that down-stairs in the movies was any better than upstairs. But now I saw that it was.[24]

Experiences similar to these reported by Wright, Farmer, and Moody occur in nearly every autobiography we have treated: in Douglass's as the youthful Frederick notes the discrepancy between the impoverished lives of blacks and the wealth of the slave-owning families; in Du Bois's when he recounts being socially rebuffed in school because of his color; in Malcolm X's as Malcolm tells how his junior high school teacher offers "friendly advice" about his unrealistic hope of becoming a lawyer. This communal experience of prejudice, whether overt or covert, finds expression in most black autobiographies.

A third key realization repeatedly mentioned in black autobiographies concerns their protagonists' determination, at some point in their lives, to fight against the oppressive forces aligned against them. Douglass's battle with Covey stands, as we have noted, as perhaps the prototypical event of black men's autobiography, serving as a rallying point for every person who must establish her or his identity through an act of resistance. Du Bois recalls the moment he decides to devote himself to the promotion of black rights through organized propaganda. As Wright tells his childhood, his life from its beginning is marked by violent conflict with whites, first by rock and bottle fights between his black gang and its white opponents. Anne Moody, who spends years working in the non-violent struggle for civil rights, finally determines to change her stance. In an angry "prayer," she tells God, "As long as I live, I'll never be beaten by a white man again. Not like in Woolworth's. Not any more. That's out. You know something else God? Nonviolence is out."[25] Even autobiographers who record no particular moment in which they determine to resist nevertheless detail lives spent battling oppression. Booker T. Washington, the least overtly aggressive of autobiographers, nevertheless devotes his life to fighting for the African American in his own way. Baldwin fights with words, Cleaver sees his rapes as insurrectionary acts, Seale forms the Black Panther Party, and Malcolm X gives the most productive years of his life to the Nation of Islam. Without exception, these autobiographers tell of selves devoted to waging the battle against the oppression of blacks.

The fourth event so often recorded in black autobiography is the writer's realization of the importance of education. Douglass recounts how he learned to read and write despite his master's strictures; Washington tells how he walked to Hampton Institute and cleaned the room to gain admittance; Wright recalls how Richard obtained books from the whites-only public library; and Malcolm X explains at length the process by which he educates himself in prison, even to detailing how he copies the entire dictionary longhand. Explicitly or implicitly, these writers and others stress education as the means by which one enters the world of ideas, the way one can know the truth about oneself and one's place in the world. Knowledge strengthens individuals in their fight against oppression and enables them to rise in the world. Learning thus helps counteract the disadvantages that often inhere in being born black in America.

Other important moments in black life could be culled from black autobiography, but these stand out because they form a cluster of experiences that decisively shape the personalities of autobiographers who have been leaders among African Americans. Given these men's and women's determination to fight oppression, the course of African American history has inevitably been marked by the struggle for freedom.

Although the critic can more easily argue the influence of history and culture upon autobiography, the impact of the genre upon the world in which it is produced can also be demonstrated, particularly black autobiography's part in shaping America's history and manner of regarding its black citizens. Douglass's *Narrative* and other slave autobiographies contributed to the tensions between North and South that resulted in the Civil War. Not only did these works shock the nation by their accounts of the horrors of slavery, but they also demonstrated that slaves were as fully human as any other people and were capable of education. A half century later, *Up from Slavery* helped lull a fearful white America into believing that African Americans would be content with unskilled labor and would press for full social equality with whites only slowly—if ever. Some historians assert that this one book did more to slow black Americans' fight for civil rights than any other. More recently, *Black Boy* alerted the country to the resentments and alienation just below the surface of many black Americans' lives, and a little more than twenty-five years ago, *The Autobiography of Malcolm X* frightened many white Americans while galvanizing blacks into action. Bobby Seale recounts, for example, that Malcolm's work helped inspire the Black Panthers and was customarily read as a kind of sacred text at Panther meetings.

Black autobiography, then, not only reflects the conditions under which its writers have lived for the last one hundred fifty years but also has helped shape their history. Moreover, the black male autobiographer, frequently locked in struggle with preceding writers and texts is, in at least some cases, combatting them because they have helped create conditions that he finds intolerable. Du Bois's hostility to *Up from Slavery* lies not only in his antipathy to the ideas it expresses but also in the constricting circumstances of his own life which he believes the earlier book's philosophy has helped perpetuate. For these writers, the battle is more than a literary exercise because the literature they dislike has power directly to affect their daily lives. By writing their own life stories, these autobiographers seek to establish their own identities, but they also intend to expose what they perceive as flaws in their predecessors' world views and to recreate the world for themselves and for those who follow them.

*   *   *

Black autobiography, then, reflects African American life and has helped shape America's perception of black culture. The relationship of the autobiographical works treated here to American autobiography in general—that is, to a tradition that has centered until recently primarily on white males—may also help explain some of this line's distinctive quality. First, the line often displays what John Adams called the "instinct of emulation," the patterning of a life on those of certain white American men, imitating precepts for success and carrying them to a degree greater than that found in the models.[26] Second, these autobiographies express the underside of the American dream by voicing what Robert Sayre calls "that fundamental, continuing contradiction in America between the idea of freedom and human fulfillment and the reality of oppression, conformity, and mean narrowness of spirit."[27] These contradictory impulses express the dilemma felt by so many African American men and women—to live in America but never to share fully in the promise of America because the potentially fortunate accident of being born American is outweighed by the real problems of being born black.

Booker T. Washington and Malcolm X are attracted to the prescriptions for success in Benjamin Franklin's *Autobiography*. Washington deliberately sets out to portray his autobiographical self as a latter-day, black Franklin whose goals of personal improvement and civic service mirror the ideals of the Founding Father. On the other hand, Malcolm X's imitation of Franklin is probably unconscious: so determined are he and the Muslims to separate themselves from the prevailing white culture that they would hardly *set out* to conform themselves to the precepts of a man instrumental in shaping that culture. Nevertheless, the Muslims' preoccupation with rigorous standards of personal conduct and with success through diligent work demonstrates the attraction of the American dream even upon those determined to reject it.

Whereas some black autobiographers imitate, knowingly or not, the model of American life created by a white, colonial society, many others reject that model, particularly in its debased forms. *The Autobiography of Malcolm X*, for example, despite its Franklinesque ideals, is famous for its attack on oppressive white society, not for any unconscious imitation of that society. *Black Boy* centers on Richard's rebellion against white oppression and his attempt to flee it; *Soul on Ice* not only savages racist America but also predicts its overthrow and the rise of a cleansed black society from its rubble. In *Dusk of Dawn*, Du Bois tries to give shape to black values that, while dismissed by the dominant white world, are nevertheless in many ways superior to its confused standards.

But whether these black male autobiographers accept in part the cultural standards and traditions of white America or reject them *in toto*, they nevertheless recognize the pervasiveness of such traditions and must deal with them. Accordingly, their autobiographies are a literature of *reaction*. As such, they well express the lives of many African American men, who also have had to accommodate themselves to living as a distinct minority in a nation that has been primarily white by virtue of numbers and by cultural domination.

To speak of these black men's autobiographies as a literature of reaction might seem to imply that this line, along with African American writing in general, stands somehow outside the mainstream of American literature. For many years, of course, black writing was either ignored or confined to the periphery of American studies, as if it were a curiosity not to be treated with the same seriousness one devoted to Hawthorne, Melville, or Faulkner. This writer completed high school, college, and a Master's degree in English without ever having been asked to read Douglass, Wright, Hurston, Ellison, Baldwin, or any other black writer. Certainly times have changed since the 1960s—a glance at a current high school American literature book shows that African American literature, along with works by Native Americans, Hispanics, Asian Americans, and women writers of all ethnic groups, is now being accorded recognition as an integral part of American literature. But while progress has been made in the revision of the canon, African American studies are still too often ghettoized, particularly in universities, where many English departments continue to offer separate courses in black writing instead of adequately incorporating it into general survey courses.

We have come to realize, especially since the advent of the liberation movements of the last twenty-five years, that American literature has spoken from the beginning with many voices, not only those of the northern European white males who settled the eastern seaboard of the continent. Puritan New England may have given earliest expression to the vision of America that we now call the "American dream"—a vision replete with images of freedom, equality, and prosperity—but no single group of Americans has ever had sole possession of that dream. African American literature, speaking for all the minority groups who have ever come to these shores, has, in its own way, helped keep the American dream alive for each succeeding generation. African American literature has done its part as a literature of reaction and protest, holding up to the nation its failure from the start to make the promises of the Declaration of Independence and the Constitution good for *all* Americans—for the religious minorities, for the poor and landless, for women, for the Native Americans, and for the blacks as well as for a certain class of white men. But by crying out for a share of the promise of America, African American literature, together with all minority literature, affirms the value of that promise, asserts that equality, freedom, and a decent life are good and that America has it within its power to grant those blessings to all its people. Even radical groups like the Black Muslims and the Black Panthers, seemingly determined to reject American culture, have tried to create in its place a separate culture within a culture that nevertheless mirrors and advocates the very values they profess to despise. Americans have always been obsessed, it seems, with the mythology of the American Dream; American literature is comprised of a welter of voices, voices often contradictory yet somehow united in their attempts to make sense about what it means to be in America and of America. Indeed, there has long existed a tradition of African American literature (including autobiographies) that celebrates black life in this country. Writers such as James Weldon Johnson, Zora Neale Hurston, Claude McKay, Langston Hughes, and Toni Morrison all express an appreciation for the vitality of black folk ways rooted in the West Indies and Africa and further enriched by black culture's exposure to American ways. These writers and others have preserved and created folk characters, folk tales, sermons, jokes, and music, thus preserving what we now recognize as part of a heritage that belongs to all Americans.

*   *   *

All the autobiographical works I have discussed are works of re-action—protest literature. Every autobiographer in this line protests the realities of the world into which he is born, and in every case, those realities are embodied in a dominating father figure. For Frederick Douglass, the "father" wears the mask of a brutal, paternalistic slavocracy; for Booker T. Washington, Douglass is the figure to be removed so that Washington can freely implement his own agenda for African Americans. But Washington in his turn is supplanted by W.E.B. Du Bois. In Richard Wright, James Baldwin, and Eldridge Cleaver, the pattern repeats itself, with Wright and Baldwin fighting the battle on two fronts: they not only combat the pervasive and abusive white world but also fight against their own fathers, victims of that world whose tortured lives make them unfit for parenthood. All these men, from Douglass in his fight with Covey to Malcolm X in his struggle with Elijah Muhammad, fight a dominating male figure—but for what end?

According to the Oedipus myth, the son displaces the father to gain access to the mother; these autobiographers, in attacking the father figures in their lives, are actually seeking, it seems to me, to displace a power structure traditionally dominated by white men. If this were accomplished, two feminine figures could be liberated to minister to the black writer. The first, the maternal figure, is America itself, which could then nourish black men with its promise of equal rights, equal justice, and equal opportunity. But only when the *pater* is removed can this *patria* be attained. These black men's Oedipal longings are directed toward their own nation. This *dura mater*, or harsh mother, whom Claude McKay calls the "cultured hell that tests my youth," can become their *alma mater*, or fostering mother, only when the blocking father figure, the white man, is removed. But because overt rebellion against whites has traditionally brought punishment and death to black men, they have found it safer to strike at the white man indirectly through his creatures, black leaders permitted by the white world to guide the black masses into paths ultimately beneficial to the dominant power structure, and black fathers whose own lives have been so blighted that they are rendered incapable of being decent fathers to their children. It is true that black men have fearlessly excoriated white culture in recent years, but they have also long directed a great deal of their pent-up rage and frustration against other blacks as well. Some black male autobiographers have sensed that even their own fathers have been used to keep them from realizing their dreams; this being so, these literary and biological fathers must be robbed of their power so that their sons may become free men.

The second feminine principle that can be freed when the oppressive father figure is removed is that of the Muse, the writer's individual creative power. We have noted that only after he had "disposed" of Richard Wright in the essay "Everybody's Protest Novel" could James Baldwin complete his own first novel, a work much less aggressively militant than Wright's—one that sought to replace Wright's deterministic notion of character with a more complex vision of human nature. The dynamic is repeated—this time with Baldwin the power to be displaced—when Eldridge Cleaver bashes Baldwin in the middle of a work altogether more pugnacious and simplistic in its vision of race relations than Baldwin's more balanced view. Both Baldwin and Cleaver seek—and find—their peculiar Muse through and after the conquest of the father figure, with the tangible result of the works of art that embody their individual vision. On a broader level, the appropriation of the Muse brings freedom, the freedom to create the self through the art of autobiography.

Since the time of the first slave narratives, African Americans who write their lives have been asserting their right to exist as free people and not as chattel; these autobiographers have, through the act of writing, emerged from the "invisibility" so long imposed upon them. Georges Gusdorf writes, "The man who recounts himself is himself searching his self through history; he is not engaged in an objective and disinterested pursuit but in a work of personal justification."[28] "Personal justification" well expresses the purpose of so much black men's autobiography, for these autobiographers have long had to overcome a double anxiety. First they must conquer the universal self-disesteem that periodically calls into question our sense that we have the right to exist let alone write our life stories. But besides this, black male autobiographers must overcome challenges directed against them individually as well as against African Americans in general—challenges against their personhood, their self-worth, their conviction that they belong as fully to and in America as any other people. If it is true that "every life, even in spite of the most brilliant successes, knows itself inwardly botched," how difficult it must be for the victims of discrimination to assert their claim to a full share of life's privileges.[29] Two voices tell them that they have failed: the inner voice in every person that accuses her or him of her or his shortcomings, and the voice of the repressive society that blames her or him for being born into a minority group. Black men's autobiography seeks to drown out both voices with the establishment of a third voice, the autobiographer's own, which asserts over and over again, "I am a human being, and I am worthy to enjoy what America has promised and still promises to all her people: the right to life, liberty, and the pursuit of happiness."

In writing their autobiographies, black authors assert their right *to be*, a right often claimed in the face of opposition of every sort. Black autobiography thus expresses more eloquently than many other bodies of life writing both the drive to lay claim to one's own life by the writing of it and the difficulties that stand in the way of such self-invention. Every autobiographer is to some extent a rebel raising the flag of independence in the face of all the forces that seek to define and restrict a sense of him or herself. Some autobiographers—Edmund Gosse in *Father and Son*, for example—openly assume an insurrectionary role; others, spiritual autobiographers like Augustine, John Bunyan, and John Henry Newman, stress instead the process by which their lives become less rebellious and more and more conformed to God's will. Yet even these writers are asserting their individuality as they trace the dealings of God with *one* of God's children. To claim "I am what I am by the grace of God" is still to say, "I am what I am."

The need to recognize how this "I am" came to be is the impetus behind the autobiographical endeavor. African American autobiography adds to our understanding of this endeavor by stressing again and again what a struggle it is to become the self one believes he or she is meant to be, and what obstacles lie in the path of self-fulfillment. Black autobiography contributes to American letters through its insistence that we look honestly at the uncomfortable realities of our history, but its importance reaches beyond any such parochial concerns. The issues raised in black autobiography are universal, for they center, ultimately, on questions of identity, the growth of the self, and the establishment of that self in the face of all others. African American autobiographers take their place in the human family not only because they claim the same rights and privileges all people desire for themselves, but because they have the questions, anxieties, and aspirations common to us all.

Notes

Introduction

1. Sidonie Smith, *Where I'm Bound* (Westport, Conn.: Greenwood, 1974).
2. Harold Bloom, *The Anxiety of Influence* (London: Oxford University Press, 1973), 5.
3. Henry Louis Gates, "In Her Own Write," foreword to Harriet Jacobs, *Incidents in the Life of a Slave Girl*, a volume in *The Schomburg Library of Nineteenth-Century Black Women Writers*, ed. Henry Louis Gates, Jr. (London: Oxford University Press, 1988), xviii.
4. Calvin C. Hernton, "The Sexual Mountain and Black Women Writers," in *Wild Women in the Whirlwind*, ed. Joanne Braxton and Andrée Nicola McLaughlin (New Brunswick, N.J.: Rutgers University Press, 1990), 195–212.
5. Hernton, "Sexual Mountain," 207. See Richard Barksdale and Keneth Kinnamon, eds., *Black Writers in America: A Comprehensive Anthology* (New York: Macmillan, 1972).
6. Bloom, *Anxiety of Influence*, 43.
7. Joanne Braxton, *Black Women Writing Autobiography: A Tradition Within a Tradition* (Philadelphia: Temple University Press, 1990).
8. Frederick Douglass, *Narrative of the Life of Frederick Douglass, an American Slave*, ed. Benjamin Quarles (Cambridge, Mass.: Belknap, 1967), 163.
9. Braxton, *Black Women Writing Autobiography*, 27.
10. Roger Rosenblatt, "Black Autobiography: Life as the Death Weapon," in *Autobiography: Essays Theoretical and Critical*, ed. James Olney (Princeton, N.J.: Princeton University Press, 1980), 170.
11. Valerie Smith, introduction to Harriet Jacobs's *Incidents in the Life of a Slave Girl*, xxviii.
12. Braxton, *Black Women Writing Autobiography*, 204.
13. Stephen Butterfield, *Black Autobiography in America* (Amherst: University of Massachusetts Press, 1974), 87.
14. Butterfield finds one source of Frederick Douglass's greatness as an autobiographer in the fact that he creates in his work a hero consistent with American notions of masculinity but free from the "chauvinist frontier

'individualism' " that has resulted in the ruthless subjection of other people. See Butterfield, Ibid., 87.

15. Robert Stepto, "Teaching Afro-American Literature: Survey or Tradition," in *Afro-American Literature: The Reconstruction of Instruction*, ed. Dexter Fisher and Robert B. Stepto (New York: Modern Language Association of America, 1978), 18.

16. Braxton, *Black Women Writing Autobiography*, 19.

17. Ibid., 31.

18. Ibid., 19.

19. Ibid., 206.

20. Ibid., 79.

21. Ibid., 203.

22. Alice Walker, *In Search of Our Mothers' Gardens* (San Diego: Harcourt, Brace, Jovanovich, 1983).

Chapter 1

1. See Charles H. Nichols, *Many Thousand Gone* (Leiden: Brill, 1963), xiv–xv, and Benjamin Quarles's introduction to Frederick Douglass's *Narrative of the Life of Frederick Douglass, an American Slave*, ed. Benjamin Quarles (Cambridge, Mass.: Belknap, 1967), xiii.

2. James Olney, "I Was Born," in *The Slave's Narrative*, ed. Charles T. Davis and Henry Louis Gates, Jr. (Oxford: Oxford University Press, 1985), 152–53.

3. Ibid., 154.

4. Quarles, introduction to Douglass, *Narrative*.

5. Sidonie Smith, *Where I'm Bound* (Westport, Conn.: Greenwood, 1974), ix.

6. Frederick May Holland, *Frederick Douglass: The Colored Orator* (rev. ed.; New York: Haskell House, 1969), 42.

7. Douglass, *Narrative*, 153. Subsequent references are to this edition and are cited by page number in the text.

8. Philip S. Foner, *Frederick Douglass* (New York: Citadel Press, 1953), 25.

9. William L. Andrews discusses the *Narrative* and the tradition of the black jeremiad and the American jeremiad in *To Tell a Free Story* (Urbana and Chicago: University of Illinois Press, 1986), 14–15, 123–24. The jeremiad takes its name from the Old Testament prophet called to the thankless task of summoning a sinful nation to repentance before God's punishment descended upon it. Andrews notes, "The *Narrative* builds a convincing case for Douglass's literary calling and his ultimate self-appointment as America's black Jeremiah." Richard Wright, whose self-portrait as heroic loner in *Black Boy* recalls Douglass's picture of himself in the *Narrative*, adopts a similar persona, particularly at the end of *American Hunger*, the work originally intended as the second part of *Black Boy*. See Wright, *American Hunger* (New York: Harper and Row, 1977).

10. This list was compiled by John F. Baylis for his introduction to *Black*

Slave Narratives (London: Collier-Macmillan, 1970) and is mentioned by Olney in "I Was Born."

11. Houston Baker, *Long Black Song: Essays in Black American Literature and Culture* (Charlottesville: University of Virginia Press, 1972), 78.

12. George M. Frederickson, ed., *William Lloyd Garrison* (Englewood Cliffs, N.J.: Prentice-Hall, 1968), 53.

13. Stephen Butterfield, *Black Autobiography in America* (Amherst: University of Massachusetts Press, 1974), 70.

14. Frederick Douglass, *My Bondage and My Freedom* (Chicago: Johnson, 1970), 282. Subsequent references are to this edition and are cited by page number in the text.

15. Butterfield, *Black Autobiography*, 68.

16. John Seelye, "The Clay Foot of the Climber," in *Literary Romanticism in America*, ed. William L. Andrews (Baton Rouge: Louisiana State University Press, 1981), 126.

17. Benjamin Quarles, *Frederick Douglass* (New York: Haskell House, 1968), 35.

18. Foner, *Frederick Douglass*, 60.

19. Baker, *Long Black Song*, 77.

20. Butterfield, *Black Autobiography*, 70.

21. G. Thomas Couser, *American Autobiography: The Prophetic Mode* (Amherst: University of Massachusetts Press, 1979), 51.

22. Steven M. Weismann, "Frederick Douglass, Portrait of a Black Militant: A Study in the Family Romance," *Psychoanalytic Study of the Child* 30 (1975), 726.

23. Joseph Campbell, *The Hero with a Thousand Faces* (Princeton, N.J.: Princeton University Press, 1949). I draw extensively from Campbell's description of the monomyth, which begins on p. 245 of his book.

24. Butterfield, *Black Autobiography*, 94.

25. Douglass, *My Bondage and My Freedom*, 190. William L. Andrews notes that, in his second autobiography, Douglass identifies himself with the devil in his fight with Covey. Andrews writes, "Douglass was sufficiently outside the boundaries of the paternalistic moral order that he could reenact Lucifer's primordial *non serviam* and become the Rebel, the essential character of the Christian devil." See *To Tell a Free Story*, 227. Andrews also calls Douglass a kind of Promethean figure, thereby identifying him with yet another heroic mythic figure.

26. Andrews, *To Tell a Free Story*, 214ff.

27. Robert L. Factor, *The Black Response to America* (Reading, Mass: Addison, Wesley, 1970), 103.

28. Seelye notes that the name "Douglass," interestingly enough, means "the black one" ("Clay Foot," 131).

29. Campbell, *Hero*, 337.

30. Andrews, *To Tell a Free Story*, 123–38. Stephen Butterfield esteems Douglass's *Life and Times* most highly of the three autobiographies because its

rhetoric, in Butterfield's opinion, is the most highly polished. See Butterfield, *Black Autobiography*, 75, 82.

Chapter 2

1. Booker T. Washington, *Up from Slavery*, in vol. 1 of *The Booker T. Washington Papers*, ed. Louis R. Harlan (Urbana: University of Illinois Press, 1972), 332. Subsequent references to this work are from this edition and are cited by page number in the text.

2. Washington, *My Larger Education*, in vol. 1 of *Washington Papers*, ed. Harlan, 424. Subsequent references are to this edition and are cited by page number in the text.

3. Robert L. Factor, *The Black Response to America* (Reading, Mass.: Addison, Wesley, 1970), 101–2.

4. Booker T. Washington, *The Story of My Life and Work*, in vol. 1 of *Washington Papers*, ed. Harlan, 56. Subsequent references are to this edition and are cited by page number in the text.

5. Factor, *Black Response*, 154.

6. Ibid., 155.

7. Houston Baker, *Modernism and the Harlem Renaissance* (Chicago: University of Chicago Press, 1987), 22ff.

8. Houston Baker, *Long Black Song: Essays in Black American Literature and Culture* (Charlottesville: University of Virginia Press, 1972), 87.

9. Charles T. Davis and Henry Louis Gates, Jr., eds., *The Slave's Narrative* (Oxford: Oxford University Press, 1985), xiii.

10. Sidonie Smith, *Where I'm Bound* (Westport, Conn.: Greenwood, 1974), 33–35.

11. Ibid., 33.

12. James Cox, "Autobiography and Washington," *Sewannee Review* 85 (1977), 242.

13. Albert E. Stone, "After *Black Boy* and *Dusk of Dawn*: Patterns in Recent Black Autobiography," *Phylon* 39 (1978), 23.

14. William L. Andrews, *To Tell a Free Story* (Urbana and Chicago: University of Illinois Press, 1986), 232–35.

15. Philip S. Foner, *Frederick Douglass* (New York: Citadel Press, 1953), 370.

16. Ibid.

17. Ibid.

Chapter 3

1. David Littlejohn, *Black on White* (New York: Grossman, 1966), 29.

2. Howells's review originally appeared in *North American Review* 173 (August, 1901) under the title "An Exemplary Citizen." The review, along

with several other favorable reviews, is reprinted in vol. 6 of *The Booker T. Washington Papers*, ed. Louis R. Harlan (Urbana: University of Illinois Press, 1972). For the Howells review, see 191–200; see also 236–37, 21, 107, 57. Subsequent references to this multivolume series of Washington's papers are referred to as *Papers* and are cited in the text by volume and page number.

3. W.E.B. Du Bois, "The Evolution of Negro Leadership," *The Dial* 31 (July 16, 1901), 54.

4. Francis L. Broderick, *W.E.B. Du Bois: Negro Leader in a Time of Crisis* (Stanford, Calif.: Stanford University Press, 1959), 67. The section of Broderick's book dealing with the Du Bois-Washington controversy is titled "The Fight Against Booker T. Washington" and is also included in Hugh Hawkins, ed., *Booker T. Washington and His Critics* (Boston: Heath, 1962).

5. Broderick, *W.E.B. Du Bois*, 69.

6. W.E.B. Du Bois, *Dusk of Dawn* (Millwood, N.Y.: Kraus-Thomson, 1975), 80. Subsequent references are to this edition and are cited by page number in the text.

7. W.E.B. Du Bois, *The Souls of Black Folk* (New York: Johnson Reprint Corp., 1968), 49. Subsequent references are to this edition and are cited by page number in the text.

8. Robert L. Factor, *The Black Response to America* (Reading, Mass.: Addison, Wesley, 1970), 292–308. Factor gives a detailed account of the conference in his book.

9. Elliot Rudwick, "The Overture to Protest: Beginnings of the Du Bois-Washington Controversy," in *The Black Man in America Since Reconstruction*, ed. David Reimers (New York: Thomas Y. Crowell, 1970), 124.

10. A full account appeared in the Boston *Globe*, July 31, 1903.

11. Factor, *Black Response*, 306.

12. Rudwick, "Overture to Protest," 126.

13. Factor, *Black Response*, 292–308.

14. Ibid., 306.

15. W.E.B. Du Bois, "The Parting of the Way," *The World Today* VI (April, 1904), 523.

16. Factor, *Black Response*, 316.

17. Ibid., 348–49.

18. Rebecca Chalmers Barton, *Witnesses for Freedom* (Oakdale, N.Y.: Dowling College Press, 1976), 190.

19. W.E.B. Du Bois, *The Autobiography of W.E.B. Du Bois* (New York: International Publishers, 1968), 421–22.

20. Although black autobiographers apart from Du Bois do not make a growing awareness of racial identity the key to their development, black novelists often use this as a primary theme. See, for example, James Weldon Johnson's *The Autobiography of an Ex-coloured Man*.

21. Booker T. Washington, *Up From Slavery*, in vol. 1 of *The Booker T. Washington Papers*, ed. Louis R. Harlan (Urbana: University of Illinois Press, 1972), 297.

Chapter 4

1. W.E.B. Du Bois, *The Autobiography of W.E.B. Du Bois* (New York: International Publishers, 1968), 394–95.

2. Louis R. Harlan, ed., *The Booker T. Washington Papers*, vol. 6 (Urbana: University of Illinois Press, 1972), 195. The review was originally published in *North American Review* 173 (August, 1901), 280–88.

3. Constance Webb, *Richard Wright* (New York: G. P. Putnam's Sons, 1968), 185, 187.

4. Richard Wright, *Native Son* (New York: Harper and Row, Perennial Classic Paperback; 1966), 392.

5. Many critics of *Native Son* have found the third part of the novel problematic; they are especially troubled by Max's long speech to the court, which sounds like Wright himself proclaiming his Communist viewpoint. Joyce Ann Joyce, who vigorously defends the third book as an artistic success and as the necessary synthesis of themes in the first two parts, offers a useful summary of the critical literature as well as an extremely detailed reading of the novel in *Richard Wright's Art of Tragedy* (Iowa City: University of Iowa Press, 1986). See chaps. 1 and 5.

6. Webb, *Richard Wright*, 197. The details of how *Black Boy* was conceived and written are from Webb's account.

7. Ibid., 208.

8. Wright uses the same strategy in *Native Son*, in which the opening scene of Bigger's killing of the rat prefigures two of the novel's themes—Bigger's rage, which causes him to lash out hysterically against forces that he perceives as threatening to him, and also the white world's view of Bigger himself, in which *Bigger* is the loathsome rodent that must be mercilessly exterminated.

9. Richard Wright, *Black Boy* (New York: Harper and Row, Perennial Classic Paperback; 1966), 281. Subsequent references are to this edition and are cited by page number in the text.

10. Webb, *Richard Wright*, 13.

11. Barrett Mandel offers a particularly lucid discussion of the implications of the inevitable fictionalization in autobiography in "Full of Life Now," in *Autobiography: Essays Theoretical and Critical*, ed. James Olney (Princeton, N.J.: Princeton University Press, 1980), 49–72.

12. For a detailed account of the differences between Douglass's versions of the fight with Covey in the *Narrative* and in *My Bondage and My Freedom*, see William L. Andrews, *To Tell a Free Story* (Urbana and Chicago: University of Illinois Press, 1986), 281ff.

13. Webb, *Richard Wright*, 409, n. 9.

14. Charles T. Davis, "From Experience to Eloquence: Richard Wright's *Black Boy* as Art," in *Chant of Saints*, ed. Michael S. Harper and Robert B. Stepto (Urbana: University of Illinois Press, 1979), 434.

15. Webb, *Richard Wright*, 53ff.

16. Edward Margolies, *The Art of Richard Wright* (Carbondale: Southern Illinois University Press, 1969), 16.

17. Davis, "From Experience to Eloquence," 429.

18. Andrews, *To Tell a Free Story*, 219ff.

19. Davis, "From Experience to Eloquence," 438; Margolies, *Art of Richard Wright*, 16.

20. George E. Kent, "Richard Wright: Blackness and the Adventure of Western Culture," in *Richard Wright: A Collection of Critical Essays*, ed. Raymond Macksey and Frank E. Moorer (Englewood Cliffs, N.J.: Prentice-Hall, 1984), 39.

21. Ibid., 40.

22. David Littlejohn, *Black on White* (New York: Grossman, 1966), 102ff.

23. Ibid., 104.

24. Some critics of *Native Son*, for example, were troubled by Wright's portrayal of the white press and the white mob in the final section of the novel. Yet Wright's fictional newspaper accounts of Bigger's crime, arrest, and trial are no more exaggerated than the racist, sensationalist newspaper coverage of the Robert Nixon murder trial in Chicago in 1938. See Keneth Kinnamon, *The Emergence of Richard Wright* (Urbana: University of Illinois Press, 1972), 121–25.

25. Littlejohn, *Black on White*, 103–4.

26. Robert B. Stepto, *From Behind the Veil* (Urbana: University of Illinois Press, 1979), 140ff.

27. Constance Webb notes the coincidence that this woman's name, Ella, is the same as Wright's mother's. It has also been suggested that this "Ella" *was* Wright's mother and that this scene is a tribute to her contribution in nurturing Wright's imaginative life. Recall also the dedication to *Native Son*: "To My Mother who, when I was a child at her knee, taught me to revere the fanciful and the imaginative," which seems to acknowledge more of her contribution than Wright shows in *Black Boy*. Michel Fabre says that the teacher's name was Eloise Crawford (*The Unfinished Quest of Richard Wright* [New York: William Morrow, 1973], 18). Perhaps Wright's memory failed him at this point.

28. Webb, *Richard Wright*, 407, n. 15.

29. Kent, "Richard Wright," 41.

30. Stepto, *From Behind the Veil*, 129.

31. Ibid., 130.

32. I agree with Robert Stepto, who comments on Wright's passage describing the bleakness of African American culture this way: "Wright is consciously and aggressively attempting to clear a space for himself in Afro-American letters." See Stepto, *From Behind the Veil*, 157.

33. Dan McCall, *The Example of Richard Wright* (New York: Harcourt, Brace, and World, 1969), 116.

34. Ibid.

35. It has been noted that Wright's account of Richard's fight with Harrison may have inspired the famous "battle royal" sequence in Ralph Ellison's *Invisible Man*.

36. Details of the publishing history of *Black Boy* and *American Hunger*

are furnished by Webb, *Richard Wright*, 207–8; by Fabre in his afterword to Wright, *American Hunger* (New York, Harper and Row, 1977), 136–46; and by John Reilly in "The Self-Creation of the Intellectual: *American Hunger* and *Black Power*, in *Critical Essays on Richard Wright*, ed. Yoshinobu Hakutani (Boston: G. K. Hall, 1982), 213–27.

37. Reilly, "Self-Creation of the Intellectual," 213–14.

38. Ibid., 214.

39. The questions remain: Why did Wright add the ending—to give a better sense of closure to the work? Why did he write it with a positive tone? With this ending, *Black Boy* read alone does not give a completely accurate idea of Wright's original tone and overall purpose.

40. Wright, *American Hunger*, 1. I wonder if this description of Chicago owes something to T. S. Eliot's description of London in *The Waste Land* ll. 60–61.

41. Critics have noted the similarity in theme between this episode and Wright's "The Man Who Lived Underground" and Ellison's *Invisible Man*.

42. Reilly, "Self-Creation of the Intellectual," 213.

43. See, for example, Horace A. Porter, "The Horror and the Glory: Richard Wright's Portrait of the Artist in *Black Boy* and *American Hunger*," in *Richard Wright: A Collection of Critical Essays*, Macksey and Moorer, ed., 55–67.

Chapter 5

1. Richard Wright, *Black Boy* (New York: Harper and Row, Perennial Classic Paperback; 1966), 18–19. Subsequent references are to this edition and are cited by page number in the text.

2. As noted in Chapter Four, this passage may be seen as an individual application and example of Wright's sweeping criticism of African American life and culture in the famous passage found just three pages later in *Black Boy*. All the emptiness Wright encountered in black life generally must have struck him with great force when, after so many years, he again met his father and saw in him the result of such cultural deprivation.

3. This photograph of Nathaniel Wright appears following p. 128 in Constance Webb's *Richard Wright* (New York: G. P. Putnam's Sons, 1968).

4. Horace A. Porter, "The Horror and the Glory: Richard Wright's Portrait of the Artist in *Black Boy* and *American Hunger*," in *Richard Wright: A Collection of Critical Essays*, ed. Richard Macksey and Frank E. Moorer (Englewood Cliffs, N.J.: Prentice-Hall, 1984), 274.

5. "Alas, Poor Richard" was originally published in *Reporter*, March 16, 1961, and was reprinted in *Nobody Knows My Name* and in *The Price of the Ticket*. All references to Baldwin's essays in this book refer to *The Price of the Ticket* (New York: St. Martin's/Marek, 1985), which collects all Baldwin's essays, and are cited by essay title and page number in the text. This quotation is from p. 274.

6. These details of Baldwin's early relationship with Wright are from

"Alas, Poor Richard." Fred L. Standley has chronicled the personal and literary relationship between the two men in a succinct and useful article that also summarizes the secondary material on their literary feud. See " '. . . Farther and Farther Apart': Richard Wright and James Baldwin," in *Critical Essays on Richard Wright*, ed. Yoshinobu Hakutani (Boston: G. K. Hall, 1982), 103. Michel Fabre writes that the fellowship was a Rosenwald Fellowship provided by the Rosenwald Foundation. See Michel Fabre, "Fathers and Sons in James Baldwin's *Go Tell It on the Mountain*," in *James Baldwin: A Collection of Critical Essays*, ed. Keneth Kinnamon (Englewood Cliffs, N.J.: Prentice-Hall, 1974), 134.

7. In devaluing the social aspect of the novel to highlight its ability to examine the complex psychology of the individual character, Baldwin seems to express the aesthetic of his time. See Morris Dickstein, "The Black Aesthetic in White America," *Partisan Review* XXXVIII, 4 (Winter 1971–72), 379ff.

8. Fabre, "Fathers and Sons," 135.

9. Recall that W.E.B. Du Bois had a similar reaction to the character of Richard in *Black Boy*. Du Bois may also have feared that Wright's self-portrait as "a loathsome brat, foul-mouthed, and 'a drunkard' " would feed the fires of white racism.

10. Baldwin's words proved prophetic: Eldridge Cleaver levels some of the same charges against Baldwin in his chapter "Notes on a Native Son" in *Soul on Ice*.

11. Nick Aaron Ford, "James Baldwin as Essayist," in *James Baldwin: A Critical Evaluation*, ed. Therman B. O'Daniel (Washington, D.C.: Howard University Press, 1977), 96.

12. Addison Gayle, *Richard Wright: Ordeal of a Native Son* (Garden City, N.Y.: Anchor/Doubleday, 1980), 281.

13. Maurice Charney, "James Baldwin's Quarrel with Richard Wright," *American Quarterly* 15 (1963): 67.

14. Fabre, "Fathers and Sons," 135.

15. Calvin C. Hernton, "Blood of the Lamb: The Ordeal of James Baldwin," in *White Papers for White Americans* (Garden City, N.Y.: Doubleday, 1966), 112.

16. Ibid.

17. Fabre, "Fathers and Sons," 136–37.

18. Hernton, "Blood of the Lamb," 112–13.

19. W. J. Weatherby, *James Baldwin: Artist on Fire* (New York: Donald I. Fine, 1989), 6–10.

20. As Stephen Butterfield notes, Richard Wright's family also used the church to "deal with their impulses to violence against the white world by . . . sublimating them in religious frenzy" (*Black Autobiography in America* [Amherst: University of Massachusetts Press, 1974], 165).

21. I refer the reader again to Fabre's essay "Fathers and Sons" for a full and convincing treatment of the subject.

22. In this essay Baldwin expresses his bafflement at whites who one minute were harassing him in a group and the next minute individually begging him to have sex with them.

23. James Baldwin, *Go Tell It on the Mountain* (Laurel Book Edition; New York: Bantam Doubleday Dell, 1985), 196.

24. Eldridge Cleaver, *Soul on Ice* (New York: McGraw-Hill, 1968), 176–90.

25. Baldwin accuses Wright of the same thing. Whether they believe the charge to be true or not, these writers seem to use it as the worst they can think to say about another black man.

26. Jervis Anderson, "Race, Rage, and Eldridge Cleaver," *Commentary* 46 (December, 1968), 68.

27. Ibid.

28. Ibid., 69.

29. William L. Andrews, *To Tell a Free Story* (Urbana and Chicago: University of Illinois Press, 1986), 227ff.

30. David Littlejohn, *Black on White* (New York: Grossman, 1966), 104.

Chapter 6

1. Paul John Eakin, "Malcolm X and the Limits of Autobiography," in *Autobiography: Essays Theoretical and Critical*, ed. James Olney (Princeton, N.J.: Princeton University Press, 1980), 183–84.

2. Ibid., 183.

3. Malcolm X, *The Autobiography of Malcolm X* (New York: Grove, 1964, 1965, 13th printing), 392. I notice that pagination in this edition differs from pagination of earlier Grove Press printings used by some critics. All references are to this edition and will be referred to by page number in the text.

4. Eakin, "Malcolm X and the Limits of Autobiography," 183.

5. Eugene V. Wolfenstein, *The Victims of Democracy: Malcolm X and the Black Revolution* (Berkeley: University of California Press, 1981), 37–38.

6. Ibid., 190.

7. Ibid., 287.

8. Historians of Malcolm's life and of the Black Muslims are united in their view that Malcolm almost worshiped Elijah Muhammad and strove for a long time to live the role of selfless adherent of his teachings. See Peter Goldman, *The Death and Life of Malcolm X* (New York: Harper and Row, 1973), 48, 89–90. See also Wolfenstein, *Victims of Democracy*, 213–30. Goldman details more than Malcolm himself does the process of gradual disillusionment Malcolm experienced. He also notes Malcolm's very human enjoyment of his public role, a dynamic downplayed in the *Autobiography*. See Goldman, 112.

9. Goldman, *Death and Life of Malcolm X*, 115.

10. Malcolm X, *Autobiography*, 409. See also Goldman, *Death and Life of Malcolm X*, 123ff.

11. For a detailed psychoanalytic approach to the process, see Wolfenstein, *Victims of Democracy*, 214ff.

12. Carol Ohmann, "*The Autobiography of Malcolm X*: A Revolutionary Use of the Franklin Tradition," *American Quarterly* 22 (1970), 131–49.

13. Goldman, *Death and Life of Malcolm X*, 92, 107, 124.

14. W.E.B. Du Bois, *Dusk of Dawn* (Millwood, N.Y.: Kraus-Thomson, 1975), 75.

15. Eakin, "Malcolm X and the Limits of Autobiography," 188.

16. Goldman, *Death and Life of Malcolm X*, 123.

17. Ibid., 31.

18. Ibid., 32–33.

19. Wolfenstein, *Victims of Democracy*, 37. Note that Wolfenstein calls Haley a *bio*graphical amanuensis, not an *auto*biographical one. This may reveal his unconscious view that the work is at least quasi-biographical because of Haley's role in helping write it.

20. Goldman, *Death and Life of Malcolm X*, 3.

21. See, for example, Robert F. Sayre, "Autobiography and the Making of America," in *Autobiography: Essays Theoretical and Critical*, 146–68.

22. James Olney, unpublished note to the author, 1987.

23. Richard Wright, *Black Boy* (New York: Harper and Row, Perennial Classic Paperback Edition, original copyright 1945), 55.

24. Anne Moody, *Coming of Age in Mississippi* (New York: Dial, 1968), 26.

25. Ibid., 285.

26. Sayre, "Autobiography and the Making of America," 152.

27. Ibid., 165.

28. Georges Gusdorf, "Conditions and Limits of Autobiography," in *Autobiography: Essays Theoretical and Critical*, 39.

29. Ibid., 39.

Bibliography

Anderson, Jervis. "Race, Rage, and Eldridge Cleaver." *Commentary* 46 (December, 1968): 63–70.

Andrews, William L. *To Tell a Free Story*. Urbana and Chicago: University of Illinois Press, 1986.

Baker, Houston. *The Journey Back*. Chicago: University of Chicago Press, 1980.

———. *Long Black Song: Essays in Black American Literature and Culture*. Charlottesville: University of Virginia Press, 1972.

———. *Modernism and the Harlem Renaissance*. Chicago: University of Chicago Press, 1987.

Baldwin, James. *The Price of the Ticket*. New York: St. Martin's/Marek, 1985.

Barton, Rebecca Chalmers. *Witnesses for Freedom*. Oakdale, N.Y.: Dowling College Press, 1976.

Berghan, Marion. *Images of Africa in Black American Literature*. Totowa, N.J.: Rowman and Littlefield, 1977.

Bloom, Harold. *The Anxiety of Influence*. London: Oxford University Press, 1973.

Bontemps, Arna. *Great Slave Narratives*. Boston: Beacon Press, 1969.

Braxton, Joanne. *Black Women Writing Autobiography: A Tradition within a Tradition*. Philadelphia: Temple University Press, 1990.

Braxton, Joanne, and Andrée Nicola McLaughlin, ed. *Wild Women in the Whirlwind*. New Brunswick, N.J.: Rutgers University Press, 1990.

Broderick, Francis L. *W.E.B. Du Bois: Negro Leader in a Time of Crisis*. Stanford, Ca.: Stanford University Press, 1959.

Butterfield, Stephen. *Black Autobiography in America*. Amherst: University of Massachusetts Press, 1974.

Byerman, Keith. *Fingering the Jagged Grain*. Athens: University of Georgia Press, 1985.

Campbell, Joseph. *The Hero with a Thousand Faces*. Princeton, N.J.: Princeton University Press, 1949.

Charney, Maurice. "James Baldwin's Quarrel with Richard Wright." *American Quarterly* 15 (1963): 65–75.

Cleaver, Eldridge. *Soul on Ice*. New York: McGraw-Hill, 1968.

Couser, G. Thomas. *American Autobiography: The Prophetic Mode.* Amherst: University of Massachusetts Press, 1979.

Cox, James. "Autobiography and Washington." *Sewannee Review* 85 (1977): 235–61.

Davis, Charles T. "From Experience to Eloquence: Richard Wright's *Black Boy* as Art." In *Chant of Saints.* Edited by Michael S. Harper and Robert B. Stepto. Urbana: University of Illinois Press, 1979.

Davis, Charles T., and Henry Louis Gates, Jr., eds. *The Slave's Narrative.* London: Oxford University Press, 1985.

Dickstein, Morris. "The Black Aesthetic in White America." *Partisan Review* XXXVIII, 4 (Winter, 1971–72): 376–95.

Douglass, Frederick. *Life and Times of Frederick Douglass.* New York: Collier, 1962.

———. *My Bondage and My Freedom.* Chicago: Johnson, 1970.

———. *Narrative of the Life of Frederick Douglass, an American Slave.* Edited by Benjamin Quarles. Cambridge, Mass.: Belknap, 1967.

Du Bois, W.E.B. *The Autobiography of W.E.B. Du Bois.* New York: International Publishers, 1968.

———. *Dusk of Dawn.* Millwood, N.Y.: Kraus-Thomson, 1975.

———. "The Evolution of Negro Leadership." *The Dial* 31 (July 16, 1901): 53–55.

———. "The Parting of the Ways." *World Today* 6 (April, 1904): 523.

———. *The Souls of Black Folk.* New York: Johnson Reprint, 1968.

Eakin, Paul John. "Malcolm X and the Limits of Autobiography." In *Autobiography: Essays Theoretical and Critical.* Edited by James Olney. Princeton, N.J.: Princeton University Press, 1980.

Egan, Susanna. *Patterns of Experience in Autobiography.* Chapel Hill: University of North Carolina Press, 1984.

Fabre, Michel. "Fathers and Sons in James Baldwin's *Go Tell It on the Mountain.*" In *James Baldwin: A Collection of Critical Essays.* Edited by Keneth Kinnamon. Englewood Cliffs, N.J.: Prentice-Hall, 1974.

———. *The Unfinished Quest of Richard Wright.* New York: William Morrow, 1973.

Factor, Robert L. *The Black Response to America.* Reading, Mass.: Addison, Wesley, 1970.

Farmer, James. *Lay Bare the Heart.* New York: Arbor House, 1985.

Foner, Philip S. *Frederick Douglass.* New York: Citadel Press, 1953.

Ford, Nick Aaron. "James Baldwin as Essayist." In *James Baldwin: A Critical Evaluation.* Edited by Therman B. O'Daniel. Washington, D.C.: Howard University Press, 1977.

Frederickson, George M., ed. *William Lloyd Garrison.* Englewood Cliffs, N.J.: Prentice-Hall, 1968.

Gates, Henry Louis, Jr. *Black Literature and Literary Theory.* New York: Methuen, 1984.

Gayle, Addison. *Richard Wright: Ordeal of a Native Son.* Garden City, N.Y.: Anchor/Doubleday, 1980.

Gibson, Donald B. *Five Black Writers*. New York: New York University Press, 1970.

Goldman, Peter. *The Death and Life of Malcolm X*. New York: Harper and Row, 1973.

Gross, Theodore L. *The Heroic Ideal in American Literature*. New York: Free Press, 1971.

Gusdorf, Georges. "Conditions and Limits of Autobiography." In *Autobiography: Essays Theoretical and Critical*. Edited by James Olney. Princeton, N.J.: Princeton University Press, 1980.

Hakutani, Yoshinobu, ed. *Critical Essays on Richard Wright*. Boston: G.K. Hall, 1982.

Harlan, Louis R., ed. *The Booker T. Washington Papers*. Urbana: University of Illinois Press, 1972.

———. *Booker T. Washington: The Wizard of Tuskegee*. New York: Oxford University Press, 1983.

Harper, Michael S., and Robert B. Stepto, eds. *Chant of Saints*. Urbana: University of Illinois, Press, 1979.

Hawkins, Hugh, ed. *Booker T. Washington and His Critics*. Boston: Heath, 1962.

Hernton, Calvin C. "Blood of the Lamb: The Ordeal of James Baldwin." In *White Papers for White Americans*. Garden City, N.Y.: Doubleday, 1966.

———. "The Sexual Mountain and Black Women Writers." In *Wild Women in the Whirlwind*. Edited by Joanne Braxton and Andrée Nicola McLaughlin. New Brunswick, N.J.: Rutgers University Press, 1988.

Holland, Frederick May. *Frederick Douglass: The Colored Orator*. Rev. ed. New York: Haskell House, 1969.

Howells, William Dean. "An Examplary Citizen." *North American Review* 173 (August, 1901): 280–88.

Jacobs, Harriet. *Incidents in the Life of a Slave Girl*. New York: Oxford University Press, 1988.

Joyce, Joyce Ann. *Richard Wright's Art of Tragedy*. Iowa City: University of Iowa Press, 1986.

Kent, George E. "Richard Wright: Blackness and the Adventure of Western Culture." In *Richard Wright: A Collection of Critical Essays*. Edited by Raymond Macksey and Frank E. Moorer. Englewood Cliffs, N.J.: Prentice-Hall, 1984.

Kinnamon, Keneth. *The Emergence of Richard Wright*. Urbana: University of Illinois Press, 1972.

Littlejohn, David. *Black on White*. New York: Grossman, 1966.

Macksey, Raymond, and Frank E. Moorer, eds. *Richard Wright: A Collection of Critical Essays*. Englewood Cliffs, N.J.: Prentice-Hall, 1984.

Malcolm X, with Alex Haley. *The Autobiography of Malcolm X*. New York: Grove, 1965.

Mandel, Barrett. "Full of Life Now." In *Autobiography: Essays Theoretical and Critical*. Edited by James Olney. Princeton, N.J.: Princeton University Press, 1980.

Margolies, Edward. "Ante-bellum Slave Narratives: Their Place in American Literary History." *Studies in Black Literature*, Autumn 1973.

——. *The Art of Richard Wright*. Carbondale: Southern Illinois University Press, 1969.

McCall, Dan. *The Example of Richard Wright*. New York: Harcourt, Brace, and World, 1969.

Moody, Anne. *Coming of Age in Mississippi*. New York: Dial, 1968.

Nichols, Charles H. *Many Thousand Gone*. Leiden: Brill, 1963.

——. "The Slave Narrators and the Picaresque Mode." In *The Slave's Narrative*. Edited by Charles T. Davis and Henry Louis Gates, Jr. Oxford: Oxford University Press, 1985.

O'Daniel, Therman B., ed. *James Baldwin: A Critical Evalution*. Washington, D.C.: Howard University Press, 1977.

Ohmann, Carol. "*The Autobiography of Malcolm X*: A Revolutionary Use of the Franklin Tradition." *American Quarterly* 22 (1970): 131–49.

Olney, James. "Autobiography and the Cultural Moment." In *Autobiography: Essays Theoretical and Critical*. Edited by James Olney. Princeton, N.J.: Princeton University Press, 1980.

——. "I Was Born." In *The Slave's Narrative*. Edited by Charles T. Davis and Henry Louis Gates, Jr. Oxford: Oxford University Press, 1985.

——, ed. *Autobiography: Essays Theoretical and Critical*. Princeton, N.J.: Princeton University Press, 1980.

Porter, Horace A. "The Horror and the Glory: Richard Wright's Portrait of the Artist in *Black Boy* and *American Hunger*." In *Richard Wright: A Collection of Critical Essays*. Edited by Richard Macksey and Frank E. Moorer. Englewood Cliffs, N.J.: Prentice-Hall, 1984.

Quarles, Benjamin. "The Breach Between Douglass and Garrison." *Journal of Negro History* XXIII (April, 1938): 144–54.

——. *Frederick Douglass*. New York: Haskell House, 1968.

Reading, J. Saunders. *To Make a Poet Black*. College Park, Md.: McGrath, 1968.

Reilly, John. "The Self-Creation of the Intellectual: *American Hunger* and *Black Power*." In *Critical Essays on Richard Wright*. Edited by Yoshinobu Hakutani. Boston: G. K. Hall, 1982.

Reimers, David, ed. *The Black Man in America Since Reconstruction*. New York: Thomas Y. Crowell, 1970.

Rudwick, Elliot. "The Overture to Protest: Beginnings of the Du Bois-Washington Controversy." In *The Black Man in America Since Reconstruction*. Edited by David Reimers. New York: Thomas Y. Crowell, 1970.

Sayre, Robert F. "Autobiography and the Making of America." In *Autobiography: Essays Theoretical and Critical*. Edited by James Olney. Princeton, N.J.: Princeton University Press, 1980.

Seelye, John. "The Clay Foot of the Climber." In *Literary Romanticism in America*. Edited by William L. Andrews. Baton Rouge: Louisiana State University Press, 1981.

Smith, Sidonie. *Where I'm Bound*. Westport, Conn.: Greenwood, 1974.

Standley, Fred L. " '. . . Farther and Farther Apart': Richard Wright and James Baldwin." In *Critical Essays on Richard Wright*. Edited by Yoshinobu Hakutani. Boston: G.K. Hall, 1982.

Stepto, Robert B. *From Behind the Veil*. Urbana: University of Illinois Press, 1979.

————. "Teaching Afro-American Literature: Survey or Tradition." In *Afro-American Literature: The Reconstruction of Instruction*. Edited by Dexter Fisher and Robert B. Stepto. New York: Modern Language Association of America, 1978.

Stone, Albert E. "After *Black Boy* and *Dusk of Dawn*: Patterns in Recent Black Autobiography." *Phylon* 39 (1978): 18–34.

Thorpe, Earl E. *The Mind of the Negro*. Westport, Conn.: Negro Universities Press, 1961.

Walker, Alice. *In Search of Our Mothers' Gardens*. San Diego: Harcourt, Brace, Jovanovich, 1983.

Washington, Booker T. *My Larger Education*. Excerpted in *The Booker T. Washington Papers*, Vol. 1. Edited by Louis R. Harlan. Urbana: University of Illinois Press, 1972.

————. *The Story of My Life and Work*. In *The Booker T. Washington Papers*, Vol. 1. Edited by Louis R. Harlan. Urbana: University of Illinois Press, 1972.

————. *Up From Slavery*. Reprinted in full in *The Booker T. Washington Papers*, Vol. 1. Edited by Louis R. Harlan. Urbana: University of Illinois Press, 1972.

Webb, Constance. *Richard Wright*. New York: G. P. Putnam's Sons, 1968.

Weissman, Steven M. "Frederick Douglass, Portrait of a Black Militant: A Study in the Family Romance." *Psychoanalytic Study of the Child* 30 (1975): 725–51.

Whitfield, Stephen J. "Three Masters of Impression Management: Benjamin Franklin, Booker T. Washington, and Malcolm X as Autobiographers." *South Atlantic Quarterly* 77 (1978): 399–417.

Wolfenstein, Eugene V. *The Victims of Democracy: Malcolm X and the Black Revolution*. Berkeley: University of California Press, 1981.

Wright, Richard. *American Hunger*. New York: Harper and Row, 1977.

————. *Black Boy*. New York: Harper and Row, Perennial Classic Paperback, 1966.

————. *Native Son*. New York: Harper and Row, Perennial Classic Paperback, 1966.

Index